This Suffering Is My Joy

This Suffering Is My Joy

The Underground Church in Eighteenth-Century China

D. E. Mungello

ROWMAN & LITTLEFIELD
Lanham • Boulder • New York • London

Published by Rowman & Littlefield
An imprint of The Rowman & Littlefield Publishing Group, Inc.
4501 Forbes Boulevard, Suite 200, Lanham, Maryland 20706
www.rowman.com

6 Tinworth Street, London SE11 5AL, United Kingdom

Copyright © 2021 by The Rowman & Littlefield Publishing Group, Inc.

All rights reserved. No part of this book may be reproduced in any form or by any electronic or mechanical means, including information storage and retrieval systems, without written permission from the publisher, except by a reviewer who may quote passages in a review.

British Library Cataloguing in Publication Information Available

Library of Congress Cataloging-in-Publication Data

Names: Mungello, D. E. (David Emil), 1943- author.
Title: This suffering is my joy : the underground church in eighteenth-century China / D.E. Mungello.
Description: Lanham : Rowman & Littlefield, [2021] | Includes bibliographical references and index.
Identifiers: LCCN 2020049493 (print) | LCCN 2020049494 (ebook) | ISBN 9781538150290 (hardcover) | ISBN 9781538173978 (pbk) ISBN 9781538150306 (epub)
Subjects: LCSH: China—Church history—18th century. | Persecution—China—History—18th century.
Classification: LCC BR1287 .M86 2021 (print) | LCC BR1287 (ebook) | DDC 282/.5109033—dc23
LC record available at https://lccn.loc.gov/2020049493
LC ebook record available at https://lccn.loc.gov/2020049494

Contents

List of Illustrations	vii
Acknowledgments	ix
Author's Note	1

1 The Underground Church in China　　　　　　　　　7

    Historical Background　　　　　　　　　　　　　　7
    The Auspicious Beginning of Catholicism in China　10
    The Eighteenth-Century Crisis　　　　　　　　　　13

2 Matteo Ripa's Attempt to Establish a School for Chinese
   Priests in China　　　　　　　　　　　　　　　　　21

    Fr. Matteo Ripa's Spiritual Vision　　　　　　　　21
    Ripa's Journey to China　　　　　　　　　　　　　23
    Ripa at the Chinese Court　　　　　　　　　　　　27
    Ripa's First School for Boys　　　　　　　　　　　31
    Opposition to Ripa's School　　　　　　　　　　　36
    Ripa Departs Beijing with Five Chinese　　　　　　40
    The Journey from Guangzhou (Canton) to London and Naples　44

3 Founding of the Chinese College for Priests in Naples　55

    Financial Struggles in Founding the Chinese College　55
    The First Chinese College Graduates Return to China　58
    Problems with Chinese Students in Naples　　　　63
    More Students Arrive from China　　　　　　　　66

	Lucio Wu as Ripa's "Perpetual Cross to Bear"	71
	Lucio's Second Flight and Imprisonment in Castel Sant'Angelo	75
4	Racial and Cultural Tensions between Chinese and European Priests	85
	Fr. Filippo Huang in China	85
	Huang's Struggles as a Missionary in Northern Shanxi	88
	Growing Tensions between Chinese and European Priests	92
	Anti-Christian Movement ("Great Persecution") of 1784	100
5	The Emergence of the Underground Church	109
	The Underground Church in Japan	109
	The Formation of Chinese Jesuit Priests	110
	Chinese Priests and Catechists in Sichuan	113
	The Formation of Chinese Underground Priests	117
	Christian Virgins (Chaste Women) in Sichuan	120
	Chinese Priests in Jiangnan	124
6	European and Chinese Forms of Martyrdom	133
	Sacrifice and Martyrdom among Chinese Priests and Catechists	133
	Indigenous Chinese Catholic Leadership	135
	Mendicant Martyrdoms	139
	Chinese Christian Martyrdoms	144
Conclusion		151
Bibliography		155
Index		165

Illustrations

MAP

China in the Qing dynasty — xi

FIGURES

	121 Martyr-Saints by Monica Lu (Liu Hebei 劉河北)	xii
2.1	Macau in the eighteenth century	26
2.2	Matteo Ripa, after Shen Yu, "Watching the Fish from Rocky Outcrop," copperplate engraving	30
4.1	Tomb of the Honorable (Filippo Maria) Huang Zhihan 黃之漢 (d. 1776) of the Congregation of the Holy Family of Jesus	99

Acknowledgments

The origins of this book go back to 1974 in Rome, when the late Fr. Edmond Lamalle, SJ, longtime director of the Jesuit Archives in Rome, helped me to locate the Yongzheng emperor's edict of 1727 in the *Archivum Romanum Societatis Iesu*. In 1975 the late Professor Wing-tsit Chan, who was always generous in responding by mail to my queries, helped me to interpret the Yongzheng emperor's edict.

Professor Michele Fatica, the leading scholar on Fr. Matteo Ripa (1682–1746) and former director of the Istituto Universitario Orientale in Naples, was instrumental in helping me to gain knowledge of Ripa that was crucial to this book. Prof. Fatica generously sent me copies of volumes I (1991) and II (1996) of his *Matteo Ripa Giornale*, an annotated edition of Ripa's famous journals. Also, at the invitation of Prof. Fatica and his former student, Dr. Francesco D'Arelli, I participated in the international symposium "Matteo Ripa e il Collegio dei Cinesi" held in Naples in 1999. In consequent years, Prof. Fatica has been a valued correspondent.

More recently, Professor Jonathan Chaves, Dr. Ad Dudink, and Prof. Robert Gimello assisted me in translating the Chinese biography of Zhou Laurentius. Prof. Claudia von Collani helped me to refine the translation of a complicated quotation from German. Professor Richard Strassberg helped provide guidance on understanding Matteo Ripa's artwork. The librarians of interlibrary loans at Baylor University helped me to secure numerous works. Dr. Xiaoxin Wu of the Ricci Institute in San Francisco assisted me in securing permission to reproduce the tombstone engraving of Father Huang Zhihan at the Zhalan Cemetery in Beijing. Prof. Louis Gendron, SJ, of Fu Jen University in Taiwan, and Father Peter Fei, director of Catholic Window Press in Taiwan, played crucial roles in helping me to secure usage permission and high-resolution images of Monica Lu's 121 Martyr-Saints painting.

I am grateful to two anonymous readers who made a number of valuable suggestions for improving the manuscript. My Rowman & Littlefield editor of eighteen years, Susan McEachern, provided her usual efficient guidance of the manuscript throughout the process of publication. My debt to all the colleagues mentioned above is immeasurable.

China in the Qing dynasty with marked sites referred to in the book.

121 Martyr-Saints by Monica Lu (Liu Hebei 劉河北) identified by individual numbers.
Source: Catholic Window Press, Taiwan.

Author's Note

The cover image of 121 Chinese martyr-saints is a remake of the original painting that was used during the canonization of the 120 martyr-saints of China in 2000. The original image appeared on the cover of the author's *The Catholic Invasion of China: Remaking Chinese Christianity* (2015). The artist, a Buddhist named Li Chien-yi, created a large painting (3.9 × 2.6 meters), which was hung at the Vatican during the martyrs' canonization ceremony on October 1, 2000. Pope John Paul II praised the martyrs as universal models of "courage and integrity." However, the painting became controversial because of the unresolved state of relations between the Communist government in Beijing and the Vatican. Beijing objected to these individuals being called martyr-saints and insisted instead that they were criminals and rebels. The controversy was sharpened because the martyrs' canonization ceremony took place on the anniversary of the founding of the People's Republic of China.

A dissatisfaction with the original painting by the Chinese Bishops Regional Conference of Taiwan led to commissioning a replacement. The famous China martyr Fr. John Gabriel Perboyre, CM, who had been omitted from the list of 120 martyrs, was added to make 121. Unlike the first painting, which is highly dramatic in tone, the second was rendered by the well-known Catholic painter Monica Lu (Liu Hebei 劉河北), with an emphasis on revealing the individual characters and social backgrounds of this diverse group of martyr-saints. Consequently, the figures were carefully drawn to indicate their unique stories of martyrdom. To this end, figure 0.1 shows the second painting, with numbers labeling each of the martyr-saints for identification purposes in the list that follows. Basic information for each martyr-saint reflects the great diversity in their ages, their roles in the Church, their occupations, and their social status. The oldest was a seventy-seven-year-old village headman and the youngest was a seven-year-old boy. Occupationally, they ranged from a literatus to servants. There were eighty-three men and thirty-eight women. They included fifteen married women, several of whom were widows, four orphaned girls, seven religious sisters, and nine chaste women (*shouzhen guniang* 守貞姑娘). Several of the martyr-saints were related either by blood or marriage. There were seven bishops (all European), twenty-six priests (only three of whom were Chinese), seven Chinese seminarians, thirteen Chinese catechists (eleven men and two women), and one European lay brother.

The painting is presently located at the Chinese Martyrs Sanctuary (Banqiao Zhonghua Xundao Shengren Chaoshengdi 板橋中華殉道聖人朝聖地) in Banqiao district, New Taipei City, Taiwan. The following list, arranged according to these numbers, contains a few lacunae when the information from various sources on certain martyr-saints was incomplete. Several of the martyr-saints on this list are discussed in this book. The abbreviations after the names indicate clerical affiliation: CM (Vincentians or Lazarists), FMM (Franciscan Missionaries of Mary), MEP (Missions Étrangères de Paris), OFM (Franciscans), OFS (Secular Franciscan Order), OP (Dominicans), PIME (Pontifical Institute for Foreign Missions), SDB (Salesians of Don Bosco), and SJ (Jesuits).

121 MARTYR-SAINTS OF CHINA

1. Saint Fr. Augustino Zhao Rong 趙榮 (1746–1815)
2. Saint Fr. John Gabriel Perboyre (Dong Wenxue 董文學), CM (1802–1840)
3. Saint Bishop Francis Serrano del Rincon (De Fangji 德芳濟), OP (1691–1748)
4. Saint Fr. Juan Alcobel Figuera (Fei Ruowang 費若望), OP (1694–1748)
5. Saint Fr. Joachim Royo (Hua Yajing 華雅敬), OP (1691–1748)
6. Saint Fr. Francesco Diaz del Rincon (Shi Fangji 施方濟), OP (1691–1748)
7. Saint Fr. Giovanni Pietro Néel (Wen Naier 文乃爾), MEP (1832–1862)
8. Saint Pietro Wu Guosheng 吳國盛, catechist (傳道員) (1768–1814)
9. Saint Giuseppe Zhang Dapeng 張大鵬, catechist (1754–1815)
10. Saint Martino Wu Xuesheng 吳學聖, catechist (1817–1862)
11. Saint Giovanni Chen Xianheng 陳顯恆, catechist (1820–1862)
12. Saint Fr. Giovanni da Triora Lantrua (Lan Yuewang 藍月旺), OFM (1760–1816)
13. Saint Giovanni Battista Luo Tingyin 羅廷蔭, peasant doctor (1825–1861)
14. Saint Bishop Pedro Sanz (Bo Duolu 博多祿), OP (1680–1747)

15. Saint Bishop Gabriel-Taurin Dufresse (Xu Dexin 徐德新) MEP (1750–1815)
16. Saint Paolo Liu Hanzuo 劉韓佐, Chinese diocesan priest (1778–1819)
17. Saint Lucia Yi Zhenmei 易貞美, catechist (1815–1862)
18. Saint Fr. Francisco Fernandez de Capillas, Liu Fangji 劉方濟, OP (1607–1648)
19. Saint Giovanni Zhang Tianshen 張天申, catechist (1805–1862)
20. Saint Agatha Lin Zhao 林昭, chaste woman (1817–1858)
21. Saint Fr. Francisco Regis Clet (Liu Gelai 劉格來), CM (1748–1820)
22. Saint Agnes Cao Guiying 曹桂英, widow (1821–1856)
23. Saint Pietro Liu Wenyuan 劉文元, lay catechist (1760–1834)
24. Saint Fr. Giuseppe Yuan (Yuan Zaide 遠在德), Chinese diocesan priest (1766–1817?)
25. Saint Paolo Chen Changpin 陳昌品, seminarian (1838–1861)
26. Saint Fr. Thaddeus Liu Ruiting 劉瑞廷, Chinese diocesan priest (1773–1823)
27. Saint Giuseppe Zhang Wenlan 張文瀾, seminarian (1831–1861)
28. Saint Jérôme (Girolamo) Lu Tingmei 盧廷美, catechist (1811–1857)
29. Saint Lorenzo Bai Xiaoman 白小滿, peasant (1821–1856)
30. Saint Mrs. Marta Wang Mande, born Luo 王曼德, 羅氏, widow (1802–1861)
31. Saint Fr. Augustus Chapdelaine (Ma Lai 馬賴), MEP (1814–1856)
32. Saint Lorenzo Wang Bing 王炳, catechist (1802–1857)
33. Saint Joachim Hao Kaizhi 郝開枝, catechist (1782–1839)
34. Saint Bishop Coadjutor Francesco Fogolla (Fu Gele 富格辣), OFM (1839–1900)
35. Saint Bishop Luigi Versiglia (Lei Wudao 雷鳴道), SDB (1873–1930)
36. Saint Fr. Callisto Caravario (Gao Huili 高惠黎), SDB (1903–1930)
37. Saint Fr. Elia Facchini (Lei Tiren 雷體仁), OFM (1839–1900)
38. Saint Fr. Teodorico Balat (De Aoli 德奧理), OFM (1858–1900)
39. Saint Tommaso Shen Jihe 申計和, OFS (1851–1900)
40. Saint Bishop Antonio Fantosati (Fan Huaide 范懷德), OFM (1842–1900)
41. Saint Francesco Zhang Rong 張榮, OFS, porter and gardener (1838–1900)
42. Saint Patrizio Dong Bodi 董博第, seminarian (1882–1900)
43. Saint Bishop Gregorio Grassi (Ai Shijie 艾士傑), OFM (1833–1900)
44. Saint Giovanni Zhang Huan 張換, OFS, seminarian (1882–1900)
45. Saint Fr. Giuseppe Mario Gambaro (An Shouren 安守仁), OFM (1869–1900)
46. Saint Sr. Maria Adolfine (Ya Dufei 雅都斐), Anne-Catherine Dierks, FMM (1866–1900)

47. Saint Filippo Zhang Zhihe 張志和, OFS, seminarian (1880–1900)
48. Saint Giovanni Zhang Jingguang 張景光, seminarian (1878–1900)
49. Saint Giacomo Zhao Quanxin 趙全信, manservant (1856–1900)
50. Saint Fr. Alberico Crescitelli (Guo Xide 郭西德), PIME (1863–1900)
51. Saint Sr. Marie Amandine, Pauline Jeuris (Ya Mangding 雅芒定), FMM (1872–1900)
52. Saint Pietro Wang Erman 王二滿, cook (1860–1900)
53. Saint Giovanni Wang Rui 王銳, OFS, seminarian (1885–1900)
54. Saint Sr. Maria Ermellina di Gesu, Irma Grivot (Ai Mingnei 埃明納), FMM (1866–1900)
55. Saint Pietro Zhang Banniu 張板紐, OFS, bishop's right-hand man (1849–1900)
56. Saint Sr. Marie de la Paix (Marianna Giuliani) Ba Xi, He Ping 巴溪, 和平, FMM (1875–1900)
57. Saint Fr. Cesidio Giacomantonio, Dong Zhexi 董哲西, OFM (1873–1900)
58. Saint Simon Chen Ximan 陳西滿, OFS, catechist (1855–1900)
59. Saint Sr. Marie de Saint Just (Anne-Françoise Moreau), Ju Side 菊斯德, FMM (1866–1900)
60. Saint Sr. Maria Chiara (Clelia Nanetti), Jia Na 嘉納, FMM (1872–1900)
61. Saint Pietro Wu Anbang 武安邦, OFS (1860–1900)
62. Saint Sr. Marie de Sainte Nathalie (Jeanne-Marie Guerquin), Na Dali 那達理 (1864–1899)
63. Saint Bro. Andrea Bauer (An Zhende 安振德), OFM (1866–1900)
64. Saint Mattias Feng De 馮德, OFS, night-watchman (1855–1900)
65. Saint Giacomo Yan Guodong 閆國棟, farmer (1853–1900)
66. Saint Anna Wang 安那, chaste woman (1886–1900)
67. Saint Andreas Wang Tianqing 王天慶 (1891–1900)
68. Saint Mrs. Lucia Wang, Wang Luqi, born Wang 王璐琪, 王氏 (1869–1900)
69. Saint Chi Zhuzi 郗柱子, catechist, 1882–1900)
70. Saint Paolo Lang Fu 郎福, seven-year-old boy (1893–1900)
71. Saint Mrs. Lang, born Yang 郎, 楊氏, mother of Paolo Lang Fu (1871–1900)
72. Saint Mrs. Mary Zhu, born Wu 朱瑪李, 吳氏, wife of village headman (1850–1900)
73. Saint Pietro Liu Ziyu 劉子玉, factory watchman (1843–1900)
74. Saint Mrs. Teresa Zhang, born He 張德蘭, 何氏 (1864–1900)
75. Saint Teresa Chen Jinjie 陳金婕, sister of Rosa Chen Aijie (1875–1900)
76. Saint Rosa Chen Aijie, 陳愛婕, sister of Teresa Chen Jinjie (1878–1900)
77. Saint Simon Qin Chunfu 秦春福, third son of Elisabetta Qin (1886–1900)

78. Saint Mrs. Elisabetta Qin, born Bian, 秦麗莎, 邊氏 (1846–1900)
79. Saint Fr. Paolo Denn (Tang Ailing 湯愛玲), SJ (1847–1900)
80. Saint Paolo Liu Jinde 劉進德 (1821–1900)
81. Saint Giuseppe Yuan Gengyin 遠庚寅 (1853–1900)
82. Saint Paolo Ge Tingzhu 葛廷柱, village headman (1839–1900)
83. Saint Giovanni Wang Kuixin 王奎新, first cousin to Giuseppe Wang Kuiju (1875–1900)
84. Saint Mrs. Anna An, born Jiao 安納, 焦氏, wife of Anna An-Xin's grandson (1874–1900)
85. Saint Maria An Linghua 安靈花, granddaughter of Anna An-Xin; catechist (1871–1900)
86. Saint Mrs. Barbara Cui, born Lian 崔芭芮, 連氏 (1849–1900)
87. Saint Mrs. Maria Guo, born Li 郭李馬, 麗氏 (1835–1900)
88. Saint Mrs. Anna An, born Xin 安安納, 辛氏, matriarch of An women (1828–1900)
89. Saint Mrs. Maria An, born Guo 安瑪利, 郭氏, daughter-in-law to Anna An-Xin (1836–1900)
90. Saint Paolo Wu Anju 吳安居, grandfather of Wu Mantang and Wu Wanshu (1838–1900)
91. Saint Giovanni Battista Wu Mantang 吳滿堂, grandson of Paul Wu Anju (1883–1900)
92. Saint Giuseppe Wang Kuiju 王奎聚, first cousin to Giovanni Wang Kuixin (1863–1900)
93. Saint Marco Ji Tianxiang 冀天祥, literatus (1834–1900)
94. Saint Paolo Wu Wanshu 吳萬書, grandson of Paul Wu Anju (1884–1900)
95. Saint Giuseppe Wang Yumei 王玉梅, Catholic village headman (1823–1900)
96. Saint Maria Qi Yu 齊玉, orphan girl at Wangla (1885–1900)
97. Saint Mrs. Maria Du, born Zhao 杜瑪李, 趙氏 (1849–1900)
98. Saint Maria Fan Kun 范坤, orphan girl at Wangla (1884–1900)
99. Saint Maria Zheng Xu 鄭緒, orphan girl at Wangla (1889–1900)
100. Saint Rémi Isoré (Zhao Xizhen 趙席珍), SJ (1852–1900)
101. Saint Pietro Zhu Rixin 朱日新 (1881–1900)
102. Saint Fr. Modeste Andlauer (Lu Maode 路懋德), SJ (1847–1900)
103. Saint Mrs. Maria Wang, born Li 王瑪麗, 李氏 (1851–1900)
104. Saint Lucia Wang Cheng 王成, orphan girl at Wangla (1882–1900)
105. Saint Maria Fu Guilin 傅桂林, chaste woman (1863–1900)
106. Saint Maria Du, born Tian 杜瑪麗, 田氏 (1858–1900)
107. Saint Maddalena Du Fengju 杜鳳菊, daughter of Marie Du-Tian (1831–1900)

108. Saint Mrs. Maria Zhao, born Guo 趙瑪利, 郭氏, mother of Rosa Zhao and Maria Zhao (1840–1900)
109. Saint Fr. Léon Ignatius Mangin (Ren Defen 任德芬) SJ (1857–1900)
110. Saint Raimondo Li Quanzhen 李全眞, brother of Pietro Li Quanhui (1841–1900)
111. Saint Pietro Zhao Mingzhen 趙明振, brother of Giovanni Battista Zhao Mingxi (1839–1900)
112. Saint Giovanni Battista Zhao Mingxi 趙明喜, brother of Pietro Zhao Mingzhen (1844–1900)
113. Saint Giovanni Battista Ma Taishun 馬太順, catechist (1840–1900)
114. Saint Giovanni Battista Zhu Wurui 朱五瑞 (1883–1900)
115. Saint Zhang Huailu 張懷祿, catechumen (1843–1900)
116. Saint Rosa Fan Hui 范惠, chaste woman (1855–1900)
117. Saint Giovanni Wu Wenyin 武文印 1850–1900)
118. Saint Maria Zhao 趙瑪利, daughter of Maria Zhao-Guo (1883–1900)
119. Saint Rosa Zhao 趙洛莎, chaste woman, daughter of Maria Zhao-Guo (1878–1900)
120. Saint Pietro Li Quanhui 李全惠, brother of Raimondo Li Quanzhen (1837–1900)
121. Saint Peter Wang Zuolong 王佐隆 (1842–1900)

Chapter One

The Underground Church in China

HISTORICAL BACKGROUND

In the foreshortened perspective of the present, the division between the official and underground Catholic church in China is often seen as originating with Communist rule in 1949; however, the longer view of history shows that the underground church dates from the eighteenth century. On the morning of June 30, 1706, in the grand imperial garden Yuanmingyuan near Beijing, the Papal Legate Carlo Tommaso Maillard de Tournon (Duoluo 多羅) was carried with elaborate ceremony on a sedan chair for his third and final meeting with the Kangxi emperor.[1] Tournon had been sent to China to formalize relations between the Vatican and Beijing, but a sticking point had emerged over the veneration of Confucius and ancestors. Underlying this problem was the intense distrust and animosity felt between the Jesuits and Tournon, who was backed by *Propaganda Fide* (Sacred Congregation for the Propagation of the Faith). Whereas the Jesuits had proposed an accommodating interpretation of the practice of the Chinese rites as a compromise to allow the precarious Christian mission in China to continue, Tournon took the hard-line position that the veneration of Confucius and ancestors was idolatrous and incompatible with Christianity. At this meeting, the Kangxi emperor bluntly told Tournon that if Christianity was incompatible with the teaching of Confucius, then Christianity could not be propagated in China. Unresolved tensions between the Chinese throne and the Vatican continued and on January 12, 1724, the Yongzheng emperor banned Christianity from being propagated in China, except in the cities of Beijing and Macau. In essence, the Kangxi emperor was claiming, like President Xi Jinping three centuries later, ultimate authority in religious practice in China. The Chinese leader's claim of authority has also been applied to other religions.

In October 1951, the newly founded People's Liberation Army (PLA) asserted control over Tibet, forcing the young Dalai Lama (Tenzin Gyatso) to become a Chinese puppet. In 1959 the PLA ruthlessly suppressed a Tibetan uprising, causing the Dalai Lama to flee to India. Not only did the Chinese government claim the right to impose itself into the highly traditional process of selecting a new Dalai Lama and Panchen Lama, but an article published in 1968 during the Cultural Revolution claimed that Mao Zedong had replaced the Buddha among the Tibetans![2] In 2007 China's State Administration for Religious Affairs (SARA) said that all reincarnations of living Buddhas in Tibetan Buddhism must receive government approval or they would be regarded as "illegal or invalid."[3]

Since its inception, the People's Republic of China has struggled unsuccessfully to control Muslims in the Xinjiang region, which is populated by twenty-five million people, of whom more than half are Muslim. As a response to terrorist attacks by Uighur militants against the Chinese in 2014, Xi Jinping initiated a program of brutal mass detentions of Muslim ethnic minorities in Xinjiang. These incarcerations have involved roughly a million Uighurs and Kazakhs.

As for Christianity, the events surrounding Tournon's embassy in 1706 precipitated the beginning of the underground church in China. The dynamics of religious persecution typically involve a government or social force that targets a segment of the population who hold beliefs that differ from the dominant values of the culture. In Europe, Christians had persecuted those who held heterodox beliefs in the sense of being minority truths and values that were not accepted by the majority and that were believed to be subversive of the dominant value system. These included members of Christian heterodoxies, Jews, Muslims, witches, and homosexuals. In eighteenth-century China the persecution involved a government with a largely Confucian ideology attacking a Catholic underground church. Since these Christian beliefs had a foreign source, they were regarded as subversive and the attacks on them were tinged with xenophobia.

In the last three centuries, periods of official acceptance of Christianity in China have alternated with periods of hostility and persecution. The Yongzheng emperor's 1724 proscription against Christianity was in effect until 1842, when Western imperialism forced the Chinese to sign the Treaty of Nanjing, opening five treaty ports to foreign traders and Christian missionaries. The ensuing colonialist exploitation of China gave rise to a new nationalist ideology in which traditional philosophies like Confucianism were replaced with Communism.

Christianity again went underground in the aftermath of the Communist victory in the Chinese Civil War of 1945–1949, when government control of Christian churches was established. Communist leaders like Mao Zedong were atheists who nevertheless felt that religion could not be abolished by administrative decree and that people could not be forced to give up their religious beliefs. Mao believed rather that religion would fade away over time with the progress of democratic socialism. Consequently, Maoists tried initially merely to control religious groups rather than destroy them.

The attack on foreign imperialism and Catholic autonomy intensified in 1950 at the time of the Korean War, when the Chinese sent PLA forces to support the North Koreans against a UN force under American leadership. To discredit the missionaries, the Chinese composed historical surveys in an attempt to document the collusion of missionaries with foreign imperialists going back to the time of the Opium War (1839–1842).[4] Stirred by patriotic feelings, some Catholics called for a break with imperialism and for the establishment of a self-governing, self-supporting, and self-propagating Chinese church. However, such sentiments were more compatible with the less hierarchical and more independent nature of Protestant churches than with the universal Catholic Church with its leadership concentrated in the Vatican.

In this hyperpartisan wartime atmosphere, Christians, and particularly Catholics, were regarded as a fifth column of the American-led UN forces attacking North Korea, particularly after Chinese soldiers died in large numbers in the Korean conflict.[5] This led to the expulsion of missionaries in 1951 and to the harsh treatment of certain Christians in China who were viewed as an extended part of the enemy on the battlefield in Korea. Chinese hostility toward Christians was reflected in the harsh treatment of the Belgian priest Dries van Coillie (Wan Guangli 萬廣禮), who was imprisoned in Beijing by the Communists for three years (1951–1954). He wrote a confessional work in which he describes the details of his imprisonment by the Communists and "the tortures it inflicts on those who believe in God."[6]

Eventually, Chinese governmental control was formalized with the 1957 founding of the Chinese Catholic Patriotic Association (CCPA), which centralized administrative control of all Christians under the Religious Affairs Bureau, later replaced by the State Administration for Religious Affairs (SARA) (*Guojia zongjiao shiwuju* 國家宗教事務局).[7] The diverging tendencies toward reconciliation and resistance led to the 1957 split between the government-sanctioned Catholic Church with its loyalty to Beijing and the underground church that was loyal to Rome.[8] Various names used for these two churches reflect subtle degrees of sympathy. The government-sanctioned Church is sometimes called the "Patriotic" church or the "official" church and at other times the "open" church. The underground church is sometimes referred to as "unregistered" or "unofficial" or "Vatican Loyalists" or "loyalists."

A central issue became who had the authority to nominate bishops—Beijing or the Vatican.[9]

When Christianity had not faded away by 1966, Mao urged a more aggressive attack against it through the Cultural Revolution, which called upon Red Guards to attack and destroy religion as part of the campaign against the "Four Olds" (old customs, culture, habits, and ideas). Throughout much of the four-hundred-year modern phase of its history in China, Christianity has been an underground church. And while the circumstances that led to its suppression have changed over time, the dynamics of practicing a forbidden faith have had notable continuities.

THE AUSPICIOUS BEGINNING OF CATHOLICISM IN CHINA

After the Jesuit missionaries first arrived in China in 1579, their initial success was followed by defeats. For more than a century, the Jesuits had notable success in converting numerous high-ranking Chinese literati, such as Xu Guangqi (1562–1633). These literati became model converts who influenced other Chinese in a culture that honored its intellectuals with scholar-official status. This was a golden age for Christian conversions in China, in which the Jesuits praised and emulated the literati as their intellectual and social counterparts. This tone of universal social and intellectual equality is expressed by Ricci in the opening words of his work *Jiaoyu lun* 交友倫 (*On Friendship*):

> I, Matteo, from the Far West, have sailed across the seas and entered China with respect for the learned virtue of the Son of Heaven of the Great Ming dynasty as well as for the teachings bequeathed by the ancient kings. Since the time that I elected the place of my lodging in Lingbiao, the stars and frosts have changed several times. In the spring of this year, I crossed the mountains, sailed down the river, and arrived in Jinling, where I beheld the glory of the capital of the kingdom, which filled me with happiness, and I thought that it was not in vain that I had made this journey.[10]

Early missionary success in China was reflected in the growing number of Christian churches. A Chinese list of church locations was compiled probably by Yang Tingyun (楊庭筠, 1557–1627) in the early seventeenth century and provided with a preface by Su Maoxiang (蘇茂相, 1567–1630), an eminent scholar-official who had passed the *jinshi* exam in 1592, the same year as Yang Tingyun, and was the governor or Zhejiang province.[11] Yang wrote a poem about meeting Su at the West Lake of Hangzhou when it was raining, reflecting their friendship.[12] This list of ninety-six *Tianzhu tang* (Lord of Heaven churches) is arranged by province, prefecture, subprefecture, district, defense command, and city.[13] However, it appears that some of the churches on this list were mission outposts that soon faded. Joseph Dehergne, SJ, compiled another list from a Chinese manuscript dating from before 1664 at the Xujiahui Library of Shanghai, which listed the locations of approximately fifty Christian churches.[14]

This golden age of conversions ended in 1724 when the Yongzheng emperor expelled the missionaries—except for those employed at the Beijing court and those permitted to reside in the far southern seaport town of Macau—and ordered that the Christian churches in China be converted to public places. Christianity became an underground church, vulnerable to the periodic anti-Christian movements that swept across China for the next century.

While still a prince and before he became the Yongzheng emperor, Yinzhen 胤禛 had formed a negative view of Christianity. He had heard numerous complaints of intramissionary disputes conveyed by his music instructor, the Lazarist Father Teodorico Pedrini.[15] As a ruler whose own ascent to the throne had been tainted by questions of usurpation, the Yongzheng emperor was particularly suspicious of Christianity as a subversive force.[16] His suspicions were further fanned by the Portuguese Jesuit João Mourão (Mu Jingyuan 穆敬遠) (1681–1726), who allied with a rival claimant to the throne, the crown prince Yintang 胤唐 (Seshe), whose branch of the imperial clan had converted to Christianity during the Kangxi period.[17] Yintang had been the most energetic of the heirs apparent in pursuing the throne.[18] Because of this affiliation, Fr. Mourão was exiled along with Yintang to the remote site of Sining in northwestern China and later executed.[19] Mourão was accused of secretly communicating with Yintang through a window in the back hall of Yintang's neighboring residence.[20] It was alleged that Yintang planned to store his possessions secretly in Mourão's house and allegedly even ordered him to open a shop in Sining as a hiding place for things and secret communications with Beijing.

In addition, the powerful Sunu 蘇努 clan, who were direct descendants of the Manchu dynasty founder Nurhaci and had their own claims to the throne, had converted to Christianity during the Kangxi period.[21] The Yongzheng emperor turned against the entire clan and punished them for what was framed as "disobedience to the Manchu Way" (*buzun Manzhou zhengdao* 不遵滿洲正道).

The Yongzheng emperor's hostility toward Christianity was embodied in his nativist outlook. His father, the Kangxi emperor, had cultivated a cosmopolitan outlook while retaining his Manchu heritage, viewing himself as a multiethnic ruler over the Manchus, Chinese, Mongols, and central Asians. Initially the Kangxi emperor was open to welcoming the missionaries, but eventually he grew frustrated with the rigid claims of the Vatican for authority over Catholics in China. However, the Kangxi emperor had broader interests and historians sometimes emphasize the technical contribution of the missionaries at the court while failing to give due weight to the Kangxi emperor's encouragement of their research into common intellectual interests. The Jesuit Joachim Bouvet (Bo Jin 白晉) was a key intermediary in this process. The emperor sent him to Europe in 1693–1699 to recruit European mathematicians for the court. For almost twenty-three years, between 1699 and his death in 1722, he supported Bouvet's research at the Beijing court on universalist themes, including Bouvet's and his fellow Figurists' research and radical interpretation of Chinese classical texts as foreshadowing Christ's revelation.[22] This led to the remarkable intellectual correspondence between Bouvet and the eminent European philosopher Leibniz.[23]

In contrast to his father, the Yongzheng emperor was more Sinified as well as more tribal and less cosmopolitan in outlook. He embraced the more exclusively Confucian principles of *jiaohua* 教化 (transformation of customs through education) and of *jiaoyang* 教養 (teaching and cultivation of the people) as a form of a more nativist "civilizing mission."[24] Since Christianity was not part of these native teachings, and was therefore a heterodox teaching, Christians in his view could not be loyal citizens.

The Yongzheng emperor's view of Christianity is presented in a 1,100-character edict, dated May 28, 1727, based on the Nine Chief Ministers of the Grand Secretariat (*Neige* 內閣) memorializing the throne.[25] The edict expresses a traditional Confucian pattern of distinguishing unorthodox teachings (*yiduan* 異端) in the sense of being parochial from the universal truths of orthodox teachings. The edict compares the honoring of the Buddha's birthday (*Fodan* 佛誕) with the Western ambassadors' honoring of their God. According to the edict, the parochial nature of both was confirmed by their reciprocal hostility: the Buddho-Daoists (Fo-Lao 佛老) were extremely vocal in their criticism of the Western teaching while the Westerners were extremely critical of the teachings of Buddho-Daoists.

The Kangxi emperor's receptivity to cosmic views had led him to encourage Jesuit research into defining universal forms of truth. These included the broader implications of Bouvet's discovery of the similarities between the binary arithmetic of Leibniz and the hexagrams of the *Yijing* (Book of Changes). They also included the Figurist interpretation of ancient Chinese texts to show their anticipation of Christianity.[26] The Yongzheng emperor by contrast viewed Christianity as well as Buddhism and Daoism as being parochial in the sense of being grounded in specific cultures. Their limited application is what made them heterodox (*yiduan*) or false, unlike Confucianism, which was true because of its universal validity. The edict cites chapter VII of the Confucian *Analects* (*Lunyu* 論語), in which the disciple Zilu 子路 asked

Confucius if he could pray for Confucius's recovery from illness. Confucius rejected the offer by saying that he had already been praying for a long time. The edict uses this example to explain that Zilu's prayers (like Christianity) were false (*xie* 邪) or untrue (*buzheng* 不正) in the sense that they had only limited application whereas Confucius's own prayers represented a universal form of truth (*zhengdao* 正道). The 1727 edict stated, "China has the teachings (*jiao*) of China [i.e., Buddhism and Daoism] and the West has the teachings of the West [i.e., Christianity]. The teachings of the West certainly cannot be applicable in China and, as for the teachings of China, how can they be applicable in the West?"

THE EIGHTEENTH-CENTURY CRISIS

Because of the precariousness of their foothold in China, many early missionaries felt compelled to be accommodating. These were mainly Jesuits whose appreciation of knowledge found a positive reception among the Chinese literati. In the process of learning about Chinese culture, the Jesuit missionaries became the chief source of information about China to Europeans. They wrote a number of highly favorable books about a nation that, apart from its lack of Christianity, was portrayed as admirable and worthy of emulation. Confucius was praised as a model of learning and morality, comparable to the Greek philosophers of classical antiquity. However, in Europe the admiration grounded in Confucian texts in the seventeenth century evolved in the eighteenth century into superficial Sinomania, with all the evanescence that fashion bears. This fashion peaked with the chinoiserie that Europeans were refashioning out of the fragments of Chinese culture that were transported in the ships of the mercantilist trading companies and from the reinterpretations of Jesuit writings about China. One of the most flagrant reinterpretations of European popular culture involved the five adaptations of the wildly popular Chinese drama *Orphan of Zhao* (*Zhaoshi gu'er* 趙氏孤兒) that appeared in the mid-eighteenth century, culminating in Voltaire's *L'Orphelin de la Chine* (1753), which completely distorted the original work in order to create a model of Enlightenment values.[27] As with the artifacts of chinoiserie, this Chinese drama was transformed into Sino-European images that had only a distant relationship to the originals. The net effect of trivializing the Chinese through chinoiserie was to regard China less seriously in both the cultural and geopolitical senses.

The dynamics of European expansion were changing the way Europeans viewed their relationship to the rest of the world. Instead of tentative explorers of the unknown, Europeans were gaining enough confidence to increasingly see themselves as conquerors of the world and purveyors of a superior culture. When an anti-Jesuit reaction in eighteenth-century Europe discredited the Jesuits and led to their dissolution in 1773, the accommodating Jesuits disappeared from China. Rome demanded that the European missionaries of the eighteenth century become less accommodating and refused to compromise on the crucial matters of Chinese rites to their ancestors and to Confucius. Their rigidity caused the early Jesuit foundations laid for the China mission to crumble and eventually forced the Church to go underground.

With the change in atmosphere from accommodating Jesuits like Ricci to unaccommodating papal representatives like Tournon, the Chinese authorities grew hostile to Christianity. As official persecution increased in the eighteenth century, the previous pace of conversions was difficult to maintain, except in an isolated province such as Sichuan. Nevertheless, the total number of Christians remained more or less stable, although it did not keep pace with China's population growth. The Jesuit Louis Le Comte's estimate of 300,000 Christians in China around 1700 was likely exaggerated.[28] More accurate was probably the estimate of 200,000 made by the China missionary Antoine Thomas, SJ, in a letter dated November 4, 1700, from Beijing to Fr. Thomas-Ignace Dunin-Szpot.[29] Estimates of the number of Christians were likely exaggerated by the inclusion of baptisms of abandoned children who were moribund. Based on the various estimates, the number of Christians seems to have declined to approximately 150,000 by the mid-eighteenth century.[30] A knowledgeable source estimated that by 1815 the number of Christians in China had risen to 221,000.[31] Given the enormous population growth of China during this time, these numbers indicated stagnation in the number of Christians. The prominent China mission historian Kenneth Scott Latourette referred to the period between 1707 and 1839 in China as a "period of retarded growth."[32]

Confronted by frightening periodic government persecutions, many Christians apostatized. With Christianity in official disrepute, the status-conscious literati and upper-class Chinese were no longer converting to Christianity, although this group had never constituted more than a small percentage of Chinese Christians. A statistic of 1636 indicated that only 0.85 percent of Christians were officials and degree holders.[33] A list initially compiled around 1669 shows that Christian churches were found in thirty-eight Chinese towns and cities.[34] By the 1720s there were 131 churches in China, with strong growth in the south.[35] However, most Chinese Christians were dispersed throughout the countryside as farmers, small merchants, and artisans. They were mostly illiterate people in villages and rural areas who composed part of the same segment of Chinese society that was responsive to heterodox and rebellious popular movements like the White Lotus. Because of public dangers and the need for priests to be constantly in transit to avoid official notice, most of the Christian ministry occurred in the homes of Christians rather than in churches. This dispersion had the effect of increasing the difficulties of the missionaries who were forced to travel farther to contact their parishioners, but it also increased the difficulties authorities faced in finding and suppressing Christian communities, thereby helping the underground church to survive.

At that point, a few far-sighted European missionaries were beginning to confront their cultural and racial prejudices toward the eighteenth-century Chinese.[36] Missionaries like Fr. Matteo Ripa (1682–1746) argued against the prevailing assumption of most European clerics that the Chinese were not yet ready to become priests and bishops. It is widely but incorrectly believed that the twin traumas of the Rites Controversy and the consequent papal suppression of the Jesuits led to the destruction of Christianity in China. It is true that the Church was brought to the brink of destruction by the expulsion of most European missionaries from China and by the severe government persecutions. Moreover, the French Revolution and Napoleonic Wars interrupted the development of priestly vocations and constricted the flow of missionaries to China for twenty years.[37] Nevertheless, these setbacks also had the positive effect of fostering the development of an indigenous Chinese church.

In 1705, only ten out of almost 140 priests in China were Chinese.[38] However, by 1815, out of 169 priests, eighty-nine Chinese outnumbered eighty Europeans.[39] Although this trend was temporarily slowed by the colonialist forces of 1842–1951, it turned out to be a long-term and necessary phenomenon. During this transition, Chinese and European priests struggled and voiced mutual accusations against one another. The criticisms of European priests are better known than the criticisms of the Chinese priests, whose protests are only now being unearthed from letters and other archival sources. This transition can be traced through several paths by which indigenous clergy were formed. These included Lazarist seminaries in Macau and Beijing, the Missions Étrangeres de Paris (MEP) seminaries in Southeast Asia, and Ripa's seminary for training Chinese priests in the Collegio dei Cinesi (Chinese College) in Naples (Naboli Zhonghua Shuyuan 納波里中華書院).

The devastating conflict over allowing Chinese Christians to continue to honor their ancestors with rites has been treated by historians as a conflict between the China Jesuits and the anti-Jesuit followers of the Papal Legate Tournon. This perspective provides a limited view of what happened because the combatants in that conflict were almost entirely Europeans. A fresh insight into the Rites Controversy can be obtained by viewing the conflict through the eyes of Chinese Christians, and particularly Chinese priests and laypeople. With the official prohibition of Christianity during the years

1724–1842 and the decline in the number of foreign priests, Christian communities were increasingly administered by Chinese priests and by catechists and Chinese congregational and confraternity leaders, including the Christian Virgins (Chaste Women).[40]

Female Chinese Catholics supported the Church by developing a distinctively Chinese organization. In eighteenth-century China there was only one traditional European Catholic cloister for women. It was the settlement of the Franciscan Order of St. Claire in Macau.[41] St. Claire of Assisi founded the order in 1212 and the Franciscans controlled its spiritual direction. However, Macau was an outpost of European Christianity where Sinicized forms of Christianity struggled to emerge. By contrast, in Fujian in the early eighteenth century, the Dominican ministry to women had given rise to the formation of a parallel group of Christian women who abstained from marriage and remained virgins.[42] These *beatas* of the Dominican Third Order devoted their lives to Christian cultivation. By 1750 there were 250 *beatas* in Fuan county. This new, uniquely Chinese organization for women grew to include 600 Christian chaste women throughout China, but especially in Sichuan and Fujian.[43] Most Christian Virgins lived with their families, but two communities of nine to ten Virgins lived in Fujian.

Differences between Chinese officialdom and European missionaries gave rise to a number of anti-Christian incidents in the eighteenth century, followed in the nineteenth century by numerous "missionary cases" (*jiaoan* 教案). These incidents should be viewed in the broader context of the ongoing struggle between Chinese and Europeans for the control of the Chinese Catholic church in which the rites were merely one of many subjects of dispute. The use of this broader context would give greater continuity and meaning to the ongoing dialogue expressed in the recent agreement of September 22, 2018, between President Xi Jinping and Pope Francis for sharing control of the appointment of bishops. In essence, this 2018 agreement is not definitive, but rather a step toward further dialogue. The underlying nature of this struggle to define the meaning of an "independent Chinese Catholic Church" (*duli zizhu ziban* 独立自主自办) has been described by one senior cleric as a debate over whether "independence" refers to the Chinese Catholic Church's independence from the Holy See or the Church's independence from Chinese political control.[44]

Father Matteo Ripa was hardly a paragon of tolerance by contemporary standards: he disliked Jesuits, Protestant "heretics," and certain Chinese officials with equal vehemence. And yet he believed in the ability of his young Chinese students to become church leaders in the same way that Europeans became leaders in the church. His almost thirteen years of service (February 1711–November 1723) as an artist in residence close to the Kangxi emperor gave him an experience that was shared by very few Europeans. This experience convinced him that his small school for Chinese seminarians needed to be moved to Naples in order to train Chinese priests whose native fluency in the language and their physical appearance as Han Chinese would enable them to be more effective missionaries in China than Europeans. His founding of the Collegio dei Cinesi (Chinese College) in Naples stands out as one of the most remarkable contributions in the attempt to create a more universal church in China.

NOTES

1. Kilian Stumpf, SJ, *The Acta Pekinensia of Historical Records of the Maillard de Tournon Legation*, vol. 1: *December 1705–August 1706*, ed. Paul Rule and Claudia von Collani (Rome: Institutum Historicum Societatis Iesu, 2015), 410–12. The above record was written by European Jesuits. For the Chinese perspective, see Chen Yuan, ed., *Kangxi yu Luoma shijie Guanxi wenshu yingyin ben* (Beijing: Palace Museum, 1932; originals now in Taipei).

2. "Mao Tse-tung Replaces Buddha in Tibet," *Renmin Ribao*, November 19, 1968. English translation in Donald E. MacInnis, *Religious Policy and Practice in Communist China: A Documentary History* (New York: Macmillan, 1972), 344–46.

3. "Reincarnation of Living Buddha Needs Gov't Approval" (Xinhua), *China Daily*, August 4, 2007.

4. MacInnis, *Religious Policy*, 132–33.

5. D. E. Mungello, *The Catholic Invasion of China: Remaking Chinese Christianity* (Lanham, MD: Rowman & Littlefield, 2015), 57–64; 88–89.

6. Dries van Coillie, *I Was Brainwashed in Peking* (Brussels: Nederlandse Boekdruk Industrie, 1969), 319.

7. The Protestant counterpart of the CCPA was the Three-Self Patriotic Movement (TSPM) (*sanzi jiaohui* 三自教會), which had been founded in 1954 and which, as with Catholics, caused a split of Protestants into official churches and unofficial house churches (*jiating jiaohui* 家庭教會).

8. Alan Hunter and Chan Kim-kwong, "Growth of the Chinese Church since 1949," in *Handbook of Christianity in China*, vol. 2: *1800 to Present*, ed. R. G. Tiedemann (Leiden: Brill, 2010), 817–19.

9. Paul P. Mariani, *Church Militant: Bishop Kung and the Chinese Catholic Resistance in Communist Shanghai* (Cambridge, MA: Harvard University Press, 2011), 206–27; Beatrice Leung, *Sino-Vatican Relations: Problems in Conflicting Authority 1976–1986* (Cambridge, UK: Cambridge University Press, 1992), 162–69; Mungello, *Catholic Invasion*, 55–69.

10. Matteo Ricci, *On Friendship: One Hundred Maxims for a Chinese Prince*, trans. Timothy Billings (New York: Columbia University Press, 2009), 87.

11. Wang Chung-min, "Yang T'ing-yun," in *Eminent Chinese of the Ch'ing Period*, ed. Arthur W. Hummel (Washington, DC: Government Printing Office, 1943), 894–95.

12. Nicolas Standaert, *Yang Tingyun, Confucian and Christian in Late Ming China* (Leiden: Brill, 1988), 26; 59.

13. This list of Catholic churches originated in Fujian province, where Fr. Aleni was active as a missionary. It is preserved in the Vatican Library in the Borgia Cinese collection and listed in Maurice Courant, *Catalogue des livres chinois . . . de la Bibliothèque nationale* (Paris: Leroux, 1910), no. 7046. Paul Pelliot lists it in his *Inventaire Sommaire des Manuscrits et imprimés chinois de la Bibliotheque Vaticaine*, rev. and ed. Takata Tokio (Kyoto: Italian School of East Asian Studies, Reference Series 1, 1995), 24.

14. Joseph Dehergne, SJ, "Les Chrétientés de Chine de la periode Ming (1581–1650)," *Monumenta Serica* 16 (1957): 1–136 & map.

15. Eugenio Menegon, *Ancestors, Virgins, and Friars: Christianity as a Local Religion in Late Imperial China* (Cambridge, MA: Harvard University Press, 2009), 118–21.

16. The accusation of usurpation is voiced by Fang Chao-ying, "Yin-chên," in *Eminent Chinese of the Ch'ing Period*, ed. Arthur Hummel (Washington, DC: Government Printing Office, 1943), 916. The Yongzheng emperor is defended against the charge of usurpation and parricide by Madeleine Zelin, "The Yung-cheng Reign," in *The Cambridge History of China*, vol. 9: *The Ch'ing Dynasty to 1800*, ed. Willard J. Peterson (Cambridge, UK: Cambridge University Press, 2002), 185–91. The most detailed description of the charge of usurpation, which argues in a balanced presentation that inclines slightly in the Yongzheng emperor's favor, is made by Pei Huang, *Autocracy at Work: A Study of the Yung-cheng Period, 1723–1735* (Bloomington: Indiana University Press, 1974), 51–59.

17. Lars Peter Laamann, *Christian Heretics in Late Imperial China: Christian Inculturation and State Control, 1720–1850* (London: Routledge, 2006), 60.

18. Fang Chao-ying, "Sunu," in *Eminent Chinese*, 693.

19. Fang Chao-ying, "Yin-t'ang," in *Eminent Chinese*, 928–29; Lo-shu Fu, *A Documentary Chronicle of Sino-Western Relations (1644–1820)* (Tucson: University of Arizona Press, 1966), 145–47; 509; Fr. Mourão's deposition to the Board of Justice of July 21, 1726, is translated in Antonio Sisto Rosso, OFM, *Apostolic Legations to China of the Eighteenth Century* (South Pasadena, CA: Perkins, 1948), 407–18.

20. Albert Chan, SJ, *Chinese Books and Documents in the Jesuit Archives in Rome: A Descriptive Catalogue. Japonica-Sinica I-IV* (Armonk, NY: M. E. Sharpe, 2002), 496–98; Lo-shu Fu, *Documentary Chronicle*, 145–47; 509.

21. Laamann, *Christian Heretics*, 60.

22. D. E. Mungello, *The Silencing of the Jesuit Figurist Joseph de Prémare in Eighteenth-Century China* (Lanham, MD: Lexington Books, 2019), 9–11.

23. See D. E. Mungello, *Leibniz and Confucianism: The Search for Accord* (Honolulu: University of Hawai'i Press, 1977), 39–68.

24. Menegon, *Ancestors, Virgins, and Friars*, 119–20.

25. *Archivum Romanum Societatis Iesu*, JapSin 168; 186–87. There is a brief identifying Latin notation dated 9/8/1912 added to the document by the archivist Fr. Léon Wieger, SJ (1856–1933).

26. Mungello, *Silencing*, 46–53.

27. Mungello, *Silencing*, 27–30.

28. Louis Le Comte, SJ, *Nouveaux mémoires sur l'état présent de la Chine* (Paris: Jean Anisson, 1697), II, 291.

29. Antoine Thomas, SJ, in a letter dated November 4, 1700, from Beijing to Thomas-Ignace Dunin-Szpot (*JapSin* 105 II, f.), 412.

30. Nicolas Standaert, *Handbook of Christianity in China*, vol. 1 (Leiden: Brill, 2001), 380–86.

31. Johannes Beckmann, "Die Lage der katholischen Missionen in China um 1815," *Neue Zeitschrift für Missionswissenschaft* 2 (1946): 221–23.

32. Kenneth Scott Latourette, *A History of Christian Missions in China* (London: Society for Promoting Christian Knowledge, 1929), 156. Cf. the discussion of the number of Christians in China in Standaert, *Handbook*, 380–86.

33. Standaert, *Handbook*, 386–91.

34. Anonymous manuscript, "Gesheng tang zhi" 各省堂誌 (A record of churches in each province), in *Xujiahu cang shulou Ming-Qing Tianzhujiao wenxian* 徐家匯藏書僂明清天主教文獻 (Chinese Christian Texts from the Zikawei Library), edited by Nicolas Standaert, Adrian Dudink, Huang Yilong, and Chu Pingyi. 5 vols. (Taipei: Fang chi 方濟 Publishers, 1996), 4: 1837–1841.

35. Standaert, *Handbook*, 562–63.

36. A recently published article by Ambrose Mong accurately blames the failure of Chinese missions on the failure to form a native clergy, but fails to take note of the eighteenth-century efforts to create Chinese priests that did occur. See Ambrose Mong, "Catholic Missions in China: Failure to Form a Native Clergy," *International Journal for the Study of the Christian Church* 19, no. 1 (2019): 30–43.

37. Beckmann, "Die Lage," 223.

38. Joseph Dehergne, SJ, "La Mission de Pékin vers 1700," *Archivum Historicum Societatis Iesu* 22 (1953): 314–15.

39. Beckmann, "Die Lage," 219.

40. Huang Xiaojuan 黃曉鵑, "Christian Communities and Alternative Devotions in China, 1780–1860" (PhD diss., Princeton University, 2006), 237.

41. Beckmann, "Die Lage," 221.

42. Menegon, *Ancestors, Virgins, and Friars*, 301–4.

43. Beckmann, "Die Lage," 220–21.

44. Jeroom J. Heyndricks, CICM, "Beijing und der Heilige Stuhl—auf der Suche nach einer gemeinsamen Basis: Zwei verwundete Partner im Dialog," *China Heute* 38, no. 3 (2019): 170–83.

Chapter Two

Matteo Ripa's Attempt to Establish a School for Chinese Priests in China

FR. MATTEO RIPA'S SPIRITUAL VISION

On April 5, 1746, two weeks after the death of Father Matteo Ripa, the Chinese seminarian Paolo Cai, the lay brothers Baldassarre Zeola and Domenico Imparato, and others carried the coffin of Father Ripa into a church in Naples.[1] The pavement in front of the high altar had been broken up to construct a sepulcher for his body, which had been placed in a wooden coffin lined with lead. Cai carried the key to the casket, which he opened. They found Ripa's body to be as fresh and handsome as it had been when he died. They touched the skin of his hands and throat and found them to be soft and flexible. Instead of the foul odor of decomposition, a pleasant odor came from his body that inspired their devotion and affection.[2] Then they rearranged the coffin and locked it with the key in preparation for the funeral.

Paolo Cai's Chinese name was Cai Wenan 蔡文安 and he was born in Longxi 龍溪 in Fujian province in 1720.[3] In March 1739 he entered the Chinese College at Naples.[4] In the following year he made his five vows to the Holy Congregation: poverty, obedience, ascent to the priesthood, serving in a foreign mission, and remaining in the Holy Foundation until death while not professing another religion or congregation.[5] He matriculated as the tenth Chinese student to enter the College.[6] Between the years 1732 and 1887, 106 Chinese students were trained as missionary-priests at the Chinese College in Naples.[7] Approximately ninety of them became priests and about eighty returned to China.[8] Only a few remained in Europe.

The founder of the Chinese College, Matteo Ripa (Ma Guoxian 馬國賢), was born in 1682 at Eboli, a small village south of Naples. He came from an obscure bourgeois family of five brothers and one sister. His father was a physician and his mother died when he was four years old. He was sent to Naples at the age of fifteen to continue his studies. In 1700, at the age of eighteen, he felt the first call from God to serve as a priest. Later in life, during the years 1743–1746, he wrote about this experience in his five-volume *Giornale*.[9] In the version edited and published in 1832 by the Holy Family priests with an aim toward initiating his canonization process, Ripa wrote:

> In the auspicious and happy year of the Lord 1700, when I was eighteen, I received the first impulse from God to pursue holy work. I do not think I could describe in detail the scarcely Christian life that I was living at that time, without shocking the young, who in their time should read this account, . . . but neither do I want to pass it by in complete silence, nor to deprive God the glory. . . . I found myself then immersed in a thousand vices.[10]

Ripa amplified on this experience in the following pages:

> In the year 1700, as I was strolling one day about the streets of Naples in search of amusement, I came to the open space before the Viceregal Palace just at the moment when a Franciscan friar, mounted on a bench, began to address the people. I was only eighteen; but though so young, I was then leading a life which I could scarcely describe without shocking the reader.
>
> Amid all my vices, however, it was fortunate for me that I always listened with pleasure to religious discourses, not indeed to derive any profit or instruction from them, but merely out of curiosity. The preacher took for his text these words of the prophet Amos, "For three transgressions of Damascus, and for four, I will not turn away the punishment thereof";[11] and he proved that there were a certain number of sins which God would forgive, but that beyond that number there is no salvation for anyone. . . . I perceived the dangerous path I was treading; and methought I saw God himself menacing me from above, while below the torments of hell lay ready to receive me. . . . Full of repentance, I resolved to devote the remainder of my life entirely to his service.[12]

Ripa's conversion experience at Naples in 1700 shaped his actions throughout his life. The experience transformed him into a man of God with a clear vision. While the experience reinforced his uncompromising tendencies, it also channeled them into a goal that transcended his personal desires. It guided his revelation that the difficulties of European missionaries in converting Chinese demanded a fundamental change in missionizing. In anticipating the eventual impediments created by Europeans dominating the priesthood in China, he decided that it was necessary to bring Chinese students to Naples to train them for the priesthood and then return them to China.[13] In an age long before the advent of international students, it was a monumental undertaking that was impeded not only by skeptical clerics, but also by certain Chinese seminarians who had difficulty living and studying for years in Europe before returning to China.

However, Ripa's approach also suffered from some fundamental flaws. In aligning himself so closely with the papal legate Tournon and those opposed to allowing Chinese to combine ancestral rites with being Christian, he resisted the need of Rome to transcend European provincialism and expand Catholicism into a truly universal religion. This is the developing process that has continued down to the present time in the effort to reconcile the Christian faith with Chinese political and cultural patterns. Ripa also suffered from a rigidity in imposing European forms of discipline on his Chinese seminarians. Some of his students were able to meld their wishes with those of Ripa, but others had more difficulty doing so and this created clashes. Most, but not all, of these conflicts were resolved, leaving in the case of one seminarian a trail of sorrow.

Given the culture of Naples and Ripa's later personal struggles, there is a strong possibility that one of the sins Ripa was repenting of in 1700 was homosexual activity.[14] In later life he appears to have sublimated his homosexual desires into the education of Chinese boys for the priesthood. Apart from his youthful sins, there is evidence of a homosexual relationship with another priest when he was twenty-six years old. In China, there was slander based on his association with his students in a cultural context that involved the tradition of *dan* 旦 (actor-escort ephebes). Finally there was the obsessive turmoil of his relationship with Lucio Wu. Ripa became a dedicated and even charismatic figure who often struggled with humility. After seminary training and consecration as a priest, he departed in 1707 for missionary work in China. He almost did not go.

RIPA'S JOURNEY TO CHINA

Unlike earlier missionaries sent to China who were organized by religious orders, such as the Jesuits or Dominicans, Ripa's group was sponsored by the Sacred Congregation for the Propagation of the Faith (*Sacra Congregatio de Propaganda Fide*) (*Tianzhujiao budao hui* 天主教布道會). Propaganda Fide had been created in 1622 to free missionary activity from the control of the Iberian monarchies and to centralize missionary administration in Rome. It consisted of a mixture of secular priests, like Ripa, as well as priests from various religious orders. A second difference between Ripa's group and earlier missionaries is that they embarked from London on a ship of the British East India Company rather than from Lisbon.[15] London was chosen because Propaganda Fide sought to avoid the influence of the Portuguese *Padroado* (as well as the related Spanish *Patronato real*), which was a royal monopoly over missionary passages that had been granted to the Portuguese monarchs by Pope Alexander VI in 1493. The beginning of the journey occurred on October 8, 1707, when Ripa and a group of missionaries knelt at the feet of Pope Clement XI to kiss him and receive his holy and paternal benediction.[16] They departed from Rome on October 13, 1707.

The mission group consisted of six members. The head of the mission was Fr. Onorato Funari, about forty-one years old, a secular priest from Fondi, but currently the *paroco* (parish priest) of San Giovanni dei Fiorentini in Rome.[17] The second eldest member of the group was Fr. Guillaume Bonjour Favre (Fabbri) (Shan Yaozhan 山遙瞻), about forty years old, an Augustinian from the city of Tolosa. The third member was Fr. Giuseppe Cerù (Pang Kexiu 龐克修) from Lucca, about thirty-six years old, of the tonsured minors (order of Franciscans). The fourth member was Domenico Perrone (Guo Zhongchuan 郭中傳), about thirty-six years old, a Neapolitan of the order of the Mother of God. The fifth member was Gennaro Amodei (Ren Zhangchen 任掌晨), twenty-six, a secular priest from San Marco Argentano in Calabria. Finally, there was Ripa, twenty-six, a secular priest from the area of Eboli, in the diocese of Salerno.

Frs. Amodei and Ripa had been acquainted since at least 1705 when they traveled together from Naples to Rome. Ripa described Amodei as stronger than him in spirit, but weaker in body.[18] Amodei's frailty forced him to take a carriage to Rome rather than walk. His frailty was exacerbated by his ascetic tendencies. Ripa said he was "endowed by the Lord with a truly solid spirit, loving all virtue, especially purity, that he cultivated with the greatest vigilance."[19] But his tendency to fast on bread and water and practice other mortifications of the flesh was so extreme that he was often too weak to study and perform necessary acts. Because of questions over whether he was well enough to make the missionary trip to China, Amodei wrote to Cardinal Giuseppe Sagripanti, prefect of Propaganda Fide, arguing that he should not be excluded over fear of his frail constitution and poor health because God was calling him to be an apostle and God in his omnipotence would give him the strength to fulfill his ministry.[20] The cardinal prefect was so impressed by Amodei's letter that he read it to Pope Clement XI, who was equally impressed and ordered that Amodei be included in the mission.

The group departed Rome and passed through Bologna on the way northward to London. On the morning of November 13, 1707, in the city of Bressanone, near Trento, they were saying mass in a church of the Capuchin fathers. Fr. Funari, who had just purified the chalice during the Eucharist, suddenly collapsed from a stroke.[21] Advised by a physician to leave the cold air of the Alps, Funari left the mission and returned to Rome. Funari's misfortune would later turn out to be auspicious for Ripa and Amodei.

The group traveled northward overland, reaching Innsbruck on November 15, then on to Frankfurt, and then by water to Cologne. In Cologne they received a puzzling letter from the secretary of state in Rome stating that the British East India vessel leaving London could only accommodate four of them and that consequently, Ripa and Amodei were ordered back to Rome.[22] Ripa and Amodei suspected there was another reason for their recall. What had happened was that their companion Fr. Favre had accused Ripa and Amodei of engaging in a homosexual relationship.[23] The details are scanty because such sexual relations at the time were *peccatum non nominandum inter Christianos* (the sin unmentionable among Christians), and even less mentionable among celibate priests. Even the abridged translation of Ripa's account by Fortunato Prandi published in 1846 reflects this prudery by not specifying that the accusation involved homosexual relations and instead refers only to "calumnious reports."[24] However, Ripa was deeply and forever seared by the accusation.

The situation was unsettled. Fr. Funari, who had returned to Rome because of his stroke, initially suggested that Ripa continue to London while Amodei returned to Rome. Then Ripa and Amodei were ordered to remain behind in Cologne until their status was clarified. When the other three members of the mission—Favre, Cerù, and Perrone—were consulted about a solution, they could not agree. When Amodei asked Ripa for his opinion on what they should do, Ripa said that they should obey blindly, remitting their cause entirely to God, while Amodei believed they should defend themselves.[25] Ripa was cast into intense despair. His desire to proceed to China was so great that the thought of having the mission denied to him caused him to weep constantly and to withdraw from his companions, abruptly leaving their dining table. Meanwhile Fr. Funari was working on their behalf in Rome to dissipate the cloud of suspicion hanging over them. He succeeded and eventually a letter came from Rome allowing them to rejoin the mission to China.[26] Consequently, Ripa and Amodei departed Cologne for Holland on December 23, rejoining the other three members of their mission and then traveling from Rotterdam to England.

Because of Protestant hostility to Catholicism, they were forced to travel under false names and to wear nonclerical clothing. In London they applied for passage with the British East India Company. However, because of the company's prohibition on carrying Catholic missionaries on its ships, it was necessary for them to assume nonpriestly identities.[27] They secured passage on the *Donegal*, a small ship only forty paces in length and ten paces in width, with a capacity of 180 tons.[28] They boarded the ship on February 11, 1708, but they had to remain on board for four months until the ship departed in

May. Conditions on board were very crowded and Ripa was forced to sleep in a makeshift bed over the powder bin. During the delay, the wives of the officers made conjugal visits, which Ripa was compelled, to his despair, to observe at close proximity.

Finally the *Donegal* departed, sailing southward in the Atlantic Ocean and came close to the shore of Brazil before turning eastward to the Cape of Good Hope, arriving in September.[29] From the Cape of Good Hope they sailed on to Bengal, arriving in February 1709.[30] There the missionaries changed ships, sailing on the *San Lorenzo* to Malacca.[31] In Malacca they switched ships to the *Nostra Signora di Cadalup* to sail to Manila, where they arrived in June.[32] In Manila the group of five missionaries was joined by Fr. Teodorico Pedrini, CM (De Like 德理格, 1671–1746).[33] The last leg of their exhausting sea journey brought them to Macau (see figure 2.1). After a land and sea journey lasting more than two years, their ship dropped anchor near an offshore island on January 6, 1710.[34]

Figure 2.1. Macau, unknown artist. Oil on canvas, 18th century. Maritime Museum Prins Hendrik, Rotterdam, The Netherlands.
Source: Universal Images Group/Art Resource, New York.

RIPA AT THE CHINESE COURT

On January 7, Fr. Pedrini, disguised as a captain, went ashore and made contact with assistants of the papal legate Carolus Thomas Maillard de Tournon (Duoluo 鐸羅), whose legation to the court of the Kangxi emperor had ended so disastrously that the emperor had confined him to house arrest in Macau.[35] After dusk on that same day, Pedrini and the other five missionaries secretly visited Tournon, bringing correspondence from the pope and the elevating cardinal's red biretta (square cap) for him. As a representative of the pope, Tournon clearly demonstrated through his Eurocentrism how far the Catholic Church was from becoming a truly universal church. He is one of the most controversial figures in the history of Christianity in China because of his rigid condemnation of Chinese ancestral and Confucian rites. By intensifying the Rites Controversy, he inflicted enormous damage on the development of the Church in China. Tournon's imperious character and inability to compromise enraged the emperor and reversed his previous tolerance of Christianity in China. Ripa was clearly an advocate of Tournon's position and spoke admiringly of the legate. This would foster hostility between Ripa and the Jesuits, who were Tournon's greatest opponents. When Ripa saw Tournon, the latter was visibly ill and died five months later, on June 8, at the age of forty-one.[36]

The arrival of six new missionaries increased suspicion among Chinese officials. In Guangzhou (Canton), the viceroy of Guangdong and Guangxi provinces, Guo Shilong 郭世隆 (1645–1716), ordered that an edict be posted at the gate of the legate's residence in Macau, commanding all Chinese serving there as domestics to depart within two days.[37] On January 25, five officials came on the pretext of visiting the new arrivals. One of the new arrivals, Fr. Favre, was residing in the convent of the Augustinian fathers and had to be brought to the legate's residence. The officials proceeded to interrogate the new arrivals individually, recording their responses to questions asking from where they had come, who had commanded them, on what ship, and for what purpose. After the officials departed, Chinese soldiers remained as guards in front of the house, where a hut was constructed for their use. Most of the Europeans, including the papal legate Tournon, were prohibited from leaving the house.

On March 4, Tournon sent a letter composed in Italian with a Chinese translation to the emperor by way of the viceroy of Guangzhou, informing him of his promotion to the cardinalate and of the arrival of the six missionaries. However, obtaining permission for the missionaries to enter China was a problem. Because the Kangxi emperor had indicated an interest in obtaining the service of Europeans trained in the arts and sciences, Tournon conveyed that three of the missionaries were skilled in the fields of mathematics (Fr. Favre), music (Fr. Pedrini), and painting (Fr. Ripa) and he offered them to the emperor's service.[38] The emperor responded favorably and on November 5, 1710, Ripa received the news that the emperor had summoned the three of them along with two Jesuit mathematicians, the German Fr. Franz Thilisch (Tillisch), SJ, and the Portuguese João Cardoso, SJ, to Beijing.[39]

Ripa was not pleased to be assigned artistic rather than missionary work, but he accepted that Tournon had offered him as a court artist in order to secure his place in China. They departed from Guangzhou on November 27 and arrived in Beijing on February 5, 1711, where they were received by the emperor at the imperial palace.[40] Ripa quickly adapted to living at the court. He described how on May 4, 1711, he joined the entourage following the Kangxi emperor to the imperial villa outside Beijing for a five-day celebration of the emperor's birthday.[41] The Europeans, along with the court grandees, made prostrations and joined in the celebratory meal.

On April 17, 1711, the Emperor asked if the skills of Pedrini in music, Thilisch in mathematics, and Ripa in painting extended to other sciences or arts.[42] Ripa had limited knowledge of optical science (perspective), but he also had some knowledge of engraving on copper sheets for printing and he volunteered his services although he was not very experienced in the art.[43] The emperor was interested in the process Ripa used in covering the copperplate with black varnish prior to engraving it and was eager to see Ripa engrave a Chinese painting.[44] Initially Ripa was assigned to the workshop of the court artists and craftsmen in the Forbidden City (Zijincheng 紫禁城) palace in the center of Beijing, where seven Chinese artists were being trained in oil painting by the Italian Giovanni Gherardi (1655–ca. 1723).[45] Although the emperor was fascinated by the European techniques of perspective, he was eager to make use of the European technique of engraving and soon conceived of plans for Ripa to develop engraving. Ripa originally regarded himself as more of a painter than an engraver, but apart from some sketches of fish, birds, and plants made on board the ship as he was traveling toward the Cape of Good Hope in 1708, no paintings by Ripa are known to have survived.[46] After about two weeks in the Forbidden City studio, he was moved to the imperial villa about four miles northwest of Beijing called the Garden of Joyful Spring (*Changchunyuan* 暢春園). The famous Yuanmingyuan 圓明園 (Garden of Perfect Clarity, sometimes called the Old Summer Palace), would later be built on adjacent land to the north of the Garden of Joyful Spring.[47] Ripa was lodged in a mansion belonging to one of the emperor's uncles. This new residence gave him access to enter the imperial residence to work in one of its workshops.

On May 23 Ripa had finished engraving a Chinese landscape and it was immediately carried, along with the original Chinese work, to the emperor for his inspection. The emperor was fascinated by the similarity between the original and the engraved reproduction. Ripa noted that the Chinese had not previously engraved on metal, but rather reproduced works by pasting drawings of the originals on wood blocks, which were then engraved and used in printing.

In June, Ripa arrived at the emperor's summer retreat in Rehe 熱河 (now Chengde 承德), commonly referred to in European writings as Jehol. The summer capital at Rehe had first been established by the Manchu founder Dorgon in 1650.[48] Weary of the humid heat of Beijing summers, Dorgon began building a summer capital in the Yan Mountains, approximately 150 miles northeast of Beijing. Rehe provided not only an escape from the Beijing heat, but also a political base from which to govern the multiethnic Qing dynasty. The Kangxi emperor's victories over the Eleuth Mongol competitor Galdan in the 1690s led him to continue the earlier construction of the palace at Rehe. When Ripa arrived in Rehe, he performed the *koutou* "bowing three times with my head to the earth" before the emperor and thanked the emperor for having sent a surgeon to help him recover from a fall from his horse.[49]

The emperor assigned Ripa the task of engraving in copper using aquafortis (nitric acid). Ripa had received one lesson in copperplate engraving from an artisan using aquafortis in Rome and, drawing from that experience, he asked for the ingredients: "white and strong vinegar, green copper, and sal ammoniac [ammonium chloride]."[50] The sal ammoniac, which was made from camel urine, was readily available. However, the Chinese vinegar was inadequate because, Ripa said, it was not made from grape wine, as in Europe. Ripa's initial prints were too pale due to the inadequate aquafortis, to the shallow lines inscribed, and to the poor quality of the ink; however, he eventually succeeded in producing good specimens.

The emperor's stays at the summer retreat in Rehe usually lasted five months, from May through September. The emperor ordered Ripa to engrave the thirty-six views of Rehe from the woodcut engravings being produced by numerous artists in the imperial printing office *Wuyingdian* 武英殿, based on the paintings of the court artist Shen Yu 沈喻.[51] The Kangxi emperor had chosen thirty-six views of the palaces at Rehe to commemorate his sixtieth birthday, which would occur in the spring of 1713. He wrote poems to accompany each of the paintings. The imperial artisan Zhu Gui 朱圭 engraved thirty-six woodcuts of these images, poems, and commentary, which were printed in 1713. These Chinese woodcuts constituted an imperial publication titled "The Emperor's Poems on the Thirty-Six Views at Bishu Shanzhuang"

(*Yuzhi Bishu shanzhuang sanshiliu jing shi* 御制避暑山莊三十六景詩). From this collection Ripa produced the *Views of Rehe* as an album of thirty-six copperplate engravings of views of the Kangxi emperor's "Mountain Retreat from the Summer Heat" (*Bishu Shanzhuang* 避暑山莊).[52] (One of these engravings is reproduced in figure 2.2.)

Figure 2.2. Matteo Ripa, after Shen Yu. "Watching the Fish from Rocky Outcrop," 1711–1713, copperplate engraving. From *Thirty-Six Views of Jehol*. London, British Museum.
Source: The Trustees of the British Museum/Art Resource, New York.

When Ripa accompanied the Kangxi emperor to Rehe in the summer of 1712, the emperor praised several of his prints as "treasures" (*baobei* 寶貝).[53] In August 1712 the emperor assigned Ripa the task of engraving Jesuit maps of his realm and assigned him two apprentices who would learn from him the art of copperplate engraving, commanding that they not share this knowledge with others.[54] One of these apprentices was Zhang Kui 張奎, whose name appears on the margins of several engravings.[55] Ripa was on very hostile terms with the Jesuits and although he mentioned the Jesuit contributions to the atlas, he failed to give them full credit for their surveys. He also diminished their contribution by saying that the emperor appointed his Propaganda Fide colleague Fr. Favre and the Jesuit Pierre Jartoux to make a geographical map of Manchuria as a follow-up to earlier Jesuit efforts.[56] In fact, this monumental atlas was based almost entirely on the Jesuit surveys of 1708–1718.[57]

Ripa described the enormous costs involved in this vast mapping project, which attests to the wealth of the early Qing empire. He explained that it involved not only the vast empire of China and Manchuria, but also thirty other contiguous realms.[58] Only Korea and Tibet were limited in delineation. Korea proved to be particularly difficult to map because although technically a tributary of China, the Koreans limited the entry of foreigners into their realm, and particularly European surveyors. Instead, the Jesuits were forced to train Manchu officials who substituted for them in surveying Korean terrain. The resulting *Huangyu quanlan tu* 皇輿全覽圖 (Complete Map of the Empire) was printed in several editions. One was in woodblock. Another edition was in copperplate in forty-four plates, produced in 1719 by Ripa at the emperor's request. Ripa described the personal interest of the Kangxi emperor in immediately seeing the results of this process in which Ripa painted a black varnish on a copper sheet before copying the map onto the sheets and then engraving them with aquafortis.[59]

RIPA'S FIRST SCHOOL FOR BOYS

The sensibility of eighteenth-century Catholics differed from our modern sensibility. This was as true for European missionaries like Matteo Ripa as it was for Chinese converts like Giovanni Evangelista Yin. This earlier sensibility was reflected in Ripa's students touching and absorbing the scent of his dead body in the casket. Our modern sensibility tends to regard such acts as morbid and repellent. Our feelings are quite different from Ripa's students. For them the touch and scent of Ripa's dead body evoked feelings of love, respect, and inspiration. The presence of a fragrant scent at the time of death was commonly associated with saintliness. Repeatedly in his journals, Ripa described the tendency of males to shed prolonged tears over disappointments. The shedding of tears was linked to spirituality. Those who lived a more religious life were often prone to weeping. Perhaps this reflected a greater sensitivity to sorrow in the world in which they lived. Physical strength in this earlier sensibility was not an athletically obsessed goal as in our modern sensibility, but rather a practical means to attain spiritual goals. The sacrifice of one's health was highly regarded as a way to achieve greater love and service to God. A diet of bread and water and other bodily mortifications harmed the body of Ripa's companion, Amodei, while developing his spirituality. Conversely, the refusal of the student Lucio Wu to submit to the dietary mortifications involved in his punishment for fleeing from the Chinese College reflected a lack of spiritual development that would lead, ultimately, to his long imprisonment and tragic end.

Ripa's effort to develop a native priesthood began at the end of 1714 in China when he received his first youth to educate.[60] According to the records of Ripa and the Chinese College in Naples, this first student's name was Giovanni Battista Kou (Gu Ruohan 谷若翰, 1701–1763).[61] In 1900, his tombstone was discovered in a diocesan cemetery in Beijing engraved with the variant name of Gu Wenyao 谷文耀, which was probably his given name while Gu Ruohan was his baptismal name.[62] Gu was the son of Christian parents and was baptized by Ripa on June 24, 1714, when he was fourteen years old.[63] He was born in Xuntian 順天 in Zhili 直隸 province.[64] When Ripa met him, he was living in the town of Gubeikou 古北口, located near the Great Wall about one hundred miles north of Beijing. It was close to the route through which Ripa passed while traveling in the Kangxi emperor's annual summer procession to and from the imperial retreat at Rehe. There was a community of about 250 Christians in Gubeikou and several devout families "gave their sons to God" to study with Ripa and prepare for the priesthood. Ripa emphasized that he received Gu with the full consent of his parents and took him to Tartaria (Tartary). The map of China in Martino Martini's *Novus Atlas Sinensis* (1655) indicates that the name Tartary was then applied to a vast unknown area stretching across northern Asia. Ripa's reference was to a subdivision of Tartary that approximated Manchuria.

The next student Ripa received was Giovanni Evangelista Yin (Yin Ruowang 殷若望, 1705–1735), who was born in Gu'an 固安 in Zhili province. Yin would become one of the Chinese students Ripa loved most. He wrote more about Yin than about any other student, except for the disastrous Lucio V (Wu Lujue 吳露爵, 1713–1763), and he expressed the greatest sadness at Yin's tragic death. The qualities that made Yin such an admirable figure were spiritual—physically he was weak. That did not matter to Ripa, for whom physical strength was a secondary consideration. Far more important was the willingness to exhaust one's physical strength in the pursuit of a spiritual goal, which is exactly what Yin ended up doing. When his parents tried to withdraw Yin from Ripa's school in 1720 at the age of fifteen, Yin engaged in a form of passive resistance by refusing to eat and became so weak that his family withdrew their demand in the face of his moral strength. Unlike the stoic hero Guan Yu of the famous Chinese folk novel *Romance of the Three Kingdoms* (*Sanguozhi yanyi* 三國志演義), who was famous for his lack of emotional display, Yin tended at times to be emotional and tearful. He voiced his desire to shed his blood in martyrdom, but his body's strength was exhausted on the path to that goal.

Ripa remained in Gubeikou until June 10 to hear confessions and to receive two more youths for educating. (A student from Beijing named Giuseppe was received by Ripa on April 14, 1719, but he left or was withdrawn by his parents soon afterward.)[65] Ripa arrived at Rehe with four Chinese youths and had a room in his lodgings partitioned into five small cubicles, each with a bed and curtain in front. Four of these cubicles were occupied by individual students and the fifth was occupied by Tommaso Wu (Wu Duomo 吳多默), "a teacher of the letters and sciences of China," who served as the boys' tutor.[66] Ripa also described Wu as "*mio scrivano, e catechista*" (my scribe and catechist).[67] The term *catechist* is a general term that covers several different roles played by trusted laypersons in China. *Chuandaoyuan* 傳道員 referred to a catechist in the sense of a religious teacher. A catechist with a more literate role as a secretary was called a *xianggong* 相公. European missionaries in China typically had such aides to assist them, particularly in speaking and writing Chinese.

When they returned to Beijing, the students and tutor were housed in Ripa's lodgings in the *Changchunyuan* (Garden of Joyful Spring), an imperial setting that was a source of prestige as well as problems to the families of the students studying there. The school was funded by yearly contributions from Ripa's brothers and other friends in Europe.[68] He invested this money in buying land, which yielded 12 percent interest per year, and houses, which yielded 18 percent per year. The principal accrued every year, reaching the sum of more than 250 Neapolitan ducats, which amounted to slightly less than 250 *taels*.[69] A tael represented uncoined silver money while the ducat was a coin. One tael (*liang* 兩) weighed 1.1 ounce or 31.25 grams.[70] It was unminted currency that contained approximately 575 grains of silver (fineness 1,000) or 1 ounce of silver, but with local variations.[71]

Ripa's school was frowned upon by certain scholar-officials as well as missionaries at the politicized and intrigue-filled court in Beijing. Critics described the room in which the boys stayed as a "scandalous harem for Gentiles and Christians."[72] One critic used purple prose in describing Ripa as emitting "an odor so depraved" that even Ripa himself might be made fetid by the intolerable scent. (Whereas a good scent was thought by Catholics to convey moral purity and saintliness, an offensive odor was thought to convey immorality and evil.) In 1765, forty-five years after these events, Fr. Filippo Huang, who was part of Ripa's group of earliest students, would note that this rumor of Ripa's homosexuality was actually voiced in a printed libel in

Latin that said, "Ripa supports so many of those youths, so that he can abuse them" (*Abbas Ripa in tantum alit illos juvenes, ut quibus possit abuti, etc.*).[73] What gave the accusation a degree of plausibility was the Chinese tradition of boy-actors that then flourished in the theater district in Beijing. Many of these *dan* 旦 (young men who played female roles in Chinese opera) also worked as escort-prostitutes and were organized into acting-escort companies by handlers who obtained the boys at a very young age from their parents for a fee.[74] These boys were trained in the art of imitating females and being companions for hire to men.

The Kangxi emperor, out of his concern for the debilitating effect boy actor-escorts might have on the martial prowess of the elite Manchu bannermen, had banned them from the Inner City of Beijing in 1671, but they were relocated to the theater district just to the south of the Qianmen Gate, where the boy-actors continued to be favorites of the scholar-officials. The boy-actors were exploited by their handlers and then cast off when their youthful features faded. Critics of Ripa's school implied that he was exploiting his pupils in a similar fashion. Others tried persuasion rather than threats to get Ripa to dismantle the school and warned of the consequences if the rumors of him abusing his students should reach the emperor's ears.[75]

Ripa was not easily intimidated and he painstakingly rebutted the accusations of sexual exploitation. He realized the seriousness of the charge because upon returning from Rehe he had seen proof of the Kangxi emperor's hostility toward homosexuality in a terrifying public display at the Garden of Joyful Spring near Beijing in 1712.[76] The court had been assembled in the street beside this imperial villa with eight high-ranking Manchu officials kneeling bareheaded with their hands tied behind their backs. Standing nearby were the imperial sons, headed by the crown prince, Yinreng 胤礽 (1674–1725), with his head still covered and with his hands tied in front of him, two kneeling eunuchs, and an important Manchu official kneeling bareheaded with his hands tied behind his back. The emperor was carried in a covered sedan chair from his apartments to the scene. Ripa described him as "enraged like a tiger, speaking harsh words and insulting this assembled group with a long admonition."[77]

Ripa said the crown prince was accused of various forms of disloyalty and misbehavior, including being "a sodomite, the most abominating of the laws of China" (*soddomita, abbominandosi sommamente dale leggi di Cina*).[78] (The European taint surrounding the word *soddomita* later fused with the Victorian sensibilities of the nineteenth century and caused Fortunato Prandi's 1844 translation of the word *soddomita* to be euphemized to "being addicted to an atrocious offense.")[79] In fact, Ripa's statement is misleading. It is more reflective of the attitudes of Beijing court circles than of life in China outside of the court. The early Manchu rulers preferred living in a more bucolic atmosphere to the urban environment of the Ming Forbidden City palace (Zi-jincheng 紫禁城) at the center of Beijing. They spent October to April at the Garden of Joyful Spring four miles to the northwest of the Forbidden City and May to September at the summer palace at Rehe. Consequently, Ripa, who lived in the emperor's palace, was exposed to a greater Manchu influence and appears to have been less familiar with Chinese culture than he would have experienced had he lived outside of the royal palace.

At the time of the emperor's public condemnation of the heir apparent in 1712 for practicing sodomy, homoeroticism was in vogue among Chinese officials, scholars, and merchants who were frequenting the boy actor-escorts in the entertainment district located only 2 kilometers (1¼ miles) due south of the Forbidden City palace in Beijing. The aversion to sodomy was far stronger among the Manchus than among the Chinese. This was particularly true of earlier Manchu rulers, such as the Kangxi emperor, who were closer to the traditional nomadic culture of the Jurchen people in Manchuria. The Manchu sensibility reflected the nomadic warriors' values that merged strength with procreative sexuality while the more urbanized, less muscular sensibility of the Chinese literati emphasized aesthetic sensitivity in which sexuality was both procreative and aestheticized. Gradually, as the Manchus became Sinicized, their intense aversion to Chinese cultural practices like sodomy would be tempered.

Yinreng's mother was a niece of the emperor's powerful uncle Songgotu and had died giving birth to Yinreng in 1674. Yinreng had been declared heir apparent in 1676 and had been raised with that special status. The emperor showed him particular favor and taught him to read while prominent officials tutored him.[80] He became an able horseman and archer. When the Kangxi emperor led campaigns against the Eleuths in 1696 and 1697, he named Yinreng regent to oversee affairs in Beijing. However, rumors of undisciplined and immoral behavior in Yinreng's palace emerged, which led to the emperor's execution of palace cooks and servants.[81] In 1703, when rumors of Yinreng's associations with threatening political figures, including Songgotu, reached the emperor's ears, Songgotu was imprisoned. In 1705 the emperor heard that children were being illegally purchased in Suzhou and brought to Beijing. Qing dynasty homoeroticism favored boys from the south (Lower Yangzi River region) who were valued in Beijing for their delicate frames.[82] Some of these youths were used for sexual purposes and linked to Yinreng.

The emperor's anger toward Yinreng was mixed with his personal affection in a way that intensified his reaction to this disappointing son and led to the public assembly that Ripa witnessed in 1712 at which Yinreng was accused of being "dissolute, tyrannical, brutal, debauched."[83] Consequently, Yinreng was dismissed as heir apparent and the six sons of Songgotu were executed. The intensity of his reaction to Yinreng's debauchery was tied to the emperor's view of bodily purity and its relationship to moral authority. He explained his anger to senior Manchu officials by saying: "Over the years I have read the histories and have always been very careful not to let women from outside wander in and out of the palace. Nor have I let pretty young boys wait upon me. I keep my body pure."[84]

After hearing that his eldest son Yinti had hired lamas to cast spells on Yinreng, the emperor's lingering fatherly affection led him to consider that Yinreng's misbehavior might have been due to demonic possession.[85] Consequently, he had pardoned Yinreng and restored him to the position of heir apparent in 1709. However, Yinreng's behavior did not improve and in 1712, he was again demoted and placed in confinement, where he remained until his death in 1725.[86] Ripa commented that Yinreng was still in custody when he left China and lamented that Yinreng had been equal to the Kangxi emperor in friendliness to Europeans.[87] When Yinreng's brother, Yinzhen 胤禛, ascended the throne in 1722 as the Yongzheng emperor, that friendliness was replaced by hostility.

OPPOSITION TO RIPA'S SCHOOL

After failing to convince Ripa to abandon his school, "Mandarins and others of the Imperial Court" tried to persuade Catholic parents at Gubeikou not to give Ripa their sons and also tried to convince some parents who had already sent their sons to Ripa to withdraw them from his school.[88] This effort gave rise to a family drama involving the parents of Giovanni Yin. Feigning illness, Giovanni's father sent Tommaso Yang, one of four Christian prefects of Gubeikou, to the imperial palace of the Garden of Joyful Spring to retrieve his son. He was accompanied by Giacomo Guo (Guo Yagu 郭雅谷? Guo Yage 郭雅歌?), who was retrieving his son Matteo Guo (Guo Matou 郭馬頭), who was also one of Ripa's students.[89] However, Giovanni did not want to return and argued, saying, "I am not a young boy of three or four years who can be tempted with a biscuit to remain in that school. I am of sufficient age; I am sixteen years old and able to distinguish good from bad. And because I know that the practices and customs of the school of Mr. Ripa are very good, I do not want to leave."[90]

Shortly afterward, Basilio Gu, the older brother of Giovanni Battista Gu (Gu Yaowen 谷耀文) (1701–1763), defended Ripa by saying, "It has been been six or seven years since my younger brother has been subject to the discipline of Mr. Ripa, and yet what bad has happened?"[91] At the beginning of the first month of the lunar new year, that is, in February 1720, the godfather of the scribe-teacher Tommaso Wu, named Cristofaro Li, a bachelor's degree holder from the town of Cian-Ciun-Iuen (?), came to the palace of the Garden of Joyful Spring and spoke to Tommaso. He said that the catechist Lorenzo Scy [Xi?] had warned him that Tommaso's life was in danger. The cause of the danger was the emperor's anger with Fr. Pedrini and the imperial threat to kill the missionary scribes like Tommaso. For this reason he urged Tommaso to immediately return to his home. Tommaso replied, "Life and death do not lie in the hands of men, but of God; even if I return to my native village, I would have to die."[92] Consequently, he refused to leave Ripa.

Nevertheless, the opposition to the school became so great that Ripa decided for the time being not to accept any new students. The student Matteo Guo departed with his father. Ripa had given his scribe Tommaso Wu permission to have his son Lucio Wu (Wu Lujue 吳露爵, 1713–1763) come to Beijing from his home in Jinshan 金山 in Jiangsu 江蘇 province to join the school, but later had second thoughts and had Tommaso write to cancel the invitation.[93] However, the letter arrived ten days after Lucio had left on a forty-day journey to Beijing. This turned out to be an ominous development because Lucio would become Ripa's "perpetual cross to bear" (*Questi è quell Lucio, ch'è stato sempre la mia croce*).[94]

After Ripa departed for Rehe to follow the emperor in 1720, he arrived at Gubeikou to rest overnight. Immediately he was greeted by a group of Christians including the father of Giovanni Yin, who asked for the return of his son.[95] This was an awkward and embarrassing request since the father had given Giovanni to God to be educated by Ripa for the priesthood. However, he said that an illness caused him to seek his son's return. Ripa released him to his father but was struck by Giovanni's great sadness and weeping. Of the three of them, only the father remained dry-eyed. The following morning when Ripa was preparing to leave for Rehe, Giovanni and his older brother came to confess and to wish him a good journey.[96] Giovanni's eyes were swollen from continual crying during the night. When Ripa asked if his father was really ill, Giovanni replied that he was not. His father had confessed the truth to him and that the real cause of his wish to withdraw Giovanni from the school was a letter he had received from Beijing, condemning Ripa's school. As soon as Giovanni had ended his confession, he uttered the form of the absolution and made in Ripa's hands a vow of perpetual chastity, expressing his intention to return to Ripa's school and to become a priest.[97]

The eighteenth-century Catholic sensibility regarded dreams as highly portentous indicators of an unseen and subconscious reality. Ripa related in his journal an event that had happened on the morning of March 26, earlier in the same year. At the school lodgings at the Garden of Joyful Spring, the teacher Tommaso Wu came to Ripa, saying that in the previous night, he had heard Giovanni Yin weeping and crying in a loud voice. Tommaso wakened him, but he continued to weep without consolation and refused to reveal the contents of his dream. Later, when Ripa spoke with him, Giovanni revealed he dreamed that during the upcoming journey of the students to Rehe, as they were passing through Gubeikou, his father stopped him and attempted to hold him back, but Giovanni fled. Then in the dream, his father suddenly fell on a bed and died. With his father's death, Giovanni was freed to continue to Rehe, but his mother grasped him by the arm and held him back. Her refusal to release him caused him to weep, but then suddenly he was freed and returned to the school. At that point Master Tommaso woke him from his dream.[98]

Now several months later, shortly after Giovanni said good-bye to Ripa in Gubeikou and returned to his home, his father suffered a fatal stroke (*apoplessia*).[99] Giovanni saw his dream as a shocking omen and his father's death as God opening a way for him to return to the school. However, as foretold in the dream, his mother would not allow him to leave, despite his entreaties. She had him fettered with iron chains to prevent him from fleeing. The sudden death of Giovanni's father brought fear to the hearts of the Christians in Gubeikou, who ascribed his death to his reneging on the promise of giving his son to God.[100] Among those affected was the father of Matteo Guo, who repented of his sin and sought to return his son to Ripa. Meanwhile, Giovanni withdrew from all contact and remained in his curtained bed where he was confined. He ate and drank only when his mother stood over him, commanding him to do so. She loved him and called in physicians, who could do nothing because, in Ripa's words, the illness resided "not in the body, but in the sick man's heart." Day by day, his weeping continued and he grew more emaciated. Finally in June, the family agreed by consensus that Giovanni should return to the school.[101] He was sent on a donkey to Rehe to rejoin his schoolmates, who joyfully welcomed his return. He quickly recovered his health.

Fellow missionaries also criticized Ripa's school and this was no doubt exacerbated by tensions with the Jesuits at the court, who exhibited proprietary tendencies toward controlling mission affairs. The Jesuits felt that other missionaries, with a less sophisticated understanding of the situation, including Ripa, were damaging the mission's delicate relations with the emperor. An unidentified missionary accuser complained about Ripa to the Monsignor Bishop of Beijing Bernardino della Chiesa, OFM (Yi Daren 伊大人). The bishop's vicar, Fr. Carlo di Orazio da Castorano, OFM (Kang Hezi 康和子) (1673–1755), passed the complaint on to Ripa. Castorano refused to identify the author, although Ripa later discovered who it was.[102]

The gossipy complaint stated that the five Chinese "*giovanetti*" (youths) and "*garzoni*" (boys) lived in Ripa's house where he came and went. Guards heard Ripa talk with them in the middle of the night and heard the "whispering laughter," which caused an obscene rumor to be spread about Ripa. The accuser complained that at the imperial summer villa at Rehe, Ripa conducted himself disgracefully by riding around in a carriage with his students to his delight, much like some of the court grandees carried boys in their carriages with whom they "satisfy their lusts."[103] Although Bishop della Chiesa and Vicar Castorano did not give credence to the slander, they believed that the consequences of the rumors were harmful to the mission. Consequently, they suggested that Ripa dismiss three of the students and keep only two, whom he would treat more as servants than students, teaching them only a few characters.[104]

Throughout his time in China (1710–1724), Ripa, like all missionaries, was affected by the Rites Controversy, whose intensity peaked around 1720. In 1715 Pope Clement XI had finalized the decree *Ex illa die*, which prohibited missionaries from allowing converts to observe Chinese ancestral and Confucian rites. This decree would have crippling effects on the development of Catholicism in China and was finally reversed in 1939. The decree was taken to China by the captain of an English vessel and given to the fathers at Guangzhou on August 10, 1716.[105] The Jesuits received copies of it and passed them on to Jesuits at the court in Beijing. They informed the Kangxi emperor, who became enraged at the European audacity to judge Chinese religious matters and suppressed the distribution of the decree.[106]

At the court, the Lazarist Father Pedrini became an object of particular imperial scorn for his role in the issuing of *Ex illa die*.[107] He had sent a letter to Rome with the erroneous information that the Kangxi emperor would tolerate a prohibition of the rites while simultaneously telling the Kangxi emperor that Rome would permit the rites.[108] On the first day of the lunar new year (February 8, 1720), following a holiday feast, two palace scribes at the French Jesuit fathers' residence entered Fr. Pedrini's room on the orders of the emperor to arrest Pedrini for failing to come to the palace that morning to kneel in reverence with the other Europeans in a customary rite in honor of the emperor.[109] The order had been given on the emperor's behalf by the scholar-official whom Ripa refers to as Ciao, a sworn enemy of Pedrini. Pedrini went with the Jesuit father Pierre Jartoux (Giartù), SJ, to the palace. Jartoux told Ripa he suspected that Pedrini might be on the verge of going to prison. Ripa's *Giornale* indicates clear sympathy for Pedrini and his association with Pedrini seems to have contributed to court criticism of his school. This controversy sharpened Ripa's hostility toward the Jesuits.

RIPA DEPARTS BEIJING WITH FIVE CHINESE

Although Ripa's greatest passion lay in missionary work, the situation at the time of his arrival in China was marked by the growing hostility of the Kangxi emperor toward Christianity and the increasing difficulties missionaries were encountering in securing permission to reside in China. Consequently, he had submitted to Tournon's assigning him to work as a painter at the Kangxi emperor's court. He was a dedicated servant of the emperor, but his greatest interest was in his school for training boys as priests. As time passed and the opposition to his missionary work increased, Ripa concluded that his school could not survive in China. It needed to be moved to Europe, but it also needed an organizational structure to support it. This is how his idea developed to found the Congregation of the Holy Family of Jesus Christ (Congregazione della Sacra Famiglia di Gesù Cristo).[110] In fact, the Collegio dei Cinesi (Chinese College) and the Congregation of the Holy Family were inseparable.

From the start, Ripa appears to have conceived of the College being located in Naples, perhaps partly because of his feelings of *campanilismo* (affinity for the customs and traditions of his home region). He resisted efforts to base the College in Rome, despite the greater resources there, because Rome was a bureaucratic maze that he tried to avoid. Consequently, he became the founder of the Holy Family. In 1832, a century after its founding, several members of the Holy Family Congregation, led initially by the congregant Vincenzo Taglialatela, combined different manuscripts by Ripa into a lengthy three-volume work in an effort to begin a process of beatification and canonization of Ripa.[111] They used this opportunity to polish Ripa's record, altering and deleting passages from his handwritten manuscripts, including other material, collating them in the 1,500-page *Storia della Fondazione della Congregazione e del Collegio de' Cinesi* (1832). However, the canonization effort later faltered.[112]

To leave China, Ripa needed imperial permission, not only for himself, but also for his five Chinese (four students and one teacher). The Kangxi emperor died on December 20, 1722, and was succeeded by the Yongzheng emperor.[113] Although the Tournon legation and the Rites Controversy had cooled the Kangxi emperor's previously sympathetic attitude toward Christianity, the missionaries were still valued at court because of their technical knowledge and translation skills. Ripa's relationship with the Kangxi emperor was not as close as the Jesuits', but his services, and particularly his engraving skills, were valued. However, the Yongzheng emperor was more hostile toward Christianity, in part because of his affinity for Buddhism and in part because certain missionaries had favored opposing candidates to the throne.

After the death of the Kangxi emperor, several missionaries, including Fr. João Mourão, SJ, joined with the Sunu family and some high officials, many of whom were either converts or sympathetic to Christianity, to support the royal brothers Yinti 胤禔 and Yintang 胤禟 over Yinzhen 胤禛 (the eventual Yongzheng emperor).[114] Yinti was favored by the emperor, but he was serving as a military commander in faraway Gansu province when his father suddenly died at the Garden of Joyful Spring and his brother Yinzhen ascended the throne as the Yongzheng emperor. Rumors swirled around Yinzhen's ascension, claiming that he had actually usurped the throne.[115] Historians have long debated the legitimacy of the Yongzheng emperor's ascension, but the weight of recent scholarship is that the rumors were generated by his political opponents as a means of discrediting him.[116]

Knowing how difficult it was to obtain permission to leave China, Ripa used a ruse in appealing to the Chinese sense of filial piety. He petitioned to leave China out of mourning for the death of his father and three uncles, even though his father had been dead for six or seven years.[117] He first appealed to the sixteenth (in order of birth to the Kangxi emperor) brother of the emperor, who previously had always favored him. He was advised to present a memorial to the tribunal of the *Du Yushi* 都御史 (censor-in-chief). Ripa, who was very sensitive to opposition, said some European missionaries (most likely Jesuits) suspected incorrectly that he was being recalled by Propaganda Fide because of the failed mission of the second papal legate, Patriarch Carlo Ambrogio Mezzabarba (1720–1721).[118] Ripa was sympathetic to Mezzabarba, but he was far more diplomatic than Pedrini, whose support for the legate's position so angered the Kangxi emperor that he had been beaten and imprisoned.[119]

Ripa consulted with the sixteenth prince, Yinlu 胤祿 (1695–1767). He suggested that Ripa speak with the thirteenth prince, Yinxiang 胤祥 (1686–1730), the so-called prince protector of the missionaries, who would be in a better position to present Ripa's petition to the emperor.[120] Yinxiang (Prince Yi) was a younger half-brother of the Yongzheng emperor. Although he had not been given important responsibilities during his father's reign, he became the most trusted advisor to the Yongzheng emperor and one of the most powerful figures of the inner court.[121] He passed the request on to the Yongzheng emperor, who granted the petition as a reward for Ripa becoming "exhausted" in serving the emperor's father and bestowed valuable gifts of porcelain and silk cloth upon him.[122] The sixteenth prince sent him two hundred pieces of porcelain, four pieces of silk, and two saddled horses along with permission to depart. The authenticity of Ripa's record has been confirmed by Han Qi, who located a memorial from the *Neiwufu Zao Ban Wai* 內務府造班外 (Imperial Household Manufacturing Department) in the First Historical Archives dated the eleventh day of the tenth month of the first year of the Yongzheng emperor's reign (October 1723).[123] The memorial states that the Yongzheng emperor granted Ripa a departure gift of a hundred pieces of white porcelain bowls in dark dragon style, forty pieces of porcelain bowls decorated with a dragon and phoenix in five colors, sixty pieces of porcelain cups with a dragon and phoenix in five colors, and four pieces of the best satin.

Obtaining permission to take his five Chinese was problematic because seven years before his request, the Kangxi emperor had issued an edict prohibiting all Chinese from leaving China. However, Ripa regarded the gifts as a favorable sign and again approached the sixteenth prince (Yinlu), who was the "first steward of the Imperial House" and whose office handled passports, with his request for passports.[124] The prince told him to submit a memorial, explaining how many horses, men, and weapons he wished to take with him, and that the memorial would be granted. Ripa immediately carried the memorial to the *Du Yushi* tribunal. Although Ripa said there was some opposition from Europeans, the memorial was approved. One of the opponents of his leaving was the procurator of Propaganda Fide, Domenico Perroni, OMD, who criticized his departure as ill-timed.[125] Perroni complained that Ripa's absence made it more difficult for those Propaganda Fide missionaries in Beijing to receive aid in case of an urgent need.

At midday on November 15, 1723, Ripa departed that "Babylon of Beijing" with the four Chinese students and their teacher.[126] Twenty-two years later, in 1745, he wrote a detailed account of their journey that was probably based on a journal he kept.[127] Ripa occupied one litter (sedan chair) while the two youngest students, ten-year-old Lucio Wu (Wu Lujue 吳露爵) and eleven-year-old Filippo Huang (personal name Huang Zhihan 黃之漢; baptismal name Huang Batong 黃巴桐), shared the other litter. The students Giovanni Evangelista Yin (Yin Ruowang 殷若望), eighteen years old, and Giovanni Battista Gu (Gu Ruohan 谷若翰), twenty-two years old, rode horses, along with the teacher and a servant. The scribe Tommaso Wu (Wu Duomo 吳多默) had been replaced by a new teacher named Gioacchino Wang (Wang Yajing 王雅敬) (ca.1693–1738).[128] Wang was a native of Chuansha 川沙 in southeastern Jiangsu province.[129] On the day of their departure the weather was hellish, with a wind so strong that it chilled them to the bone and overturned one of the litters. Ripa said it was as if the Demon, foreseeing the good that would result from this group's journey, tried to drive them backward. After the first few days, the bad weather eased.

They took the "Ambassadors' Route," so called because it was the main north-south route of foreign emissaries traveling back and forth between the entry port of Guangzhou and the capital in Beijing. Ripa's group traveled initially by land and then by water on the Grand Canal through Shandong and

Jiangsu provinces, then entered the mighty Yangzi River southward through Anhui province to Jiujiang-fu 九江府, a city bordering a two-mile-wide river with the same name. They attended mass at a church served by Fr. Joseph de Prémare (Ma Ruose 馬若瑟), a Jesuit and notable Figurist whom Ripa had met in Beijing.[130] He and Prémare were apparently on hospitable terms; they shared a meal together. Ripa and his group continued southward through Jiangxi and on December 19, after thirty-five days of travel, they arrived in the city of Nanchang-fu 南昌府. Apart from the two horses given to him by the sixteenth prince (Yinlu), the costs for the two litters and four riding-horses amounted to sixty-one taels of silver. Ripa calculated that sixty-one taels were equivalent to one hundred Neapolitan ducats.

A tael was broken down into one hundred copper coins called *fen* 分, although there were regional variations. The cost of food was higher in Beijing and also in Shandong where there was a famine.[131] They paid six or seven *fen* per person for dinner and lodging. However, it was standard practice in China to have lodgers bring their own beds, which might consist only of a bundle of rags. As they moved south, the cost of food and lodgings decreased, such that they were paying five *fen* per person each day, of which two *fen* were for a midday meal and 3 *fen* were for lodgings and dinner. Instead of bread, which was standard food in the north, they had as much rice as they wanted, various types of meat, and a green soup. Wine and fruit required extra payment.

They disembarked from the riverboat at Nanan-fu 南安府 and journeyed over the Meiling 梅嶺 mountain, where Ripa visited the leading scholar-official of that city, a relative of a friend, and stayed for dinner.[132] He also visited a Franciscan monastery run by the province of the Philippine Islands. The Franciscans invited him to stay for fifteen days, claiming that all the ships departing Guangzhou (Canton) for Europe had already left. Ripa felt it was divine guidance that caused him to decline the invitation and to move on the next morning.

The Meiling mountain straddled the border of Jiangxi and Guangdong provinces. Ripa and his five companions were carried in sedan chairs by porters and there was no sign of wagons or small carts or pack animals. As they crossed the mountain, Ripa was struck by a "a remarkable sight" (*gran meraviglia*).[133] When they had left Beijing, neither trees nor green grass had been visible, only fog. However, at the top of Meiling mountain there was a great flat plain with a perfect spring atmosphere of newly grown grass, pink open air, and flowering trees. As they approached Guangzhou, Ripa saw fields where the grain had already been harvested and the fruit on the trees had already ripened. At Shaozhou 韶州, the customs-house official examined their imperially authorized passport and immediately sped them through without paying any customs duty.[134] Fr. Orzio Maria Ferrari, MEP, from a nearby church of the Missions Étrangères de Paris, came to greet them.

After a fifty-six-day journey, they reached Guangzhou (Canton) on January 10, 1724. When they arrived, they found three English ships in the harbor that had not yet departed for Europe. They had been delayed by a dispute over payment for an expensive clock that had been confiscated by a customs official.[135]

THE JOURNEY FROM GUANGZHOU (CANTON) TO LONDON AND NAPLES

Initially, Ripa secured passage for himself and only four of the Chinese on the ship to England. Lucio Wu was to be left behind, not only because he was the youngest of the students (eleven years old) but also because Ripa had serious doubts about his aptitude, strength, and character for such a demanding undertaking. Consequently, he made an arrangement with Fr. Luigi Antonio Appiani, CM (Bi Tianxiang 畢天祥), who had previously served as the interpreter of Legate Tournon and had ties with Propaganda Fide.[136] Ripa entrusted Lucio to Fr. Appiani to have him educated in Guangzhou (Canton) at Ripa's expense.[137] Still, Ripa was not at peace with his decision. As he was saying mass on the morning of January 20, 1724, he had scarcely begun the introit with the words "*In nomine Patris, et Filii*," when he heard a voice from the depths of his soul and in the middle of his chest say in a clear and distinct reprimand: "How can I have given him to you for you to abandon him?"[138] Even as Ripa recounted these words more than twenty years later, his memory of them was acute. When he heard them, he knew that they referred to Lucio. Consequently, he decided to make every effort to secure Lucio's passage with the others.

Today we might wonder if Ripa's affection for Lucio played a role. Had Ripa been in love with the boy? Was this another instance of his latent homosexuality surfacing, as it had with Amodei? Love takes many forms. Men of his time were more prone to speak of loving another man than men today, but their sensibility was different from ours and their words had a different nuance. Whereas our age often sees same-sex love in romantic terms, the sensibility of Ripa's age saw it in predominantly emotional terms, the kind of emotion that men then more openly expressed for other men. And yet, regardless of the exact nature of his love, this relationship would turn out to have a sad ending. Betrayal is often perceived as two-sided. Twenty years later Ripa expressed his deep disappointment in Lucio's betrayal of him, but Lucio also felt that Ripa had betrayed him and moreover it was Lucio who paid the higher price for his betrayal.

On that same day that Ripa heard God's voice, he went to the captain of the ship to ask for the favor of adding Lucio as a passenger. Simultaneously, Ripa was presented with a request by the supercargo of the three ships in the harbor, whose role was to manage the merchandise on the ships, including buying and selling cargo. The leading customs official had confiscated a clock worth 2,000 ducats and refused either to pay for it or to return it.[139] He knew that the customs official's superior was planning to visit Ripa and he asked that Ripa intervene with this superior on the East India Company's behalf. Ripa did so and consequently, the customs official invited Ripa to dinner, apologetically blamed the problem on a steward, and said he would make restitution the next day. On January 22 Ripa was explaining the outcome to the supercargo when the clock arrived, to the great joy of the Englishman. Ripa and the five Chinese boarded the ship, which departed on January 24, 1724.[140]

Because of problems navigating the tide on the Pearl River (Zhujiang 珠江), they did not reach the Bocca del Tigre until February 4. After three days, they exited into the open sea and the Chinese pilot left the ship the following day. They encountered their first storm on the eighth and Ripa suffered from continual vomiting.[141] For the first month, things went well as Ripa and the five Chinese were allowed to sleep in the captain's cabin. However, Giovanni Gu fell ill and was treated by the hostile German surgeon in a way that made his condition worse. Ripa described the physician as a member of "a heretical religion," by which he meant some form of Protestantism.[142] Meanwhile Lucio gave an inauspicious sign of misfortune to come. He defecated for two nights in the middle of the floor of the captain's cabin.[143] Since this was a room used for eating and drinking as well as sleeping, the captain banned the Chinese from his cabin. Because the vessel was completely loaded, the only place for them to stay was in the area outside the cabin's door, exposed to the air, wind, and water. When it rained, they were soaked. After Lucio recovered from his digestive illness, Filippo Huang fell ill. The others remained healthy, but Ripa was concerned for their survival. When he spoke to the surgeon about treating them medically, the surgeon said he was thinking of giving them a strong medicine to make them die faster! Later, after observing their sodden state, he said, "Mister Ripa, they should all be thrown one after another into the sea, because it is impossible to keep them alive for the whole journey."[144]

Ripa described the Chinese during this ordeal as unbelievably patient. They voiced neither complaints over their condition nor regrets at embarking on the trip, but rather appeared happy and content. Ripa attributed their endurance to the Chinese teacher Gioacchino Wang, whom Ripa described as being a perfect age for such responsibility. He was about thirty years old and he had left a wife, mother, and four children behind. Ripa himself had baptized him prior to leaving Beijing.[145] Although Wang was only a neophyte, Ripa had been impressed by his conduct.

In May, the ship reached the Cape of Good Hope for a short stay. Ripa took the Chinese ashore and left them at an inn while he bought food. However, when he returned to the inn, he heard raucous laughter and loud voices from their room.[146] When he entered it, he found several Englishmen and Dutchmen amusing themselves at Giovanni Yin's expense by making the pious Giovanni embrace the daughter of the inn owner. Giovanni, in tears and trembling, had tried to flee by hiding under a bed. Immediately, Ripa took the Chinese back to the ship to stay during the layover.

On September 5, 1724, they sighted the coast of England and landed shortly afterward at Deal to make their way to London. Ripa was impressed by the improvements made in London since he had left it sixteen years before. It was better policed than previously and there were several magnificent new buildings, including St. Paul's Cathedral, which was "built by those heretics to emulate the magnificence of the Basilica of St. Peter's in Rome."[147] Their arrival in London created a stir of attention and King George I wanted to meet them.[148] They were presented at court before the king, courtiers, and ambassadors for an audience that lasted three hours. When the king grew fatigued, he invited Ripa and the Chinese to eat dinner at the table in the palace for his grandees. George's court was earthy and somewhat crude. The queen had been divorced and imprisoned for adultery, but one of the king's female favorites was at hand. Ripa and the Chinese met the Countess of Darlington (Charlotte Sophia Kielmansegg), an enormous, corpulent woman who was friendly and well read.[149] King George was quite favorable toward Ripa's group and he arranged that the Royal Customs office release their clothes and other items that they had carried from China.[150] Ripa cultivated the king's favor by presenting him with his engraving of the Jesuit atlas of China, Manchuria, and Korea. This atlas is preserved in King George III's Topographical Collection in the British Museum.[151]

Ripa may have cultivated other contacts in London as well, because a copy of his *Thirty-Six Views of Rehe* containing thirty-four of his thirty-six views is preserved in the Department of Oriental Antiquities of the British Museum. The scholar Basil Gray suggested that the architect and art patron Earl of Burlington (1694–1753) obtained this copy of the *Thirty-Six Views of Rehe* from Ripa in 1724 during his visit to England. Gray suggested that Burlington's affinity for Italian culture—by 1724 he had visited Italy twice—provided a basis for contact with Ripa. The art historian Rudolf Wittkower and others have argued that Ripa's *Thirty-Six Views of Rehe* contributed to the Chinese influence in English landscape gardens that began to appear in the 1730s.[152]

Others have disagreed and have argued that the Chinese influence in English gardens was due more to literary than visual sources.[153]

Ripa was also entertained by the East India Company merchants. They invited him into their public assembly at East India House as well as to a dinner and sent him off with soldiers to accompany him to secure their clothes from customs. The last audience of Ripa and the Chinese with the king also lasted for three hours. At midnight, the king sent Ripa off with a parcel of gold worth 300 ducats.[154] They departed London on October 5 and arrived at the Italian port of Livorno on All Saints' Day, the first of November. After boarding another English ship, they arrived in Naples on the twentieth. For Ripa, the arrival concluded a twenty-year absence from his home region.[155]

As the ship was approaching Naples, Ripa tested the individual spiritual fervor of the Chinese by asking them which of two ways of life they wished to embrace while living in Naples. The first option was to live with a standard degree of comfort. The second option was to live in poverty, going begging for food and imitating their Lord Jesus. The teacher Gioacchino Wang, who was still new to the faith and not training for the priesthood, answered that he would choose to live with standard comforts. The other two adults, Giovanni Gu and Giovanni Yin, said they wished to embrace poverty, protesting with great fervor against the first option and showing early signs of their longing for martyrdom.[156] The responses of Filippo Huang and Lucio Wu did not really count because they were too young to make such a decision. Ripa wrote in his journals twenty years later that although God had never called him to beg, his willingness to do so had served to protect him against temptation.

NOTES

1. Matteo Ripa, *Storia della Fondazione della Congregazione e del Collegio di' Cinesi*, 3 vols. (Napoli: Tipografia Manfredi, 1832), III:444–45.

2. The original text of Ripa, *Storia*, III:444–45 reads, "*ed avendo il Paolo Zai aperta la Cassa, e scoverto il volto, lo trovò così bello, e fresco, come appunto era quando spirò, ed avendo maneggiato la pelle della gola, e quella delle mani la trovò morbida, e flessible, come quanto era vivente.*"

3. Karl Josef Rivinius, *Das Collegium Sinicum zu Neapel und seine Umwandlung in ein Orientalisches Institut* (Sankt Augustin: Institut Monumenta Serica, 2004), 150. See also Francesco D'Arelli, "The Chinese College in Eighteenth-Century Naples," *East and West* 58, no. 1–4 (December 2008): 289.

4. Rivinius, *Collegium*, 150, dates his arrival March 1, 1739, while D'Arelli, "Chinese College," 307, lists his arrival as March 29, 1739.

5. Ripa, *Storia*, III:421–22.

6. Rivinius, *Collegium*, 150.

7. Rivinius, *Collegium*, 65. A partial list of these 106 Chinese students is given in an inventory of eighty Chinese students (*Elenchus Alumnorum*) printed by the Jesuit orphanage T'ou-sè-wè (Tushanwan 土山灣) at the Zikawei compound in Shanghai in 1917. It is reprinted as an appendix in Rivinius, *Collegium*, 148–53.

8. Gianni Criveller, "The Chinese Priests of the College for the Chinese in Naples and the Promotion of the Indigenous Clergy (XVIII–XIX Centuries)," in *Silent Force: Native Converts in the Catholic China Mission*, ed. Rachel Lu Yan and Philip Vanhaelemeersch (Leuven, Belgium: Ferdinand Verbiest Institute, 2009), 151.

9. Matteo Ripa, *Giornale (1705–1724)*. Introduzione, testo critico e note di Michele Fatica, vol. I (1705–1711) (Napoli: Istituto Universitario Orientale, 1991), XXV.

10. Ripa, *Storia*, I:8–9.

11. Amos 1:3.

12. Matteo Ripa, *Memoirs of Father Ripa during Thirteen Years' Residence at the Court of Peking in the Service of the Emperor of China*, selected and trans. Fortunato Prandi (London: John Murray, 1844), 1–2, based on Ripa, *Storia*, I:10–12.

13. Ripa, *Storia*, II:119–20.

14. See D. E. Mungello, *Western Queers in China: Flight to the Land of Oz* (Lanham, MD: Rowman & Littlefield, 2012), 46–53.

15. Ripa, *Giornale*, XXVI.

16. Ripa, *Giornale*, I:23. This work consists of part of Ripa's original manuscript as transcribed and annotated by Michele Fatica. An earlier version of Ripa's original manuscript was edited and published under the title of *Storia della Fondazione della Congregazione e del Collegio de' Cinesi*. 3 vols. (Napoli: dalla Tipografia Manfredi, 1832). There are slight differences between the two versions. The corresponding passage for *Giornale*, I:23 is found in *Storia della Fondazione*, I:61.

17. Ripa, *Giornale*, I:23.

18. Ripa, *Giornale*, I:3.

19. Ripa, *Giornale*, I:7–8.

20. Ripa, *Giornale*, I:23.

21. Ripa, *Giornale*, I:28. Cf. *Storia*, I:70.

22. Ripa, *Giornale*, I:30.

23. Ripa, *Giornale*, I:XXVI; LVIII.

24. Ripa, *Memoirs*, 15.

25. Ripa, *Giornale*, I:31.

26. Ripa, *Giornale*, I:32.

27. Ripa, *Giornale*, I:40.

28. Ripa, *Giornale*, I:42.

29. Ripa, *Giornale*, I:62.

30. Ripa, *Giornale*, I:114.

31. Ripa, *Giornale*, I:152.

32. Ripa, *Giornale*, I:166.

33. Ripa, *Giornale*, I:185.

34. Ripa, *Giornale*, I:188; 257.

35. Ripa, *Giornale*, I:188.

36. Francis A. Rouleau, "Maillard de Tournon, Papal Legate at the Court of Peking: The First Imperial Audience (31 December 1705)," *Archivum Historicum Societatis Iesu* 31 (1962): 265–67.

37. Ripa, *Giornale*, I:200–2.

38. Ripa, *Giornale*, I:202–3.

39. Ripa, *Storia*, I:350.

40. Ripa, *Storia*, I:369–70. Ripa's sketches are reproduced in his *Giornale*, I, between pages 50 and 155.

41. Ripa, *Giornale*, II:29.

42. Ripa, *Storia*, I:463.

43. Ripa, *Storia*, I:408.

44. Ripa, *Giornale*, II:29–30.

45. Richard Strassberg, "An Intercultural Artist: Matteo Ripa: His Engravings and Their Transmission to the West," in *Thirty-Six Views: The Kangxi Emperor's Mountain Estate in Poetry and Prints* (Washington, DC: Dumbarton Oaks, 2016), 46–47.

46. Strassberg, "Intercultural Artist," 45.

47. See figure 1 in Young-tsu Wong, *A Paradise Lost: The Imperial Garden Yuanming Yuan* (Honolulu: University of Hawai'i Press, 2001), 2. Richard Strassberg notes that the Garden of Joyful Spring is different from the later *Changchun Yuan* 長春園 (Garden of Eternal Spring), which was not constructed until 1749 and which was part of the Yuanming Yuan. Strassberg, "Intercultural Artist," 47.

48. Frederic Wakeman Jr., *The Great Enterprise: The Manchu Reconstruction of Imperial Order in Seventeenth-Century China*. 2 vols. (Berkeley: University of California Press, 1985), II:892–93.

49. Ripa, *Giornale*, II:38–39.

50. Ripa, *Storia*, I:421.

51. Han Qi 韩琦, 从中西文献看马国贤在宫廷的活动 (Matteo Ripa's activities at court drawn from Sino-Western documents) in *Matteo Ripa e il Collegio dei Cinesi*, ed. Michele Fatica and Francesco D'Arelli (Napoli: Istituto Universitario Orientale, 1999), 74.

52. Yue Zhuang, "Hatchings in the Void: Ritual and Order in *Bishu Shanzhuang Shi* and Matteo Ripa's *Views of Jehol*," in *Qing Encounters: Artistic Exchanges between China and the West*, ed. Petra Ten-Doesschate Chu and Ning Ding (Los Angeles: Getty Research Institute, 2015), 143.

53. Ripa, *Giornale*, II:82.

54. Ripa, *Giornale*, I:83–84.

55. Strassberg, "Intercultural Artist," 50.

56. Ripa, *Storia*, I:406.

57. Nicolas Standaert, ed., *Handbook of Christianity in China*, vol. 1, *635–1800* (Leiden: Brill, 2001), 762.

58. Ripa, *Storia*, I:406.

59. Ripa, *Storia*, I:408–9.

60. Ripa, *Storia*, I:495.

61. D'Arelli, "Chinese College," 306.

62. Fang Hao, 方豪. *Zhongguo Tianzhujiao shiren wu chuan* 中國天主教世人物傳 (Biographies of historical personages in the Chinese Catholic Church). 3 vols. (Hong Kong: Xianggong Gongjiao Zhenli Xuehui, 1973), II:154.

63. Ripa, *Giornale* II:141.

64. Rivinius, *Collegium*, 150.

65. Ripa, *Storia*, I:494–95.

66. Ripa, *Storia*, I:495.

67. Ripa, *Storia*, II:34.

68. Ripa, *Storia*, I:497.

69. Ripa, *Storia*, II:25.

70. Chou Chin-sheng, *An Economic History of China*. Originally published in Chinese as *Zhongguo jingji shi* 中國經濟史 (1959), trans. Edward H. Kaplan (Bellingham: Western Washington State College, 1974), 251.

71. Samuel Couling, *The Encyclopedia Sinica* (Shanghai: Kelly and Walsh, 1917), 539.

72. Ripa, *Storia*, II:7.

73. Letter of Filippo Huang to Gennaro Fatigati, May 1, 1765, in Giacomo di Fiore, "Un cinese a Castel Sant'Angelo," *La conoscenza dell'Asia e dell'Africa in Italia nei secoli XVIII e XIX*, vol. 2 (1985), 249. Huang does not identify the title of the publication containing the accusation.

74. Mungello, *Western Queers*, 25–32.

75. Ripa, *Storia*, II, 22.

76. Ripa, *Storia*, I:452–53. Jonathan D. Spence in his *Emperor of China: Self-Portrait of K'ang-hsi* (New York: Vintage, 1975), 128, describes a very similar type of public condemnation of Yinreng as occurring outside the emperor's "traveling palace" on October 17, 1708. However, Fang Chao-ying supports Ripa's date and place of this imperial condemnation as occurring at the Changchunyuan in 1712. Fang Chao-ying, "Yin-jeng," in *Eminent Chinese of the Ch'ing Period*, ed. Arthur W. Hummel (Washington, DC: Government Printing Office, 1943), 925.

77. Ripa, *Storia*, I:453

78. Ripa, *Storia*, I:453.

79. Ripa, *Memoirs*, 83.

80. Fang Chao-ying, "Yin-jeng," 924–25.

81. Spence, *Emperor of China*, 125–27.

82. Wu Cuncun, *Homoerotic Sensibilities in Late Imperial China* (London: RoutledgeCurzon, 2004), 125.

83. Spence, *Emperor of China*, 128–29.

84. Spence, *Emperor of China*, 129.

85. Spence, *Emperor of China*, 129–30.

86. Fang Chao-ying, "Yin-jeng," 925.

87. Ripa, *Storia*, I:453.

88. Ripa, *Storia*, II:9; 24.

89. Ripa, *Storia*, II:28.

90. Ripa, *Storia*, II:29.

91. Ripa, *Storia*, II:30.

92. Ripa, *Storia*, II:31.
93. Fang Hao, III:153.
94. Ripa, *Storia*, II:34.
95. Ripa, *Storia*, II:40.
96. Ripa, *Storia*, II:41.
97. Ripa, *Storia*, II:41–42.
98. Ripa, *Storia*, II:43–44.
99. Ripa, *Storia*, II:45.
100. Ripa, *Storia*, II:46.
101. Ripa, *Storia*, II:49–50.
102. Ripa, *Storia*, II:36–37.
103. Ripa, *Storia*, II:37.
104. Ripa, *Storia*, II:38.
105. Sebald Reil, *Kilian Stumpf 1655–1720: Ein Würzburger Jesuit am Kaiserhof zu Peking* (Münster, Westfalen: Aschendorff, 1978), 170–72.
106. Antonio Sisto Rosso, OFM, *Apostolic Legations to China of the Eighteenth Century* (South Pasadena, CA: Perkins, 1948), 191–92.
107. Joseph van den Brandt, CM, *Les Lazaristes en Chine 1697–1935. Notes biographiques* (Beiping: Imprimerie des Lazaristes, 1936), 2.
108. Claudia von Collani, "Legations and Travellers," in *Handbook of Christianity in China*, vol. 1, *635–1800*, ed. Nicolas Standaert (Leiden: Brill, 2001), 361–62.
109. Ripa, *Storia*, II:18–19.
110. Ripa, *Storia*, II:53.
111. D'Arelli, "Chinese College," 291; Fiore, "Un cinese a Castel Sant'Angelo," 220.
112. M. Fatica & V. Carpentiero, "Per una storia del processo di canonizzazione di Matteo Ripa: Problema di filologia e di agiografia," in *La conoscenza dell'Asia e dell'Africa*, III, ed. Aldo Gallota and Ugo Marazzi (Napoli: Istituto Universitario Orientale, 1984), 73–110; M. Fatica, "Il processo di canonizzazione di Matteo Ripa, fondatore del Collegio dei Cinesi di Napoli. L'iter di un fallimento," in *Scrivere di santi. Atti del II Convegno di studio dell'Associazione italiana per lo studio della santità, dei culti e dell'agiografia, Napoli 22–25 ottobre 1997*, ed. G. Luongo (Roma: Pubblicazioni dell'Università Cattolica del Sacro Cuore, 1998), 303–23.
113. Lin Juyuan 林铁钧, *Qingshi biannian* 清史编年 (Qing history chronicle) (北京: 中国人民大学出版社, 1988), 575.
114. Rosso, *Apostolic Legations*, 213–14.
115. Fang Chao-ying, "Yin-jeng," 916.
116. See Pei Huang, *Autocracy at Work: A Study of the Yung-cheng Period, 1723–1735* (Bloomington: Indiana University Press, 1974), 51–59; Madeleine Zelin, "The Yung-cheng Reign," in *The Cambridge History of China*, vol. 9, *The Ch'ing Dynasty to 1800*, ed. Willard J. Peterson (Cambridge, UK: Cambridge University Press, 2002), 184–91.
117. Ripa, *Storia*, II:124–25.
118. Rosso, *Apostolic Legations*, 202–11.
119. Ripa, *Storia*, II:125–26.

120. Ripa, *Storia*, II:127. Also see Eugenio Menegon, "Yongzheng's Conundrum: The Emperor on Christianity, Religions, and Heterodoxy," in *Rooted in Hope: China—Religion—Christianity. Festschrift in Honor of Roman Malek, SVD*, ed. Barbara Hoster, Dirk Kuhjmann, and Zbigniew Wesolowski, SVD (Abindgon, Oxon, UK: Routledge, 2017), 321.

121. Beatrice S. Bartlett, *Monarchs and Ministers: The Grand Council in Mid-Ch'ing China, 1723–1820* (Berkeley: University of California Press, 1991), 68–71.

122. Ripa, *Storia*, II:128–29.

123. Han Qi 韩琦, 从中西文献看马国贤在宫廷的活动 (Matteo Ripa's Activities at Court Drawn from Sino-Western Documents), in *Matteo Ripa e il Collegio dei Cinesi*, ed. Michele Fatica and Francesco D'Arelli, 71–82 (Napoli: Istituto Universitario Orientale, 1999), 79.

124. Ripa, *Storia*, II:130–32.

125. "Carità e reclusione nell'Europa del Settecento. Le disavventure carcerarie di due cinesi al seguito di Jean-François Foucquet e di Matteo Ripa," in *Scritture di Storia (Historical Writings)*, ed. Università degli Studi di Napoli "L'orientale" (Napoli: Edizione Scientifiche Italiane, 2005), 76.

126. Ripa, *Storia*, II:133.

127. Ripa, *Storia*, II:135.

128. Ripa, *Storia*, II:155. In *Storia*, III:308, this teacher's name is spelled Gioachino Kung.

129. Fang Hao, II:154.

130. Ripa, *Storia*, II:135–36.

131. Ripa, *Storia*, II:136–37.

132. Ripa, *Storia*, II:138.

133. Ripa, *Storia*, II:139.

134. Ripa, *Storia*, II:140.

135. Ripa, *Storia*, II:140–41.

136. Rosso, *Apostolic Legations*, 156.

137. Ripa, *Storia*, II:145.

138. Ripa, *Storia*, II:146.

139. Ripa, *Storia*, II:147–49.

140. Ripa, *Storia*, II:151.

141. Ripa, *Storia*, II:152.

142. Ripa, *Storia*, II:153.

143. Ripa, *Storia*, II:154–55.

144. Ripa, *Storia*, II:155.

145. Ripa, *Storia*, II:155–56.

146. Ripa, *Storia*, II:168–69.

147. Ripa, *Storia*, II:195.

148. Ripa, *Storia*, II:192–93.

149. J. H. Plumb, *The First Four Georges* (London: B. T. Batsford, Ltd., 1956; reprinted by Fontana, 1966), 41–43.

150. Ripa, *Storia*, II:194.

151. Basil Gray, "Lord Burlington and Father Ripa's Chinese Engravings," *British Museum Quarterly* 22, no. 1–2 (1960): 40.

152. Rudolf Wittkower, "English Neo-Palladianism, the Landscape Garden, China, and the Enlightenment," *L'Arte* (Istituto Editoriale Italiano Milano) 6 (June 1969): 19; 28–30.

153. Patrick Conner, "China and the Landscape Garden: Reports, Engravings and Misconceptions," *Art History* 2, no. 4 (December 1979): 429–39.

154. Ripa, *Storia*, II:194–95.

155. Ripa, *Storia*, II:198.

156. Ripa, *Storia*, II:200–1.

Chapter Three

The Founding of the Chinese College in Naples

FINANCIAL STRUGGLES IN FOUNDING THE CHINESE COLLEGE

Ripa had scarcely arrived in Naples when he was called to Rome. He did not receive a hero's welcome. He had returned from China without authorization and brought a new burden for Propaganda Fide to bear. Monsignor (later Cardinal) Carrafa had mixed feelings. He was supportive of Ripa's desire to found a Holy Congregation, but was displeased by the prospect of having to support five Chinese.[1] When the second papal legate, Monsignor Mezzabarba, had gone to China in 1720–1721, Pope Clement XI had wanted him to bring back a dozen Chinese to found a college for them in Naples. However, under the current Pope Benedict XII, the thinking in Rome had changed. The pope called Ripa to Rome for an audience.[2]

In preparation for this audience, Ripa composed a formal proposal for the establishment of a seminary in Naples for Chinese.[3] He described how he had begun training Chinese youths for the priesthood in China in 1714. Point by point he explained why this effort should be moved from China to Naples. He said the manner of European missionaries in China involved elitist practices, such as being carried in a sedan chair by porters instead of walking, of having servants, and of not mixing in gatherings of common people. They failed to convert Chinese and were forced to rely on Chinese catechists to assist them.

Another obstacle was the Chinese language, which was spoken in so many different dialects that Europeans were forced to rely on their catechists as interpreters to communicate with the people. Also, the inability to speak Chinese with native fluency made it impossible for the Europeans to hide during a persecution. By contrast, Ripa noted that the Chinese bishop, Monsignor Lopez (i.e., Gregorio López, born Luo Wenzao 羅文藻 [Luo Wenzhao 羅

文炤] [1617–1691]), had been able to move among the populace and help destitute Christians without interference.⁴ Ripa argued—in contrast to many Europeans—that Chinese catechists had the potential to become priests. In his proposal, he characterized the setting of a Chinese College as a house with a garden in Naples, in a quiet neighborhood, with five or six Chinese students and teachers of the language as well as the arts and sciences of both China and Europe.⁵

In response to the summons, Ripa departed from Naples on December 16, 1725, leaving the five Chinese in the care of Fr. Giuseppe Pisani, who was assisted by a gentleman named Liborio. He arrived in Rome five days later and presented himself to Cardinal Giuseppe Sacripanti, prefect of Propaganda Fide. The cardinal was very hostile to Ripa's proposal and "felt that it was very bad, and with holy zeal began to shout, saying among other things: the Chinese ought to come here [Rome], because we do not want to make one altar against the other, that is, one Propaganda Fide [altar] in Napoli and another in Rome."⁶ Ripa was told that Cardinal Sacripanti was unhappy about being financially burdened with five boarding-school boys. One or two days later, Ripa had further consultations with Sacripanti's subordinate, Monsignor Bartolomeo Ruspoli, at that time secretary of the Holy Congregation and later a cardinal of the Church.

As an alternative to Naples, Ripa was offered an apartment in the College of Propaganda Fide in Rome with the title of rector, independent of the rest of the college, along with a benefice.⁷ However, he realized that if the Collegio dei Cinesi were placed within the enclosure of the College of Propaganda Fide, he would be forced to follow the rules of Propaganda Fide and would not have the freedom to create a college in the way he thought best. Clearly, Ripa was an independent spirit and he wanted to be freed from the stifling bureaucratic influence of the Vatican. Consequently, he spent several fruitless months in Rome, in an exhausting process of going from one spiritual advisor to another without obtaining guidance.

Finally, on May 15 he was sent to Duke Domenico Borgia, a pious layman with great expertise as a fiscal attorney, who gave him guidance on how to proceed in founding the Congregation of the Sacred Family (Congregazione della Sacra Famiglia). Following the guidance of Duke Borgia, Ripa composed a memorial asking permission to erect the Holy Foundation in Naples.⁸ The memorial was submitted and passed up the chain of the Vatican hierarchy. Ripa was invited to submit a detailed proposal on the management and revenues of his proposed foundation. The stress of all these negotiations in Rome had a negative effect on his health, but Ripa had his supporters. When Duke Borgia, who had been so helpful in founding the Congregation of the Sacred Family, died in 1734, he left a bequest of seventy-two ducats annually for the maintenance of a Chinese student at the Collegio dei Cinesi.[9] If no Chinese were available, the support was to be used for an Indian, and if no Indian, then a European student.

In January 1726 Ripa began a series of protracted negotiations for the purchase of a foundation house in Naples. The pope promised him 5,000 ducats toward the purchase, although collecting on that promise was not so simple. Ripa signed a statement of intent to purchase a house from Giuseppe San Biagio for 5,500 ducats, although he did not yet have the means of payment in hand.[10] In June and July, he traveled to Vienna to seek additional funding from Emperor Charles VI. Ripa's well-known experiences in China had lent him a degree of prominence that, along with the worthiness of his proposal for a Chinese College, led Charles VI to grant him an annual pension of eight hundred ducats.[11]

The final approval of the Chinese College and the Sacred Foundation by all parties was ultimately received in 1729. Ripa had been away from Naples from June 1726 until March 1729, a period of two years and nine months. Upon his return he found the five Chinese in excellent health, with the two youngest, Filippo and Lucio, having grown so much that they were unrecognizable.[12] However, Ripa's absence had contributed to emerging problems with Filippo and Lucio. Lacking Ripa's guidance, their education suffered because their supervisor failed to discipline them for fear of making them unhappy.

At one point in the protracted and frustrating negotiations for a house, Ripa was overwhelmed by "a great darkness of the heart, and anguish of the soul."[13] During the vigil of the Sacred Annunciation, he convoked the five Chinese in their domestic chapel. They all knelt before the altar and made a formal declaration to the Queen of Martyrs. Ripa recited the prayer in Chinese in a loud voice. They followed with an act of lying with their faces on the ground before the image of the Queen of Martyrs. On each of the following days, they gathered every morning in the chapel, with their faces to the ground, making their individual prayers. Then Ripa recited a prayer in Chinese and the others followed him, knowing the words by heart. He voiced in prayer to the Queen of Martyrs his intense frustration in failing to complete the process of buying the house and asked for discernment.

One day shortly after the prayers, one of the Chinese (probably the pious Giovanni Yin, who had already demonstrated prophetic powers) came into Ripa's room and said, "Father, she has a good heart because our Mother Mary has already heard our prayer. She has found the house, and now there comes a gentleman, who already stands at our door, who can lead us in buying the house."[14] Ripa was astonished because he was unaware that the public engineer Michelangelo Blasio had arrived at the house using an entrance that was not visible to the Chinese and he delivered a message in Italian, which the Chinese at that point did not understand well. (Ripa communicated with them in Chinese and Latin rather than Italian.) Immediately Blasio came to Ripa and confirmed what the Chinese student had said: the Olivantani brothers were willing to offer Ripa a contract if he still wished to buy their house.

Cardinal Pignatelli had instructed the Chinese on their first tonsure, which took place on September 22, 1725.[15] Now, in 1729, Ripa received a letter from the secretary of state in Rome, conveying that Pope Benedict XIII had approved the conferring of minor orders on the four Chinese, which was done at Beneveto on May 19.[16] Given the lack of scholars in Europe who could speak in Chinese, it is not surprising that Ripa and his Chinese students were called upon in 1732 to assist with their knowledge of Chinese. This happened when the pope sent Ripa a copy of a Chinese-Latin dictionary in romanization with the request that he add the Chinese characters. This *Dictionarium Sinico-Latinum* had been compiled by Father Basilio Brollo, OFM (Basilio da Gemona) (Ye Chungxian葉崇賢) (1648–1704). The copy Ripa used is preserved in the Vatican Library.[17] Ripa and his Chinese seminarians added four thousand characters.[18] One suspects that Ripa identified the missing characters and the Chinese rewrote the characters with their native facility in calligraphy.

THE FIRST CHINESE COLLEGE GRADUATES RETURN TO CHINA

The goal of training Chinese as priests and returning them to China as missionaries was premised on the belief that Chinese priests could be more effective than Europeans in avoiding prohibitions and in ministering to Christians in China. This belief was strengthened by the 1724 prohibition of Christianity and its transformation into an underground church. The seminarians were taught Latin and Chinese characters.[19] Because of the prolonged absence from China involved in their seminary training abroad and their consequent deracination (being uprooted from their native environment), Chinese priests encountered various degrees of difficulties in reintegrating into Chinese society.[20] These difficulties were exacerbated by being sent to mission sites whose inhabitants often spoke different dialects from the region in which they had been raised. Ripa had tried to compensate for the seminarians' remote training in Naples by speaking to them in Chinese and by having a Chinese teacher to teach them to speak and write Chinese. However, Chinese teachers were not always available. After Giovanni Gu (Gu Ruohan) returned to China, Bishop Martiliat commented on his language skills by saying that although Gu understood Latin well, in comparison with the Chinese priests educated at the MEP seminary in Ayudthia, Gu was less able to speak Latin and pronounce it correctly.[21] While many Chinese priests used Latin when writing to colleagues, Gu used Chinese.

Of the first four Chinese seminarians, three returned to China. While in Europe, all four suffered varying degrees of homesickness for China. The two youngest students, Filippo Huang and Lucio Wu, appear to have suffered the greatest longing for their homeland and they caused the greatest problems for Ripa. In 1731, Filippo Huang wrote to Ripa repeatedly about his wish to leave the college.[22] However, unlike his classmate Lucio Wu, Huang eventually adapted, although the process of his spiritual formation took far longer than the other students at the Chinese College. This delayed Filippo's return to China for thirty-six years until it finally occurred in 1760. Ripa's successor as rector, Fr. Gennaro Fatigati (1707–1785), wrote in 1755 that Filippo was "of a troubled nature, fond of vanity and of honors."[23] The Sacred Congregation secretary, M. Galdo, recorded that Filippo was "erased and dismissed from the College" on June 20, 1761. However, this notation may simply have meant that he graduated and returned to China because the notation was later scratched out.[24] In fact, Filippo served in the Beijing and Shanxi missions with no less scandal or dignity than many other European missionaries, and died in 1776.[25] By contrast, Lucio never returned to China and ended his life in disgrace in Rome. The two older and more stable Chinese, Giovanni Gu and Giovanni Yin, both returned to China after eleven years. The teacher Wang, who accompanied the four students, served Ripa well until he too returned to China, departing Naples with Giovanni Gu and Giovanni Yin on September 11, 1734. Wang served as a catechist in China until his death in Beijing on July 31, 1738.[26]

By 1732, the first two Chinese College seminarians, Giovanni Gu and Giovanni Yin, were ready to be examined for the priesthood. Ripa sent a memorial to the secretary of Propaganda Fide, proposing that they be examined in the following year. He was asking that Propaganda Fide not only examine the seminarians, but also pay for the costs of transporting them to China and supporting them in their mission work there. The response from Cardinal Petra of Propaganda Fide voiced certain doubts. Ripa lamented that the cardinals did not fully understand the perilous state in which the China mission found itself.[27] The initial expulsion of the missionaries to Guangzhou (Canton) had occurred in 1724, but a further expulsion of the thirty-five missionaries to Macau took place in 1733. Ripa argued that the need to train native Chinese as priests and send them back to China to replace the expelled European missionaries was more urgent than ever. Responding in writing to Propaganda Fide's doubts, Ripa argued that Chinese priests dressed in native clothes would avoid being recognized as missionaries.[28] They would be hidden in the midst of the crowd and would be able to move fluidly through China, without exposing the mission. Ripa also added that Chinese priests should be promoted to bishops to avoid the sad destruction of the Church that had occurred in Japan due to the lack of native bishops.[29]

It was decided to have the two seminarians examined over a four-to-five-day period, after which they would depart for China.[30] Gu and Yin traveled to Rome with their teacher Gioacchino Wang.[31] Propaganda Fide provided them with three beautiful rooms in which they lived comfortably during their stay in the Vatican City. The exam began on May 13, 1734, and concluded with a ceremonial meeting on the eighteenth.[32] There were three examiners plus a returned missionary from China named Father Rinaldo Maria Teresiano. In response to their query, Ripa replied that the seminarians had completed the proscribed course of study, including philosophy, theology (scholastic and dogmatic), and moral philosophy. Gu was examined first, followed by Yin, with each exam lasting about one and a half hours. Ripa was present during the entire process. The examiners were very pleased with the seminarians' answers.

At the conclusion of the exam, each of them swore the oath administered by Cardinal Petra, prefect of Propaganda Fide, to observe the papal ruling *Ex illa die* (1715), which banned Christians from participating in Chinese rites to ancestors. Cardinal Petra was particularly pleased with the responses of Giovanni Yin and said he would like to make him a bishop. Yin replied with his characteristic intensity, surprising the cardinal by saying, "Most Eminent Lord, I wish to be a cardinal rather than a bishop." He explained to the surprised Petra: "Most Eminent Lord, I have the desire to be a Cardinal rather than a Bishop, intending not really to wear the red-colored clothes like Your Eminence, but to have my black clothes tinted red, just like my blood that I wish to spill for the love of Christ." To present-day sensibilities, Yin's reply might seem excessive and overdone, and even fawning, but to the eighteenth-century Catholic sensibility of Rome, his desire for martyrdom struck a chord and was applauded by the cardinal and others as word of it spread throughout the Vatican. On May 18, Gu and Yin knelt at the feet of Pope Clement XII to receive his apostolic benediction. The pope granted various forms of plenary indulgences to Gu and Yin. To the secular teacher Wang, he granted plenary indulgences until the third generation.

When Cardinal Petra asked Ripa to what mission in China he proposed that Gu and Yin be sent, Ripa replied the mission in Sichuan because it was administered by Monsignor Johann Müllener, CM (Mu Tianchi 穆天尺) (1673–1742).[33] Müllener was born in Osnabrück and was sent by Propaganda Fide to China.[34] He and Luigi Antonio Appiani, CM (Bi Tianxiang 畢天祥)

(1663–1732), were the first Lazarists to go to China, arriving in 1699. The Lazarists, formerly called the Congregation of the Mission, were founded by Vincent de Paul in 1625 and are sometimes called Vincentians in his honor. Whereas the Jesuits had created a loyal and tightly knit hierarchical structure that had converted massive numbers of people, acquired vast properties and wealth, particularly in South America, and gained access to powerful rulers through their scientific expertise, the Lazarists remained more committed to their original goals of devoting themselves to the salvation of poor country people.[35] In the *Common Rules for Lazarists* (1658), Vincent de Paul emphasized that Vincentians were to avoid the attractions of ambition, power, and fame. The Lazarists' religiosity proved much more suitable than the Jesuits in coping with the rising tide of eighteenth-century European anticlericalism. While Jesuits commonly prepared themselves academically for ten years, Lazarists spent only two years in a novitiate before going into the mission field. However, the Lazarists had difficulty replacing the Jesuits because the Jesuit membership at the time of their suppression has been estimated at 11,415 while the Lazarists membership in 1789 numbered only about eight hundred.

Meanwhile the Rites Controversy had caused the Kangxi emperor to demand that all missionaries wishing to remain in China swear to follow the interpretations of the Jesuit father Matteo Ricci before they could receive a *piao* 票 (certificate) of residence. Müllener and Appiani were in Sichuan from 1702 until 1706 when they were expelled for refusing to accept the *piao*.[36] In 1711 the Lazarist Müllener secretly left Guangzhou and returned to Sichuan, where he took ownership of church property on behalf of the Missions Étrangères by paying the catechist Linus Zhang for land donated by Christians of Jintang.[37] Müllener was named vicar apostolic in 1715. Although he promoted a native Chinese priesthood and ordained three Chinese priests, he rigidly defended Rome's prohibition of the Chinese rites. Two of his Chinese students went to Rome to study.[38]

Propaganda Fide issued a decree on May 25, 1734, commanding that Gu and Yin be ordained priests. Ripa's request for a European missionary to accompany them as a guide during the long journey was rejected on the grounds that Europeans were being expelled from China.[39] The monsignor nuncio in Paris was ordered to procure bookings for Gu, Yin, and Wang on a French ship to China and to pay the captain for them, expressly obliging the captain to give them one or more rooms separated from the rest of the crew. In addition to the provisions given to the sailors, they were each to receive two glasses of wine each day, plus two chickens, or the equivalent in fresh meat, every week not only during passage, but also during layovers at ports.

The Chinese were to board the French ship at the port of Cadiz, Spain. In August 1734 Propaganda Fide asked the papal nuncio of Naples to obtain passage for the three Chinese on the first ship sailing from Naples to Cadiz.[40] Propaganda Fide was willing to underwrite the complete costs of the two priests Gu and Yin, but only partial costs for the teacher Wang. Propaganda Fide allotted 150 Roman scudi to each of the priests in payment of passage with a supplementary forty scudi each from the Holy Household. They departed from Naples on September 10, 1734.[41] Nearly two years passed before any news of their arrival in China was received. Finally in August 1736, Ripa received a letter from the Jesuit Father Dominique Parrenin, SJ (1665–1741), conveying news that the three Chinese had arrived safely at Macau.[42]

The first letter from the three Chinese, dated August 31, 1735, at Macau, arrived one year later in Naples, on September 15, 1736.[43] The letter told of their departure from Cadiz on November 23, 1734, and their hundred-day navigation to the Cape of Good Hope, then onward to the islands of Mauritius, Batavia, Java, and Sumatra, finally dropping anchor in Macau on August 24, 1735. They observed great caution in going ashore because of the expulsion edict against missionaries. Dressed as sailors and accompanied by Father Archangelo Miralta, they went ashore in the captain's small boat. Miralta was procurator of Propaganda Fide from 1729 to 1750. Because of tension with the Portuguese royal monopoly, he had not been allowed to buy property in Macau but resided in a convent of Portuguese Dominicans, where the procurators remained until 1776.[44] The Chinese arrived in Macau in good health. The French captain had treated them very well, admitting them to his table and giving them a comfortable place to sleep, as had been negotiated at Paris by the papal nuncio prior to their departure.

Ripa emphasized the need to properly fund the missionaries' voyages so that they would arrive in good health and be prepared to face the rigors ahead of them. He contrasted this with the unfortunate treatment of the fifth student to enter the Chinese College—Gàbriele Bellisario from the Philippines. The grandson of a Japanese, Bellisario was born in Manila in 1713 and was received into the Chinese College in 1736.[45] Bellisario had suffered on the journey to Europe because of inadequate funding.[46] On the journey he had spat blood. Since then he had recovered his health somewhat, but Ripa would not send him to China because of a problem in his chest (tuberculosis?) that left him continually debilitated and vulnerable to relapse. He is praised by Ripa because he fit the model of someone who sacrificed his health in the service of God. He died at Naples on November 28, 1738.

Shortly after the first letter, a second letter, dated November 11, 1735, and signed by both Gu and Yin, arrived from the city of Hiang-Han-Kien (?) in Huguang province.[47] (Huguang 湖廣 was the Ming dynasty designation of a large province in central China that was divided in the Qing dynasty into Hubei 湖北 and Hunan 湖南.) The letter conveyed news of their journey and their good health. They were writing from a small riverboat that was approaching the province of Sichuan. However, within the letter was a sealed tear-soaked card written solely by Gu on November 15 that told of Yin's death. The teacher Wang wrote a separate letter saying that Yin had always been very healthy and that his death was caused by the shock of a large fish jumping out of the water and leaping into the boat, causing such a fright to Yin that he fell ill and died. However, Gu's card made no mention of such an implausible shock. He simply said that a fever overtook Yin with a little catarrh and sweating, leaving him very weak. A physician was called, who gave him medicine that made him much weaker. Yin confessed to Gu and three hours after a second medicine was administered, Gu's "dearest companion" died in the middle of the night. Yin was buried at Xiangtan 湘潭 in Hunan province while Gu proceeded to Sichuan province.[48]

PROBLEMS WITH CHINESE STUDENTS IN NAPLES

The departure of three of the original group of Chinese left the remaining two members of that group despondent. The acolytes Filippo Huang and Lucio Wu became so upset that Ripa said they "seemed to have been possessed by the Demon."[49] Probably the homesickness for China they already felt was intensified by the departure of their three compatriots. Unlike the two Giovannis, Filippo and Lucio were given no clear path to return to China because their behavior made them questionable prospects as missionaries. Consequently, they rebelled through disobedience. In 1736, Filippo and Lucio committed some unspecified grave offenses that led to Filippo fleeing from the college twice.[50] During the pre-Lenten period of Carnival in 1737, it was discovered that they had engaged in undetected sexual play with each other.[51] This was an early sign of Lucio's probable homosexuality.[52] In 1738 their plot to flee together was discovered and they were forced to submit to various humiliating punishments. Ripa attributed their misbehavior to his absence on long trips to Vienna and Rome to secure funding for the Holy Foundation. He believed that during his absence, Filippo and Lucio had been tainted by their associating with "foreigners," which stimulated their misbehavior.[53]

Filippo displayed an arrogance that Ripa punished by forcing him to stop wearing the habit of the college and instead dress in ragged and patched clothes. He also discontinued Filippo's study of theology and confined him to a room with a few spiritual texts and Chinese books to read. The room was locked in order to prevent him from fleeing. Filippo was so embarrassed by the public humiliation of wearing rags that he would not appear in the church, but rather would hear mass in a private chapel where he would not be seen.

It appears that Ripa's methods of education that had been so effective with the two Giovannis were less effective with Filippo and Lucio. Ripa failed to see that the mixture of homesickness with no clear hope of returning to China and the humiliating punishment of wearing rags caused an emotional crisis in Filippo that caused him to run away. He was brought back to the college and Ripa imposed mortifications on him from March 8 until June 18.[54] However, ultimately Filippo composed a very humble letter to Ripa in which he asked for his pardon and promised to correct his ways. Consequently, before departing for another trip to Rome, Ripa allowed him once again to study theology, which was a crucial step in becoming a missionary to China. However, Ripa continued to make Filippo wear tattered clothes.

In January 1738 Ripa received a pack of letters from Giovanni Gu that had been forwarded by Fr. Miralta, the Propaganda Fide procurator in Macau. Fr. Gu had administered thirty-six baptisms and heard 204 confessions. However, he had acquired a persistent cough and Fr. Miralta said that he was spitting blood and perhaps seriously ill.[55] Meanwhile, Ripa received news of the arrival in France of two new Chinese students for the college.[56] These fifth and sixth Chinese students arrived at the College on May 25, 1738. Domenico Zhao (Zhao Duoming 趙多明) (1717–1754) was from Chengdu 成都 in Sichuan province. He would eventually return to China in 1751, where he worked as a missionary in Huguang province.[57] Simone Zhao (Zhao Ximan 趙西滿) (1722–1778) was from Jingzhou 荊州 in Hubei 湖北 province. He would eventually return to China in 1751 and serve in Sichuan.[58]

In addition to the frustration of constant negotiations with Rome to secure payment of the promised annual pension of 800 ducats for the college, Ripa had to deal with ongoing problems with Filippo and Lucio. Filippo's unhappiness soon resurfaced when he and Andrea Medici, a student who came to the Chinese College from the Collegio Urbano in Rome, stirred up other students to complain.[59] Filippo acted erratically and failed to observe the rules, while Andrea wrote letters of complaint "filled with black calumnies and pernicious venom" against the college. The problems continued as Filippo and Lucio acted in rebellious ways that disturbed the whole college.[60] Initially the new Chinese arrivals Domenico Zhao and Simon Zhao adapted well, but Filippo and Lucio tried to taint them with critical verbal asides and negative comments conveyed in secret notes.[61]

Although the two Giovannis had obediently followed the rules of the college, Filippo and Lucio regarded the rules as tyrannical. As their frustration in failing to return to China grew, their resentment and hatred of Ripa increased.[62] They believed he was a deceitful man who was treating them like children.[63] Ripa justified his lack of awareness of the intensity of their feelings by claiming that "dissimulation [was] innate to the Chinese nation."

Then the student Gàbriele Bellisario, who lived with Filippo and Lucio, came to Ripa and informed him of their disruptive acts. Ripa confronted them with their attempts to turn the two new Chinese students against him. Eventually, Filippo and Lucio confessed of their own volition in Chinese in public in the refectory, each wearing a cross at his throat.[64]

Ripa regarded the problems with Filippo and Lucio as exceptional, but his view was unrealistic. Although the intensity of the problems with Lucio were unusual, Filippo's problems were not unique, as was shown by similar emerging problems with Domenico and Simone. Ripa's plan to develop Chinese priests was basically sound, but he underestimated the problems involved in bringing Chinese students to Europe for a long period of seminary training. Seminarians with the highly developed vocations of Giovanni Gu and Giovanni Yin could thrive in the Collegio dei Cinesi, but students with more ordinary spiritual aptitude suffered from the cultural dislocation and homesickness, particularly if their return to China was postponed indefinitely, as it was with Filippo and Lucio.

Initially Ripa appears quite intentionally to have neglected teaching them Italian because he feared that the Chinese students would acquire the bad habits of Europeans. However, by restricting them to Chinese and Latin, he was causing them to become isolated in a way that fostered unhappiness and rebellion. Regardless of Ripa's protective intentions, the Chinese inevitably began to learn Italian. By 1792, when George Staunton secured two Chinese priests from the Chinese College to serve as translators for Lord Macartney's embassy to Beijing, the priests Jacobus Li (Li Zibiao 李自標, 1760–1828) and Paulus Ke (Ke Zongxiao 柯宗孝, 1759–1825) were able to communicate with Staunton and Macartney using both Italian and Latin.[65]

Of course, Ripa was forging a new path in international seminary education and there was little experience to guide him. Another contributing factor was Propaganda Fide's insistence on compelling the Chinese seminarians to swear to follow the *Ex illa die* papal ruling that prohibited Christians from participating in ancestral ceremonies. The rigidity with which the *Ex illa die* ruling was imposed created a conflict with the Chinese students' keen sense of family loyalty. In China a less rigid application of *Ex illa die* was often adopted by Chinese priests when faced with practical realities in remote mission fields, but this flexibility was not available in a Propaganda-sponsored college so close to Rome.

Ripa lamented that although Filippo and Lucio had begun studying with him in China when they were six and one-half years old (actually Lucio was one year younger than Filippo), they were too young to have developed a vocation when Ripa took them to Europe. They had behaved well, especially Filippo, until they were fourteen years old. However, at that point, they began associating with foreigners (Europeans) and acquired bad habits. Because Ripa was absent from Naples for almost three years securing funding for the college, he was not present to prevent their exposure to these vices. From these experiences Ripa concluded two things: first, not to bring Chinese students to Europe who had not demonstrated a mature sense of vocation and, second, not to allow the Chinese students to associate with foreigners.[66] Still, Filippo seems to have been more mentally sound than Lucio. Moreover, Filippo's apologies to Ripa appear to have been filled with a more genuine sense of remorse than Lucio's apologies.

Whether the new students Domenico Zhao and Simone Zhao were infected by the critical views of Filippo and Lucio or whether they were upset by the circumstances of their residence in a foreign country, they began to cause problems. Ripa often consulted Monsignor Müllener in Macau and the Chinese priest Pablo Ju (Zhu?), to whom Domenico and Simone had sworn an oath before leaving China.[67] Ripa gave the impression that Müllener and Ju had been instrumental in securing Propaganda Fide's sponsorship of them as students for the Chinese College. When their misbehavior led Ripa to threaten to send Domenico and Simone to Rome, they submitted and asked not to be sent away. They embraced Ripa, who then tore up the letter he had been planning to send to Rome.[68] However, problems continued and Ripa complained that Domenico and Simone had joined with the "bird-brain" (*cervellino*) Andrea Medici and another student named Angelo from the same family as Gàbriele Bellisario to form a cabal (*camarilla*). The Chinese had learned enough Latin and Italian to communicate with the others and their resentments were fanned by Andrea Medici's complaints over the strictness of the rules.[69] Ripa had been reassured by having the loyal Gàbriele Bellisario live with the others until Bellisario fell gravely ill and had to be moved to a private room. When Ripa realized that Andrea's complaints were infecting Filippo and Lucio, he separated Andrea from them and petitioned to have Andrea recalled to Rome.[70] Ripa then commanded Filippo and Lucio to swear a vow to observe the rules of the college that had been authorized by the pope.

MORE STUDENTS ARRIVE FROM CHINA

In December 1738 Ripa received word that three more Chinese students for the Collegio dei Cinesi had arrived in Rome.[71] They were Giuseppe Lucio Li (Li Ruose 李若瑟) (1717–1776) from Guangdong province, Vitale Giuseppe Guo (Guo Yuanxing 郭元性) (1718–1778) of Shaanxi, and Paolo Cai (Cai Wenan 蔡文安) (1720–1782) from Fujian.[72] However, Propaganda Fide was insisting that the three new Chinese students remain in Rome until they had been thoroughly schooled in the church's official position on the Chinese rites. In addition, Propaganda Fide was insisting that the "bird-brain" Domenico Zhao also be sent to Rome so that he could be informed, along with the three new Chinese students, of the Vatican's position on the Chinese rites.[73] Meanwhile, Ripa's petition to have Andrea recalled to Rome had been approved. Consequently, Domenico and Andrea, accompanied by a college priest, Fr. Ignazio Deci, departed for Rome where Domenico was to receive instruction in the Chinese rites along with the three newly arrived Chinese.[74]

While the four Chinese students were studying in the Collegio Urbano in Rome, Simone Zhao fell gravely ill in Naples and was able to consume nothing but water for nine days. No sooner was he out of danger than tragedy struck and the fever took the life of Ripa's younger brother Lorenzo and Lorenzo's daughter. However, Ripa's greatest sorrow came with the death of his sole sister, Caterina, who had raised him after the death of their mother when he was four years of age. They died, in the nature of such plagues, in rapid order on February 19, 20, and 28, 1739.[75]

Ripa spoke frequently of God inflicting misfortunes on him. And yet, his complaints, however real, served as misfortunes that he was able to spiritually transform and sublimate into his work at the Chinese College. Meanwhile, the reports from Fr. Deci at Rome warned Ripa that he would have a heavy cross to bear because Giuseppe Li, one of the new Chinese students, was "an arrogant bird-brain and also cheeky" (*un cervellone superbo, ed impertinente*).[76] Meanwhile the "bird-brain" Domenico Zhao was demonstrating his cleverness at Rome by impressing a gathering of cardinals in reciting a prayer in Chinese in an academy of foreign languages that Propaganda Fide controlled. Zhao then filled the heads of the other three newly arrived Chinese with complaints against Ripa and the Chinese College, convincing them that it would be better to remain in Rome under the guidance of Propaganda Fide, where the food and living conditions were better than at the Chinese College in Naples.[77]

Domenico then audaciously composed a memorial, in the name of all four of them, requesting of the Cardinal Prefect Petra that they be allowed to leave the Chinese College and move to Rome. Cardinal Petra responded by calling all four of them before him with Fr. Giuseppe Cercì serving as interpreter. Petra was angry and in a loud voice scolded them for their disobedience and for their lack of appreciation for the great expense Propaganda Fide had incurred in bringing them to Europe. The four youths became frightened and fell to their knees, humbly asking the cardinal for his pardon and promising thereafter to be obedient. Soon afterward they departed Rome and arrived at the Chinese College in Naples on March 1, 1739.

Ripa was particularly angry with Domenico Zhao and Giuseppe Li for their behavior at Rome, but he punished all of them by transforming their two rooms into prison cells, removing the lamps and European-style beds and forcing them to sleep, in Chinese style, without sheets.[78] At meals they were given only common food with no wine. Seeing that their rooms were being turned into prison cells, Domenico Zhao, Vitale Guo, and Paolo Cai had a change of heart and on March 3, in the public refectory, humbly fell to their knees at Ripa's feet and asked for his pardon for all the scandal and rumors they had caused in Rome. On March 7 Domenico brought Ripa a letter of apology that he had written to the cardinal's translator Fr. Cercì. In the letter Domenico confessed that through the instigation of the Demon (*Demonio*), he had slandered the Chinese College in order to remain in Rome. The next day, Vitale and Paolo also presented letters of exculpation (*discolpa*) to Father Cercì. Of the four, only Giuseppe Li resisted apologizing, but on the very next day, the eighth, he too knelt in the refectory with the cross at his neck, confessing his sins and asking for pardon.[79] Simone Zhao, who had recovered from his illness, was zealous in criticizing Domenico and in convincing his three new fellow students from China to reform their ways, urging them to imitate the archangel Gabriel.

Meanwhile, letters from Giovanni Gu arrived from China, dated October 1737 and September 1738. His health had improved and he was able to lead a truly apostolic life, going on foot through valleys and mountains, defying hunger and thirst, sleeping outside and enduring foul weather.[80] The harvest of his apostolic efforts had been abundant. He had performed 53 baptisms and heard the confessions of 370 persons in one year and in the following year he had performed 139 baptisms and heard confessions from 560 persons. One year after Giovanni Gu had written his letter of September 18, 1740, Ripa received it. Although Giovanni was suffering from a bad case of "catarrh" (flu?), which then reached epidemic proportions in Sichuan, he had in the preceding year performed 72 baptisms and heard the confessions of 600 persons.[81]

Students of different nationalities came to study at the Chinese College. On June 18, 1739, a youth arrived, who, although appearing to be Chinese, was actually Tartar (Mongolian) and from Calmucco, home of the Kalmyk Mongols in present-day Russia. He had come to Moscow and was brought to Spain and finally to Naples.[82]

Shortly afterward, Ripa received the news of the arrival in France of the students Pio Liu, the elder (Liu Biyue 劉必約) (1718–1786), and Pio Martino Liu, the younger (Liu Chengren 劉成仁) (1718–1785), both of Sichuan.[83] They entered the college on December 8, 1739, and were the last two students to arrive during Ripa's lifetime, although the Collegio dei Cinesi continued to train Chinese seminarians until 1869, when it was transformed into the Real Collegio Asiatico (Royal Asiatic College).[84] The identical surname of Pio Liu and Pio Martino Liu and their origins and ages indicate that they might have belonged to the same family or clan. They both made their minor vows in 1741 and both returned to China as missionaries in 1755.[85] Pio Liu (the elder) served in Zhili and Shandong provinces until his death in 1786. Pio Martino Liu (the younger) served in Shaanxi province. During the great persecution of 1784, he voluntarily turned himself in to the authorities to protect his Christians.[86] Along with numerous Christians, he was exiled to Yili 伊犁 in the remote desert region of northwest China, where he died in 1785.[87]

Ripa referred to both Giuseppe Guo and Paolo Cai as being the objects of some slander that occurred in August 1740.[88] Also Paolo had a dispute with Fr. Nicolò Riccio, one of the Holy Family members, who reprimanded him with a caning. (Riccio later left the college.) Paolo recognized his error and came in humility to ask the forgiveness of Ripa in private, and later in public. Ripa grew to have a special fondness for Paolo, whom he "loved more than all the others because he was the most fervid, and observed the rule, that might vex most of the others."[89] After the death of Pope Clement XII, there was a long conclave in Rome lasting several months and ending in the election of Pope Benedict XIV in August 1740, who confirmed the annual pension of 800 ducats to the Collegio dei Cinesi.[90]

Ripa's health began to fail in August 1742 when he suffered from a painful colic. In that month he had the consolation of receiving another letter from Giovanni Gu dated September 25, 1740, which conveyed the happy news of 103 baptisms during the preceding year. However, the troubling Rites Controversy caused Ripa to temper his praise for the work of his former student. Propaganda Fide was rigid in its insistence that Chinese Christians not be permitted to participate in ceremonies honoring their ancestors on the grounds that they were a form of idolatry. Although Ripa had expressed nothing but praise for Giovanni Gu's suffering as a missionary in remote areas of Sichuan and the numerous baptisms and confessions he had made and heard, he now voiced his displeasure after receiving a letter on September 29, 1745, from Monsignor Luigi Maria Maggi, OP (Lu Wenren 陸文仁) (d. 1743). Maggi was a missionary in Sichuan who had succeeded Monsignor Müllener as the bishop of Sichuan and administrator of Huguang and Guizhou provinces.[91] As a representative of Propaganda Fide, he voiced complaints about Father Gu's handling of the rites. Gu was allowing the Chinese to use the Eight Permissions to modify the *Ex illa die* ruling.[92] The different points of view in this dispute reflected a tension between the European and Chinese priests.

When the papal legate Carlo A. Mezzabarba had been presented at the Chinese court in 1720, the Kangxi emperor was so enraged over *Ex illa die* of 1715 that Mezzabarba issued the Eight Permissions (Eight Concessions) on December 20, 1720, in an attempt to temper the ruling and assuage the emperor's anger. However, the emperor adamantly rejected *Ex illa die* and refused to allow the papal representative permanent residence in China. The issue involved a debate between the theological pragmatists and purists. Whereas Bishop Della Chiesa was pragmatic and tolerant on the rites, his vicar general Carlo di Orazio da Castorano, OFM, was a strict opponent. When the papal ruling *Ex illa die* had arrived in 1716, Castorano had insisted on promulgating it.[93] Later, imperial opposition forced him to flee from Shandong to Beijing in the persecution of 1730–1734.[94] In 1732, when the bishop of Beijing Francisco da Purificaçâo da Rocha Fróes (d. 1733), who was forced to reside in Macau due to the imperial expulsion of the missionaries, included some of the Eight Permissions in his pastoral letter, Castorano went to Rome and succeeded in having the Eight Permissions prohibited. This incident was another manifestation of the ongoing conflict between the practical realities that missionaries faced in China versus the rigid theological views of Rome.

Although Ripa had lived in China for nearly thirteen years, he had worked at the emperor's court in Beijing, rather than in the mission field. It is unlikely that he had sufficient experience to understand the problems that missionaries like Father Gu were facing in the remote countryside of China. Ripa's primary apostolate among the Chinese was as a court artist and with the seminary preparation of young men. He tended to have the mentality of a schoolmaster. He was very devoted to his pupils, but he was a strict disciplinarian who emphasized following the rules and inflicted humiliating punishments on those who broke them. Although the punishments appear overly harsh by contemporary standards, they were quite common in eighteenth-century Europe. Moreover, there is little evidence that Ripa practiced physically abusive corporal punishment. He got along well with those pupils, like Giovanni Gu, Giovanni Yin, and Paolo Cai, who submitted to his demands, but he had difficulties with those like Filippo Huang, Lucio Wu, Domenico Zhao, and Giuseppe Li, who resisted his heavy-handed discipline. However, all of these seminarians, except for Lucio, eventually returned to China and served as missionaries.

Ripa pressed ahead with his plans. He anticipated that in two years, Vitale Guo and Domenico Zhao would be ready to be sent to China.[95] They were currently studying moral philosophy (ethics), and not yet able to undertake scholastic dogmatics because of their physical problems. Guo, in particular, showed promise and was praised by Fr. Fatigati. Guo and three others were examined in Rome in 1750 and Pope Benedict XIV praised Guo, saying that he had the qualities to become a future archbishop of Sichuan. Guo was indeed eventually nominated as pro-vicar of Shanxi province.[96] Vitale and Zhao departed for China on July 26, 1751.[97]

Ripa had a complicated view of the Chinese. Unlike many eighteenth-century European clerics, he had no doubt that the Chinese were capable of becoming priests and bishops. But the Chinese he dealt with most closely were mere students in faraway Europe whose occasional opposition he was in a position to suppress. However, when they returned to China, these priests began to diverge from Ripa's strict views on the rites. This was true of Fr. Giovanni Battista Gu, who had been much admired in Europe. However, when he served in Sichuan in the area of Jiangjin 江津 in 1734–1746, he was criticized by the Apostolic Vicar of Sichuan, Bishop Müllener, and by his successor Bishop Luigi Maria Maggi, OP. Ripa knew Müllener and was in agreement with him and with Maggi on their criticism of Fr. Gu's handling of the Chinese rites with parishioners.[98] However, the Holy Family congregant Fr. Domenico La Magna, whom Lucio Wu was originally to have accompanied in returning to China, dissented. La Magna firmly defended Gu and harshly criticized Bishop Maggi as being an inept administrator.

While Bishop Müllener thought that Gu was a good priest, he was opposed to granting him any authority. Bishop Maggi was even more critical and complained to Ripa about Gu's arrogance in tolerating the practice of the Chinese rites among his parishioners. Maggi projected his criticism of Gu as an individual priest onto the entire Chinese nation, which became a form of cultural and racial bias akin to racism. Maggi wrote, "The pride [arrogance] of the Chinese, and their esteem of it is a vice characteristic of that nation" (*la superbia de' Cinesi, e stima di se è un vizio proprio di questa Nazione*). Ripa blamed this arrogance for causing Chinese priests to feel justified in using the Eight Permissions to circumvent the papal ruling *Ex illa die* to sustain the continued practice of the superstitious rites to ancestors.[99] Ripa was also less conscious of his own pride as a European. Consequently, instead of compromising with an ingrained Chinese cultural trait (ancestral reverence), he followed Propaganda's rigid interpretation of Christian theology to treat ancestral reverence as a theological error that could be corrected through a disciplined form of education.

LUCIO WU AS RIPA'S "PERPETUAL CROSS TO BEAR"

At dawn on April 5, 1739, Ripa received in public the priestly vows of the "two bird-brains" (*due cervelloni*), Filippo Huang and Lucio Wu.[100] One year later, on March 19, 1740, he had the consolation of hearing their first mass after their ordination as priests on the previous day.[101] However, Ripa faced a dilemma with Lucio. Although the college had made a commitment to have him return to China as a missionary, Ripa felt that Lucio was too immature to serve there alone. Consequently, he proposed to his Holy Family confreres that they send Lucio to China in the company of the Holy Family congregant Fr. Domenico La Magna (1717–1773), with whom he would remain until he was judged mature enough to serve independently.[102] The college then sent the names of Lucio and Fr. La Magna to Propaganda Fide in Rome as missionaries chosen to go to China. Later it was decided to hold Lucio back and send only La Magna, who departed from Naples for Genoa on September 26, 1743.[103] The decision to hold Lucio back was not made by Ripa alone. The Rules and Constitution (*Regole e Costituzioni*) of the congregation and college of the Holy Family had been approved by Pope Clement XII in 1736.[104] They stipulated that a candidate for mission abroad should be subjected to an evaluation process involving not only a report of the college rector (Ripa) on the "character, conduct, and customs" of the candidate, but also a secret ballot by the members of the Holy Congregation.[105] Their negative decision would have tragic consequences because it triggered a sense of betrayal in Lucio's troubled mind, followed by a series of desperate acts. With his hopes of returning to China once again frustrated, he viewed the Chinese College increasingly as a prison in which he was sentenced to an indefinite confinement.

Ripa's motives for withdrawing his support of Lucio as a missionary to China are unclear. In a letter of June 25, 1744, to Propaganda Fide, he requested that Lucio not be invited to go to China because he gave "examples of being not yet mature."[106] In his journals, Ripa tried to justify his decision, although it is unclear whether he was justifying his behavior to God or to himself. He recited a litany of Lucio's "many offenses, incorrigible deeds" that included damaging the door lock of his room so that it could not be opened by the superior and making false keys to open other rooms.[107] Lucio apparently used these false keys to collect new surplices, five soutanes and six pairs of shoes, and luxurious clothes. This might indicate kleptomania or merely rebellion, but it was certainly irrational behavior. Given the small size of the Chinese College, it is hard to see how such thefts could go unnoticed. When his thefts were discovered, he shut himself up for several hours in the changing room, from which he fled the college and could not be found. Eventually Ripa discovered that he was staying in a house of the diocese of Monte Casino called San Vittore. He was exercising ecclesiastical functions and acting as a curate and exceeding his ordinary title of missionary.

Ripa was embarrassed and dismayed by the dishonor Lucio was bringing on the Collegio dei Cinesi, but clearly there was also a deep personal sense of responsibility and disappointment. Before leaving China, Ripa had felt that Lucio was too young and intellectually deficient and had decided to leave him, but then twice heard a command from God to take him. Consequently,

Ripa felt that he had failed in some way to fulfill what had been commanded by God. On April 3, 1745, a troubled Ripa wrote an apologetic letter to the abbot of Monte Casino, asking him to confine the fugitive Lucio and hold him until arrangements could be made for his return to the Chinese College.[108] After Lucio gave signs of his repentance, Ripa sent the Holy Family congregant Fr. Carlo Nardi to fetch him and Lucio was brought back to the college on May 3.

But clearly the matter was not resolved. Lucio's father, the teacher-catechist Tommaso Wu, gave his son to God in a distinctively Chinese way that blended an obligation of filial piety with priestly vocation. Separated from his family for so many years, Lucio's bond of filial obligation may have weakened. In addition, his call to the priesthood never fully developed. By 1745, Lucio had been away from his homeland for twenty years. He had left it when he was twelve years old and he was now thirty-two. He had been too young to have had a clear sense of his vocation when he left China. His homesickness and unhappiness at the Chinese College appear to have overwhelmed him and impeded his development of a mature sense of vocation in Naples. Several of his fellow Chinese seminarians at the Chinese College also experienced difficulties, but all of them were regarded as sufficiently advanced in their vocations to be sent eventually to China. Lucio was the one exception and when the Chinese College denied him the opportunity to return to China, he felt trapped and reacted out of desperation.

On the night of July 14, 1745, Lucio fled the college a second time.[109] The act was premeditated. Before fleeing the college, he had forged testimonials from fake witnesses with counterfeit seals of the archdiocese of Naples to use when needed. He was running away, but he had no clear idea to where. He had been trained as a priest and he tried using his training to survive. The first news of his whereabouts came from Ripa's cousin Giuseppe, a priest in Rome, who recognized Lucio among the pilgrims when he washed their feet at the Piazza de Trinità de Pellegrini on August 24.[110] When Fr. Giuseppe asked him why he had come to Rome, Lucio answered that he was visiting holy places, but said that he would soon be returning to Naples. He refused to go to the pope's table under the pretext of being ashamed because his clothes were inappropriate. He then disappeared. Lucio then wandered throughout the Papal States, visiting Macerata, Loreto, and Ancora.[111]

Lucio was finally discovered in Senigallia, a port on the Adriatic Sea more than two hundred miles north of Naples. He had been arrested for having given counterfeit documents to the clerical authorities and for having celebrated mass in that city without being an authorized priest.[112] On September 25 and 28, he was interrogated by Ferdinando Giuliani, vicar of the bishop of Senigallia.[113] There is a record of the interrogation.[114] The interrogator posed the questions in Latin and Lucio responded in Italian. Unlike previously, he no longer used the fictitious name of Giuseppe Ugar, but instead gave his name as Giuseppe Lucio Vu of the Chinese city of Nanjing. The prison records from his later imprisonment at Castel Sant'Angelo in Rome show that he would increasingly discontinue using Lucio as his name and prefer Giuseppe Vu.[115] Since Ripa always referred to him as Lucio rather than Giuseppe, one wonders if this was Lucio's way of creating a new identity in an attempt to separate himself from his past association with Ripa. In the interrogation, he gave his age as thirty-six and said he had resided at the Chinese College for twenty years, studying Latin, philosophy, and theology. He said he was a secular priest, ordained by Cardinal Spinelli, archbishop of Naples. Oddly, he could not remember if his ordination had been four or five years earlier. This was only one of several lapses of memory. He said he had been arrested thirty days before, in the middle of the night. In a dubious claim of innocence, he said he did not know nor could he imagine the reason for his detention.

When the interrogator asked him about the papers that were confiscated from him after his arrest, Lucio claimed he could not remember their contents. When he was shown the papers, he admitted they were the papers. He explained that in the twenty days prior to his second flight from the Chinese College, he had forged these two certificates, using a nail to inscribe the shield of the archbishop of Naples, and forged the signatures of the archbishop of Naples as well as Monsignor Cioffo, vicar general of Naples.

There was a second brief interrogation on September 28.[116] The vicar then wrote to Ripa, explaining that Lucio was incarcerated and enclosing a letter from Lucio to Ripa. Lucio described his unhappy condition and, once again, in servile fashion, begged for mercy and promised to amend his behavior. This was a deeply troubled soul, completely alone and trapped in a place and circumstances far from home.

Ripa in self-justification lamented that although he had hoped to send Lucio as a Holy Congregation missionary in China when his studies were completed, his conscience had kept him from doing so because of Lucio's "excesses" (*eccessi*).[117] One suspects that the word "excesses" was a euphemism for mendacities. Lucio had left a trail of falsehoods when he fled to Monte Casino for nine months and then, after being forgiven and brought back, had fled again seventy-four days later, on July 14, 1745. Nevertheless, Ripa said he was loath to abandon him because of the great effort that had been made in bringing him to Naples and educating him in the Chinese College. In addition, there appears to have been something else—an obsession and sublimated quasi-sexual attraction to a boy that over the years became a paternal bond with all the complex feelings that fathers have for wayward sons. But these are feelings that Ripa could not confront. Instead, he complained about the costs involved in educating Lucio, one of eight Chinese youths on whom Propaganda Fide had spent a total of 1,300 Roman scudi to educate. (Actually, as of 1745, eleven Chinese students had studied in the Chinese College.)

Lucio recognized in his letter that he had done something evil. He expressed the hope that God would pardon him and that he could return to the college. However, Ripa was conflicted. With his judgment possibly affected by his approaching death, he lost his sense of proportion and exaggeratedly claimed that Lucio's crimes were serious enough to send him to the galleys or at least to a long imprisonment.[118] He had violated the five vows of the Congregation of the Holy Family that had been approved by the Holy See and that were renewed every year in a public ceremony in the Chinese College's church. But such was Ripa's lingering affection for this wayward son that he believed his faith and his responsibility as father superior obliged him to forgive Lucio.

LUCIO'S SECOND FLIGHT AND IMPRISONMENT IN CASTEL SANT'ANGELO

Ripa sent an elderly priest, Fr. Giuseppe Andrada, to Senigallia to secure Lucio's release and to bring him back to Naples. On December 5, 1745, the vicar general of Senigallia wrote to Ripa, saying that he had released Lucio to Fr. Andrada with a document of the sentence, obliging Lucio to present himself at the Chinese College under pain of excommunication.[119] However, Ripa received a letter dated two days later (December 7) from Fr. Andrada saying that two days after leaving Senigallia with Lucio, in the coastal city of Loreto, Lucio had suddenly expressed the wish to say confession. Forced to search for a confessor, they found one in the Jesuit penitentiary. Lucio completed his confession and while Andrada was being confessed, Lucio suddenly bolted and could not be found.

On December 20 he was sighted at Macerata, and on January 1, 1746, he was arrested at Foligno.[120] He was interrogated by the vicar Bernabucci on February 1. Fr. Andrada conveyed to Ripa that Lucio was incarcerated and warned that Lucio was hoping to flee to Geneva.[121] Ripa feared that Lucio might be trying to find a way to return to China and he worried about the consequent damage to the reputation of the Chinese College that might result.[122] Moreover, Ripa was presented with a bill for payment of prison costs for food and a bed for each of Lucio's incarcerations. On February 7, 1746, Ripa wrote to Propaganda Fide. After conveying how well an Indian youth named Lazaro was doing in the Chinese College, he shared the disturbing news that Lucio was incarcerated in Foligno, where he was toying with the idea of fleeing to Geneva. Ripa does not seem to have confronted the possibility that Lucio had become mentally deranged and was no longer capable of rational thinking.

Ripa felt betrayed by Lucio and turned against him. He became obsessive in requesting the incarceration of his old student. Ripa's irrational demand that Lucio be sentenced to the pontifical galleys was rejected by the Vatican as disproportionate to the crime.[123] He removed Lucio's name from the list of students at the Chinese College.[124] Lucio complained that his prison food allowance was inadequate, but he had become persona non grata to Ripa.

How did Lucio view his flight? One fragment of evidence is the record of his statement made at the interrogation by the vicar Bernabucci on February 1, 1746, at Foligno.[125] Lucio had said he no longer wanted to remain at the Chinese College because of the severity of the punishments and mortifications he was forced to undergo. This included being forced to eat a dish of dog and cat meat instead of regular food. The punishment of being fed dog and cat meat was still fairly widespread in colleges, seminaries, and monasteries in the Italian peninsula at the end of the eighteenth century. Lucio defended himself, claiming that he had been a good and obedient student. Was this statement, like his previous promises to Ripa to reform, merely the result of his desperation to escape punishment or did he sincerely believe what he said? It is difficult to say whether Lucio was still capable of distinguishing truth from falsehood. Ripa believed that Chinese culture accepted a greater degree of mendacity than was tolerated in Europe. However, Lucio's deceitfulness far exceeded what was typical among his fellow Chinese students. Ripa had hesitated to bring Lucio to Europe because of a weakness in both his intellect and character. Had his isolation in Europe caused his mental frailties to devolve into derangement?

Ripa said his twenty-six-year relationship with Lucio began in China on April 22, 1720.[126] There were distinct qualitative differences among the eleven students who had arrived at the Chinese College by the time of Ripa's death. Giovanni Gu and Giovanni Yin were outstanding students and trailblazers for Chinese College missionaries in China. Paolo Cai was also highly praised by Ripa. Ripa spoke of his love for all three of them. Pio Martino Liu the younger later died from his service to God in China. Filippo Huang, Domenico Zhao, and Giuseppe Li were not model students. They proved troublesome for Ripa, who referred to the three of them as well as Lucio as "bird-brained." Domenico, Giuseppe Li, Vitale Guo, and Paolo Cai all got into trouble in Rome when they petitioned Propaganda Fide to remain in Rome rather than go to Naples. However, their transgressions were within the range of normal and all of them eventually were sent to China as missionaries—except for Lucio.

The lives of Ripa and Lucio were bound together in the culminating trauma of Ripa's death. The stress of Lucio's flight combined with Ripa's sixty-three years of age to precipitate the beginning of his physical decline on November 22, 1745.[127] An abrasion on his leg created an eschar (slough produced by gangrene), requiring him to lie still. He developed jaundice, suffering spasms in his chest that gradually became longer and more dangerous. On March 18, 1746, he took Holy Communion from the Viaticum. On the twentieth he was given extreme unction. He died with the whole community gathered around his bed on their knees—the priests, novices, Chinese students, boarders, and brothers.

As Ripa lay dying, the Chinese College was informed that the Bishop of Foligno had been ordered by Propaganda Fide to compile an indictment against Lucio. Two days after Ripa's death, a letter from Cardinal Niccolò Lercari, the secretary of Propaganda Fide, arrived in Naples informing the Holy Congregation that His Holiness, Benedict XIV, had ordered Lucio to be brought to Rome, where he was less likely to escape.[128] Lucio was consequently imprisoned in the Castel Sant'Angelo. After Lucio spent several months as a cooperative prisoner, Propaganda Fide wrote to the archbishop of Naples, Giuseppe Spinelli, asking him to inquire whether the Holy Congregation was willing to take him back.[129] However, Ripa's successor, Fr. Gennaro Fatigati, did not share the ambiguities of Ripa's viewpoint and sent a very negative assessment of Lucio to the archbishop. Fatigati wrote to Propaganda saying that there was no basis on which to make him repent because the Chinese priest was "truly a depraved spirit with depraved habits." If Lucio were to return to the Holy Congregation, Fatigati felt he could not be sent to China and that he would once again take flight. Instead Fatigati advised that Lucio should remain in prison and be well guarded.

Lucio spent the remaining eighteen years of his life in prison. His name appeared intermittently on the prison rolls. After an initial period of good behavior did not secure his release, he lapsed into his more usual traits, but documentation is scant. A report dated July 8, 1750, by Monsignor Caracciolo of Santobono, Commissioner of the Sea, and addressed to the secretary of Propaganda Cardinal Lecari claimed that Lucio lived *"una vita scandalosa"* (a scandalous life) for a priest.[130] He loved the vice of gambling with cards and when he lost, he became enraged. His rage led to physical fights in which he would be injured so badly that he could not rise from his bed. At times, his status as a prisoner changed and for a period he seems to have lived outside of the Castel Sant'Angelo. His request to leave Rome during the jubilee of 1750 was denied by the Propaganda Fide cardinals. In a 1758 appeal to these cardinals, he wrote of having been "a supernumerary young person in the Chinese language of the Vatican Library."[131] Thereafter he remained confined but relatively unrestricted within the Castel Sant'Angelo.

In later years, Lucio had health problems and was allowed to reside for a time on the outskirts of Rome. There are records of him writing to Propaganda Fide twice, requesting financial aid for personal care. The first request was granted. His final request, dated February 28, 1763, asked for aid to deal with a severe case of rheumatism causing pain to his entire body and making him unable to lift his arm.[132] The request was denied. He died in Rome in August 1763.

In 1747 Pope Benedict XIV created two sections in the Chinese College. One was for Chinese and Indian students and the other was for students in the Middle East under Turkish domination. The college enrollment was small, never surpassing fifteen students on average. The college produced 173 alumni (106 Chinese and 67 from the Middle East) during its 156 years of existence. Since the religious orders in China did not collaborate in sending Chinese students to Europe, most of the students were recruited from areas where Chinese College alumni worked.[133] The Shanxi and Shaanxi vicariate sent twenty-seven students, Hubei and Hunan sent twenty-one, Guangdong sent twenty, and Jiangxi sent thirteen, while only eight came from Hubei, five from Sichuan, and four from Fujian, plus a few from Beijing and Macau. Most of the priests trained at the Chinese College were sent to the vicariate of Shanxi-Shaanxi (about forty-five) and Hubei-Hunan (about forty) while six priests worked in Guangdong and five in Beijing.

The end of the Collegio dei Cinesi was the result of the secularizing forces of the new Italian state that were hostile to the Catholic Church. An incident occurred when six young Chinese boys who were brought to the Chinese College in 1886 resisted, with one exception, becoming priests.[134] The anticlerical Italian government and its supporters exploited the incident to justify the suppression of the Chinese College on the grounds of "yellow human bondage" (*tratta gialla*). Although the Italian government lost a long and bitter legal dispute with the Congregation of the Holy Family in the courts, the parliament passed a law in 1888 that changed the ownership of the college as well as its name and purpose.[135] The Italian government changed the Chinese College from a seminary for Chinese students into an educational institution for the study of the most important languages of the East and to prepare students to work in consulates, trade, scholarly research, and education. It was renamed the Royal Asiatic Institute.[136] The Congregation of the Holy Family was dissolved.

NOTES

1. Matteo Ripa, *Storia della Fondazione della Congregazione e del Collegio di'cinesi*. 3 vols. (Napoli: Tipografia Manfredi, 1832), II:203–4.

2. Ripa, *Storia*, II:206.
3. Ripa, *Storia*, II:206–9.
4. Song Liming 宋黎明, "Luo Wenzhao haishi Luo Wenzao?—wei zhongguo shouwei guoji zhujiao Luo zhujiao zhengming 罗文炤还是罗文藻?—为中国首位国籍主教罗主教正名," *Haijiaoshi yanjiu* 海交史研究 3 (2019): 40–51.
5. Ripa, *Storia*, II:211.
6. Ripa, *Storia*, II:218–19.
7. Ripa, *Storia*, II:255–56.
8. Ripa, *Storia*, II:256–58.
9. Ripa, *Storia*, III:55.
10. Ripa, *Storia*, II:269–71.
11. Ripa, *Storia*, II:281.
12. Ripa, *Storia*, II:376.
13. Ripa, *Storia*, II:387–91.
14. Ripa, *Storia*, II:389–91.
15. Ripa, *Storia*, II:260.
16. Ripa, *Storia*, II:401–2.
17. Paul Pelliot, *Inventaire sommaire des manuscrits et imprimés chinois de la Bibliothèque Vaticane*, rev. and ed. Takata Tokio (Kyoto: Italian School of East Asian Studies, 1995), 63. Also see Yu Dong, *Catalogo delle Opere cinesi Missionarie della Biblioteca Apostolica Vaticana (XVI–XVIII sec.)* (Vatican: Biblioteca Apostolica Vaticana, 1996), 17.
18. Ripa, *Storia*, II:458–59.
19. Ripa, *Storia*, II:34; 36.
20. R. G. Tiedemann, "The Controversy over the Formation of an Indigenous Clergy and the Establishment of a Catholic Hierarchy in China, 1846–1926," in *Light a Candle: Encounters and Friendship with China*, ed. Roman Malek, SVD, and Gianni Criveller, PIME (Nettetal: Institut Monumenta Serica, 2010), 342.
21. Robert Entenmann, "Chinese Clergy and Their European Colleagues in Sichuan, 1702–1800," in *Silent Force: Native Converts in the Catholic China Mission*, ed. Rachel Lu Yan and Philip Vanhaelemeersch (Leuven: Ferdinand Verbiest Institute, 2009), 80. Entenmann refers to Joannes-Baptista Kou (Giovanni Battista Gu) by his given name of Gu Yaowen 谷耀文 instead of his baptismal name, Gu Ruohan 谷若翰.
22. Ripa, *Storia*, II:451.
23. Giacomo Di Fiore, "Carità e reclusione nell'Europa del Settecento. Le disavventure carcerarie di due cinesi al seguito di Jean-François Foucquet e di Matteo Ripa," in *Scritture di Storia* (Historical Writings), ed. Università degli Studi di Napoli "L'orientale" (Napoli: Edizione Scientifiche Italiane, 2005), 83.
24. Francesco D'Arelli, "The Chinese College in Eighteenth-Century Naples," *East and West* 58, no. 1–4 (December 2008): 292n41.
25. Di Fiore, "Carità," 84.
26. D'Arelli, "Chinese College," 291n33.
27. Ripa, *Storia*, III:20–21.
28. Ripa, *Storia*, III:35.

29. Ripa, *Storia*, III:186.
30. Ripa, *Storia*, III:27; 30–31.
31. Ripa, *Storia*, III:44.
32. Ripa, *Storia*, III:45–47.
33. Ripa, *Storia*, II:48.
34. Joseph van den Brandt, CM, *Les Lazaristes en Chine 1697–1935. Notes Biographiques* (Beiping: Imprimerie des Lazaristes, 1936), 1–2; Joseph de Moidrey, SJ, *La Hiérarchie catholique en Chine, en Corée et au Japon (1307–1914)* (Shanghai: Tousèwèi Orphanage, 1914), 125.
35. Seán A. Smith, "Surrogate Fathers: The Lazarists as Jesuit Successors in the Eighteenth Century, 1759–1814," *Journal of Ecclesiastical History* 69, no. 1 (2018): 61–66.
36. Appiani was chosen by his relative, the papal legate Tournon, as an interpreter and accompanied him to Beijing in 1705. As a consequence of Tournon's alienation of the Kangxi emperor, Appiani was imprisoned in Beijing and expelled to Guangzhou in 1707. He remained in prison, first in Beijing and later in Canton, for nineteen years and nine months, then was released in 1726, whereupon he continued to reside in Canton. In 1732 he was expelled to Macau with all the other missionaries. He died in 1742 in Macau, where he is buried.
37. Robert Entenmann, "Linus Zhang Feng (1669?–1743): A Catholic Lay Evangelist in Early Qing Sichuan," in *China: New Faces of Ethnography*, ed. Bettina Gransow, Pal Nyiri, and Shiaw-Chian Fong (Münster: Lit. Verlag; Piscataway, NJ: Transaction Publishers, 2005), 142.
38. Entenmann, "Chinese Clergy," 79.
39. Ripa, *Storia*, III:32–33; III:50.
40. Ripa, *Storia*, III:56–57.
41. D'Arelli, "Chinese College," 306.
42. Ripa, *Storia*, III:185.
43. Ripa, *Storia*, III:187–89.
44. Eugenio Menegon, "Interlopers at the Fringes of Empire: The Procurators of the Propaganda Fidei Papal Congregation in Canton and Macao, 1700–1823," *Cross-Currents: East Asian History and Culture Review* 25 (December 2017): 33–35.
45. Karl Josef Rivinius, *Das Collegium Sinicum zu Neapel und seine Umwandlung in ein Orientalisches Institut* (Sankt Augustin: Institut Monumenta Serica, 2004), 150.
46. Ripa, *Storia*, III:190–91; III:419.
47. Ripa, *Storia*, III:192.
48. Gianni Criveller, "The Chinese Priests of the College for the Chinese in Naples and the Promotion of the Indigenous Clergy (XVIII–XIX Centuries)," in *Silent Force: Native Converts in the Catholic China Mission*, ed. Rachel Lu Yan and Philip Vanhaelemeersch (Leuven: Ferdinand Verbiest Institute, 2009), 153–54.
49. Ripa, *Storia*, III:195.
50. Di Fiore, "Carità," 77.
51. Ripa, *Storia*, III:201.
52. Di Fiore, "Carità," 49.

53. Ripa, *Storia*, III:204.
54. Ripa, *Storia*, III:205.
55. Ripa, *Storia*, III:225.
56. Ripa, *Storia*, III:207.
57. D'Arelli, "Chinese College," 306.
58. D'Arelli, "Chinese College," 307.
59. Ripa, *Storia*, III:274.
60. Ripa, *Storia*, III:299–300.
61. Ripa, *Storia*, III:308.
62. Ripa, *Storia*, III:310–11.
63. Ripa, *Storia*, III:309–10.
64. Ripa, *Storia*, III:312.
65. Rivinius, *Collegium*, 57.
66. Ripa, *Storia*, III:206.
67. Ripa, *Storia*, III:310–11.
68. Ripa, *Storia*, III:312.
69. Ripa, *Storia*, III:312–13.
70. Ripa, *Storia*, III:314–15.
71. D'Arelli, "Chinese College," 307.
72. Ripa, *Storia*, III:322.
73. Ripa, *Storia*, III:322.
74. Ripa, *Storia*, III:323.
75. Ripa, *Storia*, III:323–24.
76. Ripa, *Storia*, III:324–25.
77. Ripa, *Storia*, III:325–26.
78. Ripa, *Storia*, III:327–28.
79. Ripa, *Storia*, III:329.
80. Ripa, *Storia*, III:337–38.
81. Ripa, *Storia*, III:346.
82. Ripa, *Storia*, III:333.
83. Ripa, *Storia*, III:338; D'Arelli, "Chinese College," 307.
84. Michele Fatica, "Per una Mostra Bibliografica ed Iconografica su Matteo Ripa, il Collegio dei Cinesi e il Real Collegio Asiatico (1682–1888)," in *Matteo Ripa e il Collegio dei Cinesi. La Missione Cattolica in Cina tra I Secoli XVIII–XIX*, ed. Michele Fatica and Francesco D'Arelli (Napoli: Istituto Universitario Orientale, 1999), 23.
85. Ripa, *Storia*, III:343; Rivinius, *Collegium*, 151.
86. Criveller, "Chinese Priests," 155.
87. On Yili, see Joanna Waley-Cohen, *Exile in Mid-Qing China: Banishment to Xinjiang, 1758–1820* (New Haven, CT: Yale University Press, 1991), 185–86.
88. Ripa, *Storia*, III:339–41.
89. Ripa, *Storia*, III:340.
90. Ripa, *Storia*, III:347.
91. Moidrey, *Hiérarchie catholique*, 125.
92. Ripa, *Storia*, III:416–17.

93. Nicolas Standaert, ed., *Handbook of Christianity in China*, vol. 1, *635–1800* (Leiden: Brill, 2001), 361.
94. Standaert, *Handbook*, 332.
95. Ripa, *Storia*, III:418.
96. Criveller, "Chinese Priests," 155.
97. D'Arelli, "Chinese College," 307–8.
98. Criveller, "Chinese Priests," 153–54.
99. Ripa, *Storia*, III:418–19.
100. Ripa, *Storia*, III:330–31.
101. Ripa, *Storia*, III:345.
102. Ripa, *Storia*, III:367.
103. Ripa, *Storia*, III:408.
104. Ripa, *Storia*, III:167–68.
105. "Regole e Costituzioni," part I, chapter II, IV, p. 129, quoted in D'Arelli, "Chinese College," 287.
106. Di Fiore, "Carità," 78.
107. Ripa, *Storia*, III:411.
108. Ripa, *Storia*, III:412.
109. Ripa, *Storia*, III:413.
110. Ripa, *Storia*, III:413 refers to Giuseppe Ripa as Matteo's "*fratello*" (brother), but he was actually a "*cuchino*" (cousin). See Fiore, "Carità," 79n65.
111. Di Fiore, "Carità," 79.
112. Ripa, *Storia*, III:420–21.
113. Di Fiore, "Carità," 79–80.
114. See the transcription of the interrogation in Giacomo Di Fiore, "Un cinese a Castel Sant'Angelo," *La conoscenza dell'Asia e dell'Africa in Italia nei secoli XVIII e XIX*, vol. 2 (Napoli: Istituto Universitario Orientale, 1985), 233–35.
115. Di Fiore, "Un cinese," 269.
116. Di Fiore, "Un cinese," 236.
117. Ripa, *Storia*, III:422–23.
118. Ripa, *Storia*, III:424–26.
119. Ripa, *Storia*, III:426–27.
120. Di Fiore, "Carità," 81.
121. Ripa, *Storia*, III:429–30.
122. Ripa, *Storia*, III:431–32.
123. Ripa, *Storia*, III:424–25; Di Fiore, "Carità," 81–82.
124. Ripa, *Storia*, III:435.
125. Di Fiore, "Carità," 85–86.
126. Di Fiore, "Un cinese," 237.
127. Ripa, *Storia*, III:439–40.
128. Ripa, *Storia*, III:437–38.
129. Di Fiore, "Carità," 82–83.
130. Di Fiore, "Un cinese," 270.
131. Di Fiore, "Carità," 84.

132. Di Fiore, "Carità," 85.
133. Criveller, "Chinese Priests," 151.
134. Criveller, "Chinese Priests," 163.
135. Criveller, "Chinese Priests," 150.
136. Rivinius, *Collegium*, 97–99.

Chapter Four

Racial and Cultural Tensions between Chinese and European Priests

FR. FILIPPO HUANG IN CHINA

Filippo Huang returned to China in 1762 after a thirty-eight-year absence. He had been twelve years old when he departed with Ripa's little group of students in 1724 and now he was fifty, but unlike his companion student Lucio Wu, he had succeeded in returning. Since his departure, the Chinese court had expelled the missionaries from the provinces and the authorities had pursued anti-Christian policies that forced Christianity to become an underground church. Faced with such pressure and the absence of priests, numerous Christians apostatized. The situation was particularly acute in Shanxi province, to which Huang was assigned. The combined vicariate of Shanxi-Shaanxi-Gansu, with its vast spaces and high mountains, was remote. In 1703 the Jesuit Father Jean de Fontaney had described the mission of Shaanxi as "the most harsh and the most laborious in China and the one most destitute of all human consolation."[1]

The ecclesiastical structure in China had been shaped by the conflicts between the Portuguese crown's claims of control called the *Padroado* and the opposing claims of Propaganda Fide. Initially, from 1576 China had only one diocese, which was based in Macau.[2] The dioceses of Nanjing and Beijing were added in 1690. After the suppression of the Society of Jesus in 1773, the direction of most mission work in China was taken over by Propaganda Fide, which preferred to create vicars apostolic. In order to circumvent the territorial prerogatives of Portugal in the appointment of bishops, the vicars apostolic were appointed as bishops whose territory was located in remote and defunct dioceses outside of China. This allowed Propaganda Fide to have direct control over these bishops.

The missionaries dependent on Propaganda Fide were spread throughout ten provinces: Zhili (Beijing), Nanjing, Fujian, Sichuan, Yunnan, Shanxi, Shaanxi, Huguang (subdivided into Hubei and Hunan), Shandong, and Guangdong.[3] When Gansu province was created in 1666, it became part of the vicariate of Shaanxi and remained so until it became autonomous in 1878.[4] Only three of the original nine vicariates instituted by Innocent XII were autonomous, namely, Fujian, Shaanxi, and Sichuan. The heads of these three vicariates oversaw the other six vicariates. The arrangements with Propaganda Fide were complicated, as the vicariates were administrated by different religious orders with different degrees of funding by Propaganda Fide.

With the expulsion of most European priests early in the eighteenth century and with the suppression of the Jesuits, Chinese priests came to constitute the majority of the clergy in China by the second half of the eighteenth century.[5] Some Chinese priests were trained by European missionaries in China, at the seminary of the Société des Missions Étrangères de Paris in Siam, or in the seminary in the Philippines. European seminaries for Chinese were established at the Propaganda College in Rome and at the Collegio dei Cinesi in Naples (abbreviated as CCN). The CCN priests were assigned to several vicariates. The first two CCN missionaries, Giovanni Evangelista Yin (Yin Ruowang) and Giovanni Battista Gu (Gu Ruohan), were assigned to Sichuan. Yin died en route to Sichuan and Gu later moved on to Zhili. Pio Minor Liu (Liu Chengren), Vitale Guo (Guo Yuanxing), and Lucio Li (Li Ruose), together with the catechist Tommaso Wang, served in Shaanxi, which was administered by Italian Franciscans. Paolo Cai (Cai Wenan) and Simone Zhao (Zhao Ximan) worked in Huguang. Cai later went to Guangdong. Pio elder Liu (Liu Biyue) served in Shandong. Filippo Maria Huang (Huang Batong) served in Zhili and Shanxi.

Of the eleven Chinese priests trained at the Chinese College by Ripa during his lifetime, ten returned to China as missionaries. Sixteen letters written by Filippo Maria Huang from China between 1762 and 1775 reveal how Christianity continued under the leadership of these Chinese priests.[6] The letters by Huang, as well as journals by other Chinese missionaries, clearly contradict the belief that the Christian mission in China was temporarily destroyed after the death of the Kangxi emperor in 1722.[7]

Filippo Maria Huang can best be understood in counterpoint to Lucio Wu. At their respective ages of eleven and ten, they were the youngest members of Ripa's group who traveled from China to Europe in 1724. Their common childhood years bonded them through a number of experiences, whether sharing a litter in departing from Beijing or in their early experiences at the Chinese College. They were the most rebellious of the first eleven Chinese students. Both fled the college at different times and both suffered the humiliating punishments imposed on them after their return. And yet there were crucial differences between them.

Lucio's character was unstable in a way that led to his imprisonment and death in Rome. Filippo's character was more stable, although he was required to remain at the college in Naples from 1724 until 1762 while his counterparts returned to China far sooner. Unlike Lucio, Filippo repented. In 1765 he wrote to his superior Fatigati: "The Lord made me stay in Europe for a period of 40 years—was that perhaps without his purpose? But in this I am unable to take pride, to take pride in my abundant weaknesses, in obstacles . . . now I wish I should be saved, that with saving others, to ask the Lord for me, and to ask that you as his penitents also pray to God for me."[8] Filippo never forgot his youthful companion Lucio, whose tragic fate had a profound influence on Filippo's life. In 1767 he wrote "the mercies of the Lord are very great upon me! Mr. Lucio Wu is dead and God knows where his soul has gone, and I am still alive, for which there is a need to be thankful for so many benefits."[9]

Filippo Maria Huang (Huang Batong 黄巴桐) (hereafter referred to by his surname Huang) was born in Zhili province in 1712 and was received into Ripa's instruction in China in November 1719 at the age of seven.[10] He departed in Ripa's group from Guangzhou in January 1724. He made his priestly vows in 1739 and remained away from China for thirty-eight years. Consequently, when he departed Cadiz on the *Finlandia* of the Royal Company of Sweden in April 1762 to return, he was far past the ideal age of a new missionary. Given the average longevity of people at that time and the relatively few years left in Huang's life to serve as a priest, the Chinese College seems, in part, to have been fulfilling a commitment as well as performing an act of kindness to send him home.

Huang's long stay in Naples gave him a proficiency in Italian that is conveyed in his correspondence. Whereas most Chinese College priests developed a proficiency in Latin, Huang was unusual in developing a proficiency in both Latin and Italian. Huang's ship arrived in Macau in July. Because of the Swedish captain's fear that Huang would be discovered circumventing the Chinese restrictions on transporting Chinese missionaries to China, Huang disembarked from the ship dressed in European clothing with a sword at his hip.[11] His disguise was effective and he was not recognized as a priest. He presented his letter from Propaganda Fide to the Propaganda procurator, Fr. Emiliano Palladini (1733–1793), who was also a congregant of the Holy Family.

Huang was present in Macau to observe the traumatic confiscation of Jesuit property by the Portuguese authorities. The suppression of the Jesuit order had begun in Portugal in 1759. It was led by Sebastião José de Carvalho, who was a trusted advisor to the Portuguese King Joseph I.[12] Carvalho was a man of the Enlightenment who was determined to make the state dominant over the church. In this brutal process, almost 850 Jesuits were either jailed or expelled from Portugal. Although the Jesuits in China were spared because of their secular knowledge, those in Africa, India, and Macau were not. Huang described how in Macau in July 1762 the Jesuits were imprisoned and the colleges of San Giuseppe and San Paolo were confiscated. A range of goods from expensive furniture to trumpets were auctioned while costly rare books from the Jesuit library were sold "for a morcel of bread."[13]

Huang went on to Guangzhou, where he fell ill and was confined to bed for two months because of fever. During his confinement, three of his "old companions" (*miei antichi compagni*) from Naples visited the same house for fifteen days.[14] These included Fr. Vitale Giuseppe Guo (Guo Yuanxing 郭元性) and Fr. Paolo Cai (Cai Wenan 蔡文安), who had both returned in 1751, as well as Fr. Giovanni Evangelista Zhang (Zhang Yuewang 張月旺), who had returned in 1760.[15] When Huang departed for Beijing, Guo and Cai went to Macau to get their subsidies while Zhang went to his mission in Nanxiong-zhou 南雄州 (also pronounced Namyong-zhou) in Guangdong province.

Huang waited for the autumn to depart in order to take the Propaganda subsidies to Beijing. His three-month journey to Beijing was fraught with fear of being discovered as a Christian missionary. He finally arrived at the Propaganda Fide house in Beijing on April 18, 1763. There he stayed with the discalced Augustinians fathers Sigismondo a S. Nicola and Giovanni Damasceno. Fr. Sigismondo was a favorite of the Qianlong emperor because of his ability to make clocks. Both priests spent their days working in the palace, except for Sundays and feast days, when they held services in the church. Palladini had assigned Huang to a mission in Datong-fu 大同府 in Shanxi province. However, Fr. Giovanni Battista Gu, who had been in Beijing since 1747, had died in February. Consequently, Huang asked Palladini if he should remain there to replace Gu in ministering to the Christians in Beijing. While in Beijing in 1764, Huang saw his former classmate Fr. Pio Martini Liu, the younger (Liu Chengren 劉成仁), who had returned in 1755. Thereafter Huang rarely made contact with his former classmates from the Chinese College because of the enormous distances that separated them, the dangers of communications being discovered by the authorities, and the limitations of the mission couriers.

HUANG'S STRUGGLES AS A MISSIONARY IN NORTHERN SHANXI

In his letters, the dominant complaint Huang voiced repeatedly was the lack of funds. Propaganda Fide funds to missionaries were channeled through

Palladini, the procurator in Macau. However, their delivery was irregular, causing contention and forcing missionaries at times to rely on their own resources. Fr. Pio Liu the younger complained to Huang that he had not received his subsidy for two years.[16] On the journey from Guangzhou to Beijing, Huang had been forced to rent a litter with two mules to carry him. The mules, medical expenses, food, and customs duties cost three hundred Roman scudi or three hundred Spanish patacas (*pattache spagnole*). The China missionaries used several different monetary units, most of which consisted of silver. Huang referred to scudi, ducats, patacas, and taels.

The scudo was a silver coin used by several Italian states. Huang made numerous references to Roman scudi and Neapolitan scudi. The scudo had parallels in the Spanish escudo and Portuguese escudo. The pataca was also a silver coin, of which there were Portuguese, Spanish, and Mexican forms. The ducat was originally a Venetian gold coin, but by the sixteenth century also appeared in a silver form. The equivalent values of these coins varied slightly and were compared to the predominant Chinese monetary unit, which consisted of unminted silver. A Chinese tael (*liang* 两) contained 1.1 ounce or 31.25 grams of silver. However, silver is a precious metal and there were variations in value. The equivalences between taels and European currencies were not precise, but expressed with slight variations, depending on the time and circumstances. One scudo was worth approximately two-thirds of a tael. Huang refers to twenty taels as being equivalent to thirty Spanish patacas.[17] He refers to forty taels being equivalent to about seventy Neapolitan scudi, and to fifty taels amounting to eighty Neapolitan scudi.[18] He refers to twenty taels as being equivalent to twenty-seven Neapolitan scudi.[19] Huang referred to the Qianlong emperor giving ten thousand taels for the rebuilding of the Nantang, the famous church of the Portuguese fathers that was destroyed by fire in 1775.[20] However, the number ten thousand (*wan* 萬) was often used in a figurative way in China for "many" rather than a literal number.

A second prominent subject of Huang's letters was the number of baptisms and communions that he administered. He took particular joy in baptizing seven members of his family on the festival day of Saints Peter and Paul on June 29, 1763, in Beijing.[21] They included his two nephews (sons of his brothers), as well as their wives, their two grandchildren, and a five-year-old son as well as a brother-in-law.[22] (Huang appears to have omitted his brother-in-law in his reference to the "seven" baptized, possibly because he was not a member of the Huang family and had a different surname.) In another letter, Huang wrote that he baptized a forty-four-year-old sister-in-law, with two daughters and three sons.[23] Huang described the Christians of Beijing as poor. In a revealing statement about the emergence of a distinctive Chinese church, Huang described how the Chinese Christians were circumventing the pope's strict ban on the Chinese rites. Many priests were allowing the use of stone tablets for the deceased, allowing the title of saint (*sheng* 聖) for Confucius, and allowing visits to the Confucian temple where the disciples prostrated themselves. Given Rome's rigidity and lack of appreciation for Chinese filial piety, these sorts of minor transgressions were both inevitable and significant.

At the end of his letter, Huang added that he had just received a letter from three Christians in the city and prefecture of Datong, which lay north of the Great Wall in northeastern Shanxi province (see map 1). This was the mission site that Palladini had assigned to Huang. Their very passionate and affectionate letter said they had not seen a priest for three years.[24] Because Huang had not received any funds from Palladini since arriving in Beijing, he was forced to borrow fifty taels (sixty Roman scudi) to survive. Still, seven months after returning to Beijing, he had decided to sell some European things in his possession and depart on the nine-day journey to Datong at the end of August. Huang described his assigned mission area as very vast, requiring eight or nine days to traverse. In past times there had been more than a thousand Christians there, but now because of persecution, they numbered no more than five or six hundred, dispersed in sixteen villages and towns. A large section of his mission was in Tartary.

Despite the persecution that Christians were suffering in China, Huang was optimistic and filled with hope for the Church. One sees how his years at the Chinese College had nurtured the seeds of martyrdom that became such a powerful force among Chinese Christians. Unlike many clerics and officials, Huang was sympathetic to the Jesuits. He spoke of how the public arrest of the Jesuit fathers in Macau and the harsh manner in which they were transported to a Portuguese ship for deportation inspired gentiles to join the faith.[25] He described how in the middle of the night, each one of the Jesuits was marched to the ship between two Portuguese soldiers armed with guns and bayonets. These Jesuits were said to be rebels against their Portuguese king, but Huang felt the Portuguese mistreatment of them dishonored the Catholic religion. Huang wondered how many other missionaries were being humiliated in similar fashion.

This willingness of Chinese to suffer as Christians is reflected in Huang's account of a youth named Tomaso Gao, a twenty-one-year-old son of a gentile mandarin with six brothers and a sister, none of whom were Christians.[26] Because of his father's opposition, Gao fled to Beijing from his home in Taiyuan-fu in Shanxi province. In Beijing, he was baptized by a Jesuit known to Huang. His father came searching for him and took him back to Taiyuan-fu, where he demanded that his son abjure Christianity. When he demurred, his father confined him to a room. Eventually Tomaso fled again to Beijing, where he convinced a Jesuit to help him become a priest. The Jesuit offered to take him to Macau to study at the seminary there. However, because of the expulsion of the Jesuits from Macau, the Jesuit could not follow through on his offer. Consequently, two catechists brought the inconsolable youth to Huang. He asked to follow Huang to Datong-fu and to be his servant so that he might learn Latin and become a priest or at least a catechist of the Holy Family. After consulting with Fr. Pio Liu the elder and Fathers Sigismondo and Damasceno, all of whom were agreeable, Huang eventually accepted Gao as his assistant on August 11, 1763.

Huang did not describe how Gao assisted him, but the roles of lay leaders in China had been well defined by the eighteenth century. These roles had first developed in the missions of India and Japan and then been regularized in Vietnam during the sixteenth and seventeenth centuries.[27] By Huang's time, secretary-catechists (*xianggong* 相公) were distinguished from teacher-catechists (*xiansheng* 先生). Secretary-catechists composed letters and documents in Chinese and were essential aides to European missionaries whose Chinese skills, particularly in composition, usually fell far short of fluency.[28] Teaching-catechists were crucial in assisting Chinese missionaries who were often assigned missions that required extensive and exhaustive traveling to remote Christian communities.[29] The functions of a *xiansheng* were sometimes described as "the master who explains the doctrine" (*jiangdao xiansheng* 講道先生) and "the master who explains the principles of the doctrine" (*jiang daoli xiansheng* 講道理先生). The term *xiansheng* is used extensively in the thirty-two-page manual *Chuanjiao zhinan* 傳教指南 (Guide to the Mission) published in 1905.[30] This work describes another important lay role in the Chinese Catholic Church, namely, the *huizhang* 會長 (head of the community).[31] Unlike the priests and catechists who only visited most small Christian communities, the *huizhang* resided in the community and functioned in a role of authority. There were variations on this term, including *laohuizhang* 老會長 (elders) and *nannü huizhang* 男女會長 (male and female heads of the community).

On July 1, 1763, Huang departed from Beijing to his mission in Shanxi province, accompanied by three Christians from that region. They traveled through mountainous terrain and on July 11 arrived at Tai ttung fu (Datong-fu), where Huang spent eight days administering the sacrament to eighty Christians and baptizing thirty adults and children.[32] The villages of his mission were so obscure that many of them can no longer be identified.[33] They proceeded to Hunyuan-zhou 渾源州, where Huang stayed for six days, administering the sacrament to thirty persons and baptizing seven persons, then on to Pa ttaj (?) where he spent seven days administering the sacrament to forty persons and baptizing fifteen adults and children. Finally, accompanied by another Christian, he proceeded by mule on a three-day journey to

Kuei hhua Ccing (Guihuaqing?), which would be his place of residence. The town contained about eighty Christians, all of whom were Tartar (Mongol) merchant families. It was located north of the Great Wall and most of its inhabitants were Tartars except for a few Chinese merchants. Huang described most of the Christians there as very fervent. In the first ten months in his vast mission region, he baptized one hundred children and adults and administered the sacrament of penitence and communion to six hundred persons. He described his fear of being seized by the police as incredible.

In May 1764, Huang returned to Beijing, departing from Datong, to receive the Propaganda Fide subsidy from Fr. Sigismondo.[34] There he also received mail from Europe and was saddened to learn that his classmate, Pietro Andrea Wu (Wu Baiduo 吳佰鐸), who entered the Chinese College in 1754, had died in 1763 before he was able to return to China. Wu was from Guangdong province and Huang had met Wu's mother when he passed through Guangzhou in 1763.

Because of Huang's health problems in 1765, which were aggravated by the very cold weather in northern Shanxi, the vicar apostolic (bishop of Miletopolis), Msgr. Francesco Maria Magni, OFM (Fan 范) (1723–1785), offered him the mission of Kiang Ceu (Jiangzhou 絳州—modern Yunchengshi 運城市) in southwestern Shanxi—as more suitable. Huang declined the offer for reasons that he later explained in confidence to Fr. Fatigati.[35] The mission at Jiangzhou had been established by the Collegio dei Cinese priest Fr. Giuseppe Lucio Li (Li Ruose 李若瑟), who had returned to China in 1755. Based on a letter from two Jiangzhou catechists that Fr. Sigismondo had shared with him in Beijing, Huang saw that the Christians there were in a constant state of discord. The catechists' letter had accused Li of drunkenness, abusive language, and scandalous behavior toward women.[36] Huang described an incident in which they wrote that a father returned home to find Fr. Li alone in a room with his daughter, a severe violation of Chinese propriety. The father expelled Li from his house and prohibited Li to have any further contact with his daughter, including even the rite of confession. Because of these difficulties, neither Fr. Giuseppe Li nor Fr. Liu the younger wished to serve there.

GROWING TENSIONS BETWEEN CHINESE AND EUROPEAN PRIESTS

Huang's differences with the Propaganda Fide procurator Fr. Emiliano Palladini reflected broader tensions between European and Chinese missionaries that were emerging with the development of an indigenous church in China. These tensions resulted from the attempt to create a universal church in China while its mentality was still anchored in Europe. As Chinese catechists and priests began to play a greater role in the Church, they came into increasing conflict with a European clerical hierarchy funded from Europe. Fr. Huang complained that the missions of Shanxi and Shaanxi were dominated by European Franciscans. He wrote, "The European missionary gentlemen are eternally hostile to the Chinese priests, and wherever they are, they do not want Chinese priests, consequently there is a great daily strife, quarrels, dissension, abuse, etc."[37] Huang criticized Propaganda Fide for not correcting this impediment to the development of the Christian church in China. This problem was reflected in Huang's claim that European missionaries were given larger stipends than Chinese missionaries. Huang spoke of the Europeans receiving 120 Spanish coins (patacas) annually while the Chinese received only seventy.[38]

Huang wrote to his superior Fatigati that the annual Propaganda subsidy (converted from seventy Spanish patacas to seventy Roman scudi) was completely insufficient.[39] He explained that a servant whom he fed and who cooked for him cost forty Neapolitan scudi annually. He asked how he could feed and clothe himself, rent a dwelling, buy utensils for the house and for cooking, and pay for medical treatment on such limited funds? In addition, how would he be able to maintain a mule to visit his Christians, to buy food and lodging for the journey, to buy sacred utensils for the mass, and to obtain wine? Since grapes were not grown in Kuei hhua Ccing (Guihuaqing?), he had to obtain wine from Taiyuan-fu, a twelve-day journey away. He calculated that 158 scudi were needed to pay these expenses each year. Since he had sold all the crystal and clocks that he had carried from Europe to cover these expenses, he had no idea how he would manage in the future. While Huang was limited to an annual subsidy of seventy Spanish patacas, the European priests Fr. Giovanni Damasceno and Fr. Angelo complained that their individual subsidies of two hundred Spanish patacas each year were not enough.[40] Unless their subsidies were increased, they were forced to borrow money and pay interest of 2.5 percent per month. When Huang wrote to the procurator about the need for more funds, Palladini told him to save money by remaining closer to his residence and not travel to minister to his Christians.[41]

Faced with the lack of funds, Chinese priests sought to raise money by other means; however, Palladini criticized them for doing so. Fr. Giovanni Battista Gu had developed a friendship in Beijing with an Archimandrite Moscovite of the Russian Orthodox Church.[42] Gu sold him a map for fifty taels. Later the Archimandrite took the map to the church of the French Jesuits and showed it to Fr. Pierre de Goville, SJ (Ge Weili 戈維理), who said the Archimandrite had been swindled. The latter refused to reveal the seller's name and Goville only later discovered it was Fr. Gu. Palladini indignantly presented this as a case of immorality, but Gu needed the funds to survive as a missionary. Moreover, the differences here between the European and Chinese perspective were as much cultural as moral.

Did Propaganda give less funding to Chinese missionaries than to European missionaries because they believed Chinese as natives could survive on fewer funds in their homeland than European missionaries? If so, Palladini should have been less critical in saying, "What I am able to say in matters involving the reverend Chinese priests, is that they demonstrate an excessive passion for illicit trade and extreme fondness for profit."[43] Palladini criticized Huang for excessive spending in maintaining three donkeys, for twice giving money to his brother, for "lavishly" (*lautamente*) supporting his nephews, and for excessive spending of his impoverished parishioners' money. In addition, Huang sold a piece of land that had been given by his parishioners as a benefice to the church. When the parishioners protested, Palladini said Huang claimed he had the right to do as he wished.

Palladini also criticized Fr. Vitale Giuseppe Guo (Guo Yuanxing 郭元性) who returned to China from Naples in 1751. Palladini claimed Fr. Guo indulged in "a useless and inexcusable residence of two years in Macau and Canton," spending more than three hundred taels on articles of clothing.[44] Moreover, Palladini complained that Guo squandered the subsidy of the Holy Congregation and held back the consignments for missionaries.

Palladini claimed that his criticism of Huang was supported by Fr. Sigismondo and described incidents that occurred in Beijing that Sigismondo communicated to him in Macau. Palladini also criticized Huang's family, including his older brother, who threatened to take away a mule from the stall because he had not received a loan from the European missionaries in Beijing.[45] Palladini also accused Huang's nephew of stealing money from the Propaganda house. Palladini asked, "How could [Huang] agree as a priest to love relatives?" By this he meant that Huang's love for his relatives exceeded his love for the mission. He wrote that Huang's love of relatives made him unfit for the mission house of Beijing. Clearly Palladini's grievances were, at least in part, based on cultural differences and on Palladini's lack of appreciation for Chinese filial piety.

Sigismondo sent Palladini's admonition to Huang, who responded promptly and briefly from Datong-fu on May 27, 1764. Huang wrote that he had read the admonition with "a great horror and flood of tears."[46] He bluntly accused Palladini of being a hypocrite who "had bought large cases of cloth to transact business and of being a whoremonger" (*che V. S. Rever.ma abbia comprato grandi cassoni de panni per negoziare, e d'ésssere un puttaniere)*!

The enmity with Palladini appears to have begun soon after Huang's arrival in Guangzhou in 1762. It involved not only the insufficiency of funds that Palladini sent to Huang, but also Palladini's disrespectful treatment of him. Huang's long education at the Chinese College and his fluency (written as well as spoken) in Chinese, Italian, and Latin gave him an intellectual status that was by no means inferior to Palladini, who served as a financial agent for Propaganda. And yet Palladini offended Huang by treating him as an inferior. In 1765 Huang gave one notable example that enraged him. At that point, Huang was fifty-three years old and Palladini was only thirty-two. And yet Palladini in a letter referred to Huang using the condescending term "son" (*filio*) as if Palladini were acting in the superior role of a "father" (*padre*).[47] The enmity was two-sided. In 1765 Huang denied that he had publicly referred to or even thought of referring to Palladini as a "whoremonger and merchant" (*puttaniere e mercandante*).[48] But in fact, Huang had used similar words in a written statement quoted above in rebutting Palladini's criticisms in 1764.

The enmity that Huang felt for the European missionaries was not simply a personal grievance. It was shared by other Chinese priests and the Europeans reciprocated it. In defining the nature of their mutual enmity, cultural and racial differences become blurred in ways that are difficult to disentangle. In Huang's case, the enmity manifested itself in the vicariate of Shanxi and neighboring Shaanxi province to the west, which were administered by the Franciscans. Huang's letters made frequent reference to Msgr. Magni, who was vicar apostolic of Shanxi and Shaanxi until 1777, when he was forced to retire because of poor health. He was replaced by Magni's coadjutor bishop Nathanael Bürger, OFM (Min 閔) (1733–1780).[49] Msgr. Bürger became a particular object of Huang's enmity.

In 1762, when Huang had first arrived in China, Fr. Vitale Guo (Guo Yuanxing) warned him about the European priests' bias against Chinese priests and their feelings of superiority over the Chinese.[50] Guo urged Huang to join in writing a petition to the Holy Congregation, asking that the Chinese missionaries be separated from the Europeans in the same way that eastern Tongking (northern Vietnam) and Fujian had been given to the Spanish Dominican fathers.[51] At first Huang felt that Guo's complaints were exaggerated, but by 1768, he had come to agree with them. Huang was particularly annoyed with how the Franciscans had circulated letters of criticism of the Chinese fathers to all the missionaries and even the neophytes, causing them to lose face among their flocks. In a mocking manner he asked, "Is this then the love (*carità*) that the glorious Saint Francis [the founder of the Franciscans] bestowed?"[52] Huang, who was not prone to humility, proudly noted that he had been examined by the pope in person in 1750.

Huang also criticized Franciscan missionaries in Beijing, in particular, Eusebio di Cittadella (Ye Zongxiao, Chengxian 葉宗孝，承先) (1716–1785), a

Propaganda missionary. He drew an unflattering portrait of Fr. Eusebio as a priest of about fifty years old who was prone to violent anger and a satirical tongue.[53] Twice Huang saw him threaten Chinese Christians with violence, first threatening to slap a servant on the face with a prosciutto and threatening to strike another servant with a large cudgel. He criticized Fr. Eusebio's ability to speak Chinese and mockingly claimed he spoke "the Turkish language better than he does Chinese!" Fr. Eusebio did not understand his penitents and they did not understand him. Huang cited an incident from July 10, 1768, in which he was called by a mortally ill parishioner whom Fr. Eusebio had just confessed. The parishioner said she had not understood a word Fr. Eusebio had said. Huang later asked Fr. Fatigati if such confessionals were valid. Huang was not merely criticizing Fr. Eusebio's language skills, but voicing criticism of all the European missionaries of Beijing, and especially Propaganda missionaries.

Huang also criticized Fr. Sigismondo of S. Nicola, a discalced Augustinian who had acquired a great reputation working on clocks in the imperial palace in Beijing for thirty years. At his death on December 29, 1767, it was revealed that he left behind numerous unpaid debts that became the responsibility of his associate, the discalced Augustinian vice-procurator, Father Gio Damasceno.[54] Huang criticized Sigismondo and Damasceno for living in an extravagant manner, collecting the money from the people and paying large amounts of interest to their creditors.

Huang's complaints about European disparagement of Chinese priests were echoed by others. In his *Journal*, the highly praised Sichuan priest Andreas Li complained that a procurator of the Missions Étrangères in Canton said there was nothing written by Li that he would believe.[55] In spite of Li's many years of remarkable service as a priest in Sichuan, Rome failed to name Li vicar apostolic. Instead, it named Fr. François Pottier, who had been consecrated as a priest only two and a half years earlier, as vicar general.[56] When Pottier arrived in Sichuan in 1756 at the age of thirty, he was given authority over Li, who was twice his age. In China that would have created a great loss of face for Li, but he appears to have submitted quietly to the situation. Shortly after his arrival, Pottier accused Li of laxity in administering the sacraments. Pottier noted that Chinese priests believed French missionaries treated them as domestics rather than as spiritual collaborators.

Huang wrote to Fatigati that some of his Christians were very good and some were very bad, but he believed that if he offered them compassion rather than dominance, they would become good Christians.[57] He had used the *Spiritual Exercises* of St. Ignatius of Loyola—once in In Ppa Liang and again in Kuei hhua Ccing (Guihuaqing?), teaching in the European manner of using noise and shouting to demonstrate the enormity of sin, the harshness of the flames of hell, and the eternity of its duration. Huang said that the fear he instilled in their hearts caused their sobbing to become so loud that it drowned out his voice. However, the catechists assured Huang that the people understood his preaching. After the neophytes were baptized, Huang taught them to say the *Pater Noster*, *Ave Maria*, the *Credo*, and the Commandments of God and nothing more. Two or three years later a European missionary came to Huang's mission area and spent six or seven days before departing, but the people did not understand the words he spoke. This failure of European missionaries to communicate in Chinese had been one of the reasons that Ripa had argued for the need to raise up Chinese priests.

From 1763 until 1774, Huang lived a harsh life in northern Shanxi. Serving there from the ages of fifty-one to sixty-two, he was no longer young, and yet he was called to minister as a priest in a remote region where his five hundred Christians were so dispersed that it took two months to visit them all. The terrain was rough and Huang either walked or rode a mule in making his rounds. The region was so isolated that he did not see another priest (and therefore could not make his own confession) for three years (1763–1766). His letters are continuous pleas for funds and complaints about delayed payment of promised funds. Before leaving Naples, his superior Fatigati had promised to support him with forty Neapolitan scudi each year for the rest of his life plus alms for masses that he celebrated.[58] However, in 1774 he wrote that he had received neither the annual charitable subsidy from the Chinese College nor the alms for the thousand masses he had celebrated from 1760 to 1774.[59]

During Huang's missionary service in northern Shanxi, there were periodic persecutions. On Easter 1768 in the small town of Pa Ttaj, Huang celebrated two masses, one for men and one for women, in which he gave homilies and distributed Holy Communion.[60] The room was crowded with people and there was great spiritual jubilation. Afterward, Huang retired to his hut to say the holy breviary but was interrupted by "a bad Christian with the surname Ma" who berated him and snatched the breviary from his hands. Ma threatened to drag him to the tribunal of a gentile judge because he had caused him to lose face by not absolving him for his sins and not giving him communion like the others. However, a catechist along with some other Christians appeared and forced Ma to leave. Huang confessed to Fatigati that he had become afraid and wanted to leave Pa Ttaj immediately. However, the Christians protected him and he was able to say holy mass on the third day of Easter and then in the midst of the "weeping and tears and sobbing of the Christians," he mounted his mule and left for Im Ppan Liang.

Huang was preparing to return to his residence at Kuei Hua Ccing (Guihuaqing?) when in the middle of the night, two Christians sent by a catechist from the town of Taj Ttung (Datong?) arrived to inform him of a rebel insurrection and great persecution in the town of Yu Zu. Eighteen Christians had been dragged to the tribunal, and a leader had been tortured in the legs (perhaps with the *jiagun* 夾棍, i.e., ankle press) and died, while others apostatized the faith. Fr. Nathanael Bürger, the vicar general, fled in the middle of the night, leaving the sacred vestments behind. Instead of returning to his residence at Kuei Hua Ccing (Guihuaqing?), Huang on the following morning left for Taj Ttung (Datong?), arriving after three days at the house of the catechist Hei. However, the normally hospitable Hei was so fearful that he did not want Huang to stay at his home. In the chapel where Huang usually said mass, all sacred images, crucifixes, and religious books had been removed and the sacred vestments were buried in the ground. Huang left the town of Taj Ttung (Datong?) on his mule and after eight days of travel he arrived at Beijing on April 22.

The bitterly cold and windy weather of northern Shanxi eventually took its toll on Huang's aging body. In 1765 he wrote of suffering for two years from a chronically ulcerated leg that impeded his traveling. Elsewhere he added that he had a sickness that affected both legs and arms, giving him swollen hands and forcing him to be confined to bed for four months while yellow fluid drained from his body.[61] In 1767 he wrote that his physical strength was weakening. Meanwhile his fellow Chinese College alumnus Fr. Pio Minor Martino Liu (Liu Chengren 劉成仁) in neighboring Shaanxi province was afflicted with a dangerous infirmity of bleeding.[62] After contracting tuberculosis, Huang was forced to return to Beijing in 1774.[63] His worsening hand tremors made it increasingly difficult to write letters.[64] However, Beijing was more expensive than Shanxi and Huang complained that he had not received the annual charitable subsidy from the Holy Congregation in Naples for four years and he was having trouble maintaining himself. In a last letter, he was forced to stop writing because of hand tremors.[65]

Huang died on April 26, 1776, at the age of sixty-five *sui* (sixty-four by European reckoning). He was the only member of the Holy Family of Naples to be buried at the Zhalan 柵蘭 (Shala) cemetery, the oldest Christian cemetery in Beijing (see figure 4.1). Its origins date from the death of Matteo Ricci on May 11, 1610. After a four-day funeral ceremony, the Spanish Jesuit Diego de Pantoja, with the assistance of the Chinese convert Li Zhizao, had submitted a memorial to the Wanli emperor requesting a burial site for Ricci.[66] The request was granted and Pantoja chose a site just outside the western side of the city wall. Nearly one year later, candle-carrying Christians as well as officials and literati followed the crucifix and Ricci's body in a procession from the Nantang westward to the gravesite at Zhalan.[67]

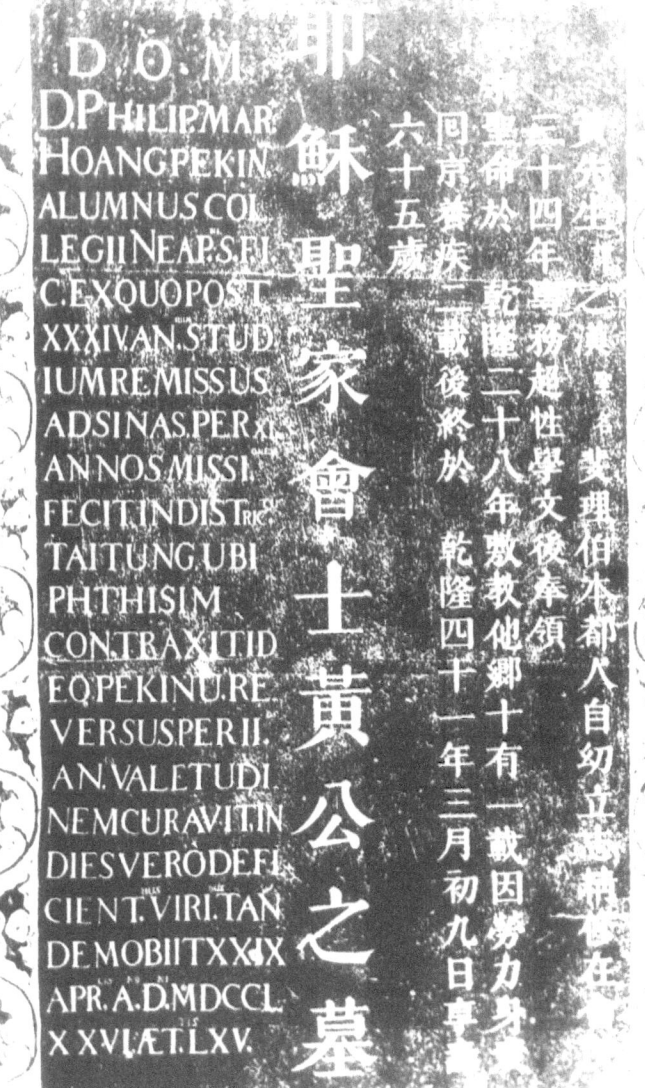

Figure 4.1. Tomb of the Honorable (Filippo Maria) Huang Zhihan 黃之漢 **(d. 1776) of the Congregation of the Holy Family of Jesus. Zhalan** 柵欄 **Cemetery, Beijing.**

Source: Reproduced by permission from Edward J. Malatesta and Gao Zhiyu, eds., *Zhalan: Departed, Yet Present, the Oldest Christian Cemetery in Beijing* (Macau: Instituto Cultural de Macau & Ricci Institute, University of San Francisco, 1995).

In 1654 the Shunzhi emperor granted Fr. Adam Schall's request for a westward enlargement of the cemetery. In the following years numerous Christians were buried there; however, the exact list is incomplete because of gravestones without epitaphs and because of the desecration of the cemetery by the Boxers in 1900.[68] The Boxers desecrated the graves and scattered the remains across the yard. Afterward, seventy-seven tombstones were gathered and placed in the exterior walls of the church on the Zhalan. In 1966 the Red Guards again desecrated the cemetery. When the cemetery was restored in 1984, sixty-three steles were set up in rows. Stone rubbings of these sixty-three steles have preserved the epitaphs. The gravestone rubbing of Father Filippo Maria Huang contains both Chinese and Latin epitaphs.[69]

THE ANTI-CHRISTIAN MOVEMENT ("GREAT PERSECUTION") OF 1784

After Fr. Huang Batong's death, anti-Christian persecutions continued in the vicariate of Shanxi and Shaanxi, which confirmed the wisdom of Fr. Ripa's proposal to train native priests. The early Qing dynasty from 1644 until the death of the Qianlong emperor in 1799 was marked by the conquest of vast areas in central Asia. Although the Manchus adopted many features of the traditional Chinese state, they were preoccupied with maintaining their conquests and suspicious of foreign threats to imperial stability. This suspicion of foreign elements created misunderstandings and a failure to distinguish the different nature of the foreign threats. In the region of Shaanxi this caused two very different groups—Muslims and Christians—to be misperceived as a united movement. Imperial anxiety had been heightened by a Muslim uprising in the neighboring province of Gansu in the 1770s. There was a large Muslim population in Shaanxi and the governor, Bi Yuan 畢沅 (1737–1797), was cautious in pacifying them.[70] The Chinese priests trained in Naples had been more able than European priests to avoid detection by the authorities, but the Muslim uprising brought greater scrutiny to all the Christian priests in the Shanxi-Shaanxi area and led to their persecution.

In May 1784, a group of four newly arrived European Franciscans destined for Shaanxi—Giovanni da Sassari, OFM (b. 1742), Giuseppe Mattei da Bientina, OFM, Luigi Landi da Signa, OFM, and Giovanni Battista da Mandello, OFM (b. 1746)—had been forced to flee Macau. As Propaganda Fide missionaries, they had been obliged to refuse to recognize the Portuguese monarch's authority over them embodied in the so-called *Padroado* (royal monopoly). When the Portuguese authorities in Macau tried to send them back to Europe, they fled to Guangzhou, where they found refuge in the house of Msgr. Francesco Giuseppe della Torre (Duoluo 哆囉), who served as Propaganda Fide procurator from 1781 to 1785. Msgr. della Torre was highly respected for his character, but he suffered from a weak body and would die in a prison in Beijing in 1785.⁷¹ The departure of these four Italian Franciscans for Xi'an would cause problems because, as an imperial edict to the Grand Council of December 22, 1784, clarified, Europeans in China were restricted to Beijing and to the Macau-Guangzhou region and were prohibited from residing in other provinces.⁷²

The procurator had expected that Christians would be coming from Shaanxi to escort the four Franciscans. When these guides did not appear, he turned to Fr. Pietro Cai (Cai Ruoxiang 蔡若祥 or Cai Boduolu 蔡伯多祿) for assistance. Pietro Cai (1739–1806) had been born in Longqi 龍溪 county in Fujian. Like his older brother, Paolo Cai, Pietro had studied at the Chinese College in Naples, residing there in 1761–1767. Fr. Pietro had joined his brother Paolo at the mission in Huguang (southwestern Hubei) and during the years 1771–1783 served as a very effective missionary.⁷³ Fr. Paolo complained about serving in a poor and mountainous area among crude Christians who spoke a different dialect and he had often asked the procurator, Palladini, to transfer him to his native Fujian, but Fr. Pietro seems to have been more willing to adapt.⁷⁴

In 1783 the procurator, della Torre, recalled Fr. Pietro to Guangzhou to assume the delicate task of organizing the journey of the Franciscans to missions in Shanxi and Shaanxi provinces. Fr. Pietro arranged for the four missionaries to be escorted by Chinese Catholics through Huguang province. After departing in 1784 from Canton, the four Franciscans experienced numerous difficulties on their northward journey to Xi'an. Unlike the Chinese priests trained at the Collegio dei Cinesi, their knowledge of Chinese was very undeveloped and their physical features marked them as foreigners. In Hubei, a subdivision of Huguang province, a Christian apostate named Liu Xi 劉喜 attempted to rob the priests.⁷⁵ Liu's father by adoption, a Christian named Liu Zongxuan 劉宗選, tried to escape punishment for himself and his son by denouncing the missionaries, claiming that they were traveling to Shaanxi to help the rebellious Muslims.⁷⁶ Consequently, the four Franciscan priests were arrested in August 1784 in Hubei and sent to Beijing for trial. Unaware that Pietro Cai was a Christian priest, the emperor personally ordered an investigation. When Beijing issued an order for the arrest of Cai and an assisting catechist, Bartolomeo Xie, they went underground in Canton.⁷⁷ In spite of a large reward for his capture, Cai evaded arrest. The Portuguese authorities in Macau sent Cai and the catechist Xie to Goa. After 1785 Chinese officials abandoned the manhunt.

On October 4, 1784, the governor of Shaanxi, Bi Yuan, received an imperial edict from Beijing indicating a fear that these four Christian priests arrested in Huguang province were on their way to Xi'an to join the Muslim rebels in a secret plot against the government. This suspicion was strengthened by the erroneous belief that Christians and Muslims shared the same religion.[78] Bi Yuan's attitude toward the Christians was much less accommodating than toward the Muslims because their numbers were smaller and they tended to be identified with the subversive White Lotus Society. Bi Yuan consequently undertook a persecution that destroyed many of the missions in Shaanxi and Shanxi and temporarily drove most of the missionaries out of the region.

News of the arrest of the four priests in Huguang was urgently conveyed to the Christians in Xi'an by Fr. Francesco Zeng (Zeng Qinggui 曾清貴), who had been trained at the Collegio dei Cinesi in 1754–1767. Fr. Zeng was a native of Xi'an and had been in charge of the mission there.[79] Assigned by Propaganda to travel to Guangzhou to obtain important documents, he had departed for Canton, accompanied by his nephew, Zeng Xuekong 曾學孔. While en route, Zeng learned of the arrest of the four priests and immediately wrote to Fr. Pio Liu the younger (Liu Chengren 劉稱仁), a priest at Xi'an who had also studied at the Chinese College in Naples (1739–1755).[80] In the persecution that followed, Fr. Pio was arrested in January 1785 for being a priest and was condemned to exile in Yili 伊犁, a remote area in northwestern China (present-day Xinjiang province). However, the hardships of the journey were too much for the sixty-seven-year-old priest, who died two days after departing for Yili.

Late in 1784 Jiao Zhengang 焦振鋼 and Qin Lu 秦祿 were arrested in Huguang. Jiao seems to have been from Xi'an in Shaanxi while Qin was from Qixian 祁縣 in Shanxi.[81] They were both Christian merchants who bought furs and hides in the northern provinces and traveled annually to Guangzhou to sell them. Jiao belonged to an old Catholic family; he had already suffered for his faith by allowing the vicar apostolic Mgr. Giovanni Antonio Buocher, OFM (1701–1765), to stay at his house. Jiao and Qin were both prominent members in their Catholic parishes and were trusted to carry the mail and annual European subsidies between Guangzhou and the northwest. When they were arrested, they were discovered to be carrying letters (four in Chinese and ten in European languages) that aroused suspicion, particularly since no one in the interior provinces could read European languages.[82] All four priests to whom the Chinese letters were addressed had studied in Naples, which indicates the important role that Chinese College priests were by that point playing in the China mission. Their names and the years they studied in Naples were Fr. Francesco Zeng (Zeng Qinggui 曾清貴) (1754–1767), Fr.

Pietro Cai (1761–1767), Fr. Filippo Liu (Liu Kaidi 劉開迪) (1770–1775), and Fr. Cassio Giuseppe Dai (戴德冠) (1756–1764).

The imperial edict of December 31, 1784, voiced Beijing's fear of Chinese Christian priests.[83] Native Christians were required to recant and to turn over their religious books and objects, which were to be destroyed. Chinese who brought missionaries into China were to be banished to Yili. The title of *shenfu* 神父 (religious father, i.e., priest) was prohibited. Chinese who used the title *shenfu* were regarded as serving a foreign power and punished severely. They were said to have been tempted by financial gain and were banished to Yili to serve as slaves to the Eleuths. Their family property was to be confiscated. The edict attributed the presence of Western priests in the interior provinces to European traders in Guangzhou who plotted with the Chinese to enter the inner provinces secretly. Local officials were to be held responsible for their lack of supervision of these activities and punished accordingly.

Some officials, such as Fukangan 福康安, were more perceptive in analyzing the relations between Muslims and Christians. Fukangan is famous as much for his outstanding military leadership as for his unscrupulous theft of public funds to enrich himself, second only to the unscrupulous advisor to the Qianlong emperor, He Shen.[84] Fukangan, who served as governor-general of Gansu and Shaanxi in 1784–1788, wrote a memorial to the emperor in February 1785 in which he saw no evidence of communication between the Christians and Muslims.[85] He noted that the Muslim prohibition on eating pork, one of the distinguishing characteristics of Muslims in China, was not shared by Christians. He also added that the Ten Commandments of the Christians were neither unreasonable nor unorthodox by Chinese standards.

During the persecution of 1784, thirty-three missionaries and native priests were arrested, seven of whom were priests of the Collegio dei Cinesi.[86] Fr. Gaetano Xu (Xu Geda 徐格達) (1748–1801), and Fr. Dominico Liu (Liu Minge 劉明我) (1747–1828) were sentenced to perpetual forced labor in exile. Fr. Xu was brought to Beijing where he was dragged on the ground, tortured, branded on the forehead, and sent into exile in Yili, where he died.[87] Fr. Filippo Liu (Liu Kaidi 劉愷弟) (1752–1785) was branded on the face and died in exile in Yili. Fr. Pio Liu (the younger) and Fr. Cassio Giuseppe Dai (Dai Deguan 戴德冠) (1737–1785) were arrested in Beijing and died there. Fr. Simone Carlo Liu (Liu Jialu 劉嘉綠) (1742–1820) and Fr. Emanuele Ma (Ma Gongsa 馬功撒) (1740–1797) were arrested in Shaanxi. They were all Chinese martyrs of the faith.

In response to the persecution that began in China in 1784, an eminent cleric in Rome made some innovative proposals for dealing with the problems in the China mission. Stefano Borgia, secretary of Propaganda Fide, submitted two documents to the Special Congregation of China (Congregazione Particolare della Cina) in 1787.[88] Borgia's first proposal emphasized the need to raise up a native clergy. He blamed the 1784 persecution on the lack of native priests and blamed the earlier destruction of Catholicism in Japan on a similar deficiency. Borgia claimed that foreign missionaries entering China were harmful because they violated the laws of the country, which local Catholics needed to obey. Borgia harshly criticized foreign bishops ministering in China, a criticism that would be voiced repeatedly until the twentieth century. The bishops could not be effective because they were unable to master the difficult Chinese language. Moreover, the bishops were restricted in their movements. The bishops of the dioceses of Macau, Beijing, and Nanjing were unable to leave their cities to visit their flocks in the countryside. Borgia's second proposal involved the need to celebrate mass in Chinese rather than Latin.[89] Borgia's proposals were rejected mainly because of the European missionaries in China who opposed the nomination of local bishops. However, the opposition was not monolithic. There were unsuccessful attempts in 1817, 1818, and 1819 to have Fr. Matthew Luo (1751–1832) elected bishop in Sichuan.[90] Borgia's proposal for native bishops was finally realized in 1926 in the appointment of six Chinese bishops in a ceremony in Rome.[91] His proposal for saying the mass in Chinese was realized with Vatican II (1961–1965).

Borgia's proposals were influenced by the ideas of Matteo Ripa and the Chinese College in Naples. During his term as secretary and later prefect of Propaganda Fide (1770–1804), Borgia wrote numerous letters to G. Fatigati and others at the Chinese College. He appears to have been a Sinophile who delighted in the gifts of paintings, tea, porcelains, and other Chinese artifacts given to him by Chinese priests. He showed warm hospitality to the Chinese College seminarians who stayed over at Borgia's hometown of Velletri when they traveled between Naples and Rome.

NOTES

1. Joseph Dehergne, SJ, "Les Missions du nord de la Chine vers 1700," *Archivum Historicum Societatis Iesu* 24 (1955): 276.

2. Joseph de Moidrey, SJ, *La Hiérarchie catholique en Chine, en Corée et au Japon (1307–1914)* (Shanghai: Tousèwèi Orphanage, 1914), 254; Nicolas Standaert, "Ecclesiastical Administration," in *Handbook of Christianity in China*, vol. 1, *635–1800* (Leiden: Brill, 2001), 576.

3. Giacomo Di Fiore, *Lettere di Missioneri della Cina (1761–1775)* (Napoli: Istituto Universitario Orientale, 1995), 65–66.

4. Dehergne, "Missions du nord," 275.

5. Nicolas Standaert, "The Creation of Christian Communities," in *Handbook of Christianity in China*, vol. 1, *635–1800* (Leiden: Brill, 2001), 565.

6. Di Fiore, *Lettere di Missioneri*, 140–372.

7. One recent example of this erroneous belief is found in Christopher M. S. Johns, *China and the Church: Chinoiserie in Global Context* (Oakland: University of California Press, 2016), 25 & 40.

8. Letter of Filippo Huang to Gennaro Fatigati, dated at Kui-hua-ch'eng, May 1, 1765, in Di Fiore, *Lettere di Missioneri*, 240.

9. Letter of Filippo Huang to Gennaro Fatigati, dated at Datong-fu, April 22, 1767, in Di Fiore, *Lettere di Missioneri*, 304.

10. *Elenchus Alumnorum decreta et documenta quae spectant ad Collegium Sacrae Familiae Neapolis* (Shanghai: T'ou-sè-wè Orphanage printers, 1917).

11. Letter of Huang to Fatigati, September 29, 1762, in Di Fiore, *Lettere di Missioneri*, 140.

12. William V. Bangert, SJ, *A History of the Society of Jesus*, rev. ed. (St. Louis: Institute of Jesuit Sources, 1986), 366–72.

13. Huang to Fatigati, September 29, 1762, 143.

14. Huang to Fatigati, August 20, 1763, in Di Fiore, *Lettere di Missioneri*, 167.

15. Huang to Fatigati, May 22, 1766, in Di Fiore, *Lettere di Missioneri*, 280.

16. Huang to Fatigati, May 22, 1766, 279.

17. Huang to Fatigati, August 20, 1765, in Di Fiore, *Lettere di Missioneri*, 172.

18. Huang to Fatigati, May 1, 1765, in Di Fiore, *Lettere di Missioneri*, 242.

19. Huang to Fatigati, April 22, 1767, in Di Fiore, *Lettere di Missioneri*, 302.

20. Huang to Fatigati, October 4, 1775, in Di Fiore, *Lettere di Missioneri*, 372.

21. Huang to Nicolò Borgia, September 10, 1764, in Di Fiore, *Lettere di Missioneri*, 219.

22. Huang to Fatigati, April 20, 1763, in Di Fiore, *Lettere di Missioneri*, 173.

23. Huang to Borgia, May 1, 1765, in Di Fiore, *Lettere di Missioneri*, 200.

24. Huang to Fatigati, April 20, 1763, in Di Fiore, *Lettere di Missioneri*, 175.

25. Huang to Fatigati, April 20, 1763, 176.

26. Huang to Fatigati, April 20, 1763, 177–78.

27. Emanuele Raini, "Catechisti e capi laici delle comunità nella storia della chiesa in Cina," *Urbaniana University Journal* 2 (2019): 98.

28. Raini, "Catechisti," 111–12.

29. Raini, "Catechisti," 112–14.

30. Anonymous, *Chuanjiao zhinan* 傳教指南, Hejian Shengshitang 河間勝世堂, Hejian, 1905.

31. Raini, "Catechisti," 115–16.

32. Huang to Fatigati, September 10, 1764, in Di Fiore, *Lettere di Missioneri*, 213.

33. Di Fiore, *Lettere di Missioneri*, 239n1.

34. Huang to Fatigati, September 10, 1764, in Di Fiore, *Lettere di Missioneri*, 214.

35. Huang to Fatigati, May 22, 1766, in Di Fiore, *Lettere di Missioneri*, 278.

36. Huang to Fatigati, Beijing, August 20, 1763, in Di Fiore, *Lettere di Missioneri*, 169–70.

37. Huang to Borgia, September 10, 1764, in Di Fiore, *Lettere di Missioneri*, 220.

38. Huang to Fatigati, May 1, 1765, in Di Fiore, *Lettere di Missioneri*, 242.
39. Huang to Fatigati, May 1, 1765, 241.
40. Huang to Fatigati, May 1, 1765, 243–44.
41. Huang to Fatigati, May 1, 1765, 242.
42. Emiliano Palladini to Naples, undated, arrived November 1766, in Di Fiore, *Lettere di Missioneri*, 270–71.
43. Palladini to Naples, undated, 271.
44. Palladini to Naples, undated, 272.
45. Palladini to Naples, undated, 273.
46. Palladini to Naples, undated, 274.
47. Huang to Fatigati, May 1, 1765, in Di Fiore, *Lettere di Missioneri*, 249.
48. Huang to Fatigati, May 1, 1765, 248–49.
49. Moidrey, *Hiérarchie catholique*, 29–30.
50. Huang to Fatigati, July 26, 1768, in Di Fiore, *Lettere di Missioneri*, 326–27.
51. Di Fiore, *Lettere di Missioneri*, 65.
52. Huang to Fatigati, July 26, 1768, in Di Fiore, *Lettere di Missioneri*, 327.
53. Huang to Fatigati, July 26, 1768, 327–28.
54. Huang to Fatigati, July 26, 1768, 328.
55. Robert Entenmann, "Chinese Clergy and Their European Colleagues in Sichuan, 1702–1800," in *Silent Force: Native Converts in the Catholic China Mission*, ed. Rachel Lu Yan and Philip Vanhaelemeersch (Leuven: Ferdinand Verbiest Institute, 2009), 87.
56. Entenmann, "Chinese Clergy," 85–87.
57. Huang to Fatigati, May 1, 1765, in Di Fiore, *Lettere di Missioneri*, 239–240.
58. Huang to Borgia, May 1, 1765, in Di Fiore, *Lettere di Missioneri*, 259.
59. Huang to Fatigati, October 29, 1774, in Di Fiore, *Lettere di Missioneri*, 370.
60. Huang to Fatigati, July 26, 1768, in Di Fiore, *Lettere di Missioneri*, 320–321.
61. Huang to Fatigati, May 22, 1766, in Di Fiore, *Lettere di Missioneri*, 277.
62. Huang to Fatigati, April 22, 1767, in Di Fiore, *Lettere di Missioneri*, 303.
63. Edward J. Malatesta, SJ, and Gao Zhiyu, eds., *Zhalan: Departed, Yet Present, the Oldest Christian Cemetery in Beijing* (Macau: Instituto Cultural de Macau & Ricci Institute, University of San Francisco, 1995), 228–29.
64. Huang to Fatigati, October 29, 1774, in Di Fiore, *Lettere di Missioneri*, 370–71.
65. Huang to Fatigati, October 29, 1774, 372.
66. Thierry Meynard, SJ, *Following the Footsteps of the Jesuits in Beijing: A Guide to Sites of Jesuit Work and Influence in Beijing* (Saint Louis, MO: Institute of Jesuit Sources, 2006), 23.
67. Edward J. Malatesta, SJ, "Zhalan from 1610 to 1949," in *Zhalan*, ed. Malatesta and Gao, 32.
68. Yu Sanle, "Zhalan from 1949 until 1994," in *Zhalan*, ed. Malatesta and Gao, 98.
69. Malatesta and Gao, *Zhalan*, 228–29.
70. Fang Chao-ying, "Pi Yüan," in *Eminent Chinese of the Ch'ing Period*, ed. Arthur Hummel (Washington, DC: Government Printing Office, 1943), 624–25; Bern-

ward Henry Willeke, OFM, *Imperial Government and Catholic Missions in China during the Years 1784–1785* (Saint Bonaventure, NY: Franciscan Institute, 1948), 76–77.

71. Willeke, *Imperial Government*, 19.

72. In *Gaozong chun Huangdi shilu* 高宗純皇帝實錄, Qianlong 49, 11th month, 11th day, *wuchen* (December 22, 1784), (ch. 1218, 18a–20a), translated in Willeke, *Imperial Government*, 176.

73. Willeke, *Imperial Government*, 26.

74. Eugenio Menegon, "Wanted: An Eighteenth-Century Chinese Catholic Priest in China, Italy, India and Southeast Asia," *Journal of Modern Italian Studies* 15, no. 4 (2010): 507–9.

75. Willeke, *Imperial Government*, 35.

76. Willeke, *Imperial Government*, 37.

77. Menegon, "Wanted," 508–10.

78. Imperial Edict on the Arrest of Four Missionaries, in *Gaozong chun Huangdi shilu* 高宗純皇帝實錄, Qianlong 49, 8th month, 20th day, *guimao* (October 4, 1784), (ch. 1213, 11b–12a), translated in Willeke, *Imperial Government*, 170.

79. Willeke, *Imperial Government*, 78.

80. Willeke, *Imperial Government*, 78n, confuses Fr. Pio Liu the younger (Liu Chengren) (1718–1785) with Fr. Pio Liu, elder (Liu Biyue 劉必約) (1718–1786), both of whom studied at the Chinese College in Naples in 1739–1755.

81. Willeke, *Imperial Government*, 27.

82. Willeke, *Imperial Government*, 84.

83. Edict to the Grand Council, December 31, 1784, in *Gaozong shilu*, ch. 1219, 5a–6a, translated in Willeke, *Imperial Government*, 181–82.

84. Knight Biggerstaff, "Fu-k'ang-an," in *Eminent Chinese of the Ch'ing Period*, ed. Arthur W. Hummel (Washington, DC: Government Printing Office, 1943), 253–55.

85. Memorial of Fukangan, February 20, 1785, in *Wenxian congbian* 文獻叢編 (Collection of selected palace documents, published by the Palace Museum, Beiping, no. 15–17, 1930–1934), translated in Willeke, *Imperial Government*, 185–86.

86. Gianni Criveller, "The Chinese Priests of the College for the Chinese in Naples and the Promotion of the Indigenous Clergy (XVIII–XIX Centuries)," in *Silent Force: Native Converts in the Catholic China Mission*, ed. Rachel Lu Yan and Philip Vanhaelemeersch (Leuven: Ferdinand Verbiest Institute, 2009), 158.

87. Criveller, "Chinese Priests," 157.

88. Criveller, "Chinese Priests," 165–66.

89. Criveller, "Chinese Priests," 167–68.

90. Fortunato Margiotti, "La Chiesa Cattolica al traguardo della maturità," in *Sacrae Congregationis de Propaganda Fidei Memoria Rerum. 350 anni a servizio delle missioni 1622–1972*, vol. 3, ed. Josef Metzler (Rom-Freiburg-Wien: Heider, 1975), 513–14.

91. D. E. Mungello, *The Catholic Invasion of China: Remaking Chinese Christianity* (Lanham, MD: Rowman & Littlefield, 2015), 44.

Chapter Five

The Emergence of the Underground Church

THE UNDERGROUND CHURCH IN JAPAN

At the time of the expulsion of missionaries in China in 1724, the disastrous expulsion of missionaries in neighboring Japan was well known. In Japan when Christianity was outlawed and the *ebumi* (trampling on a Christian plaque as a sign of apostasy) was introduced in 1629, Christians were forced to choose between conversion to Buddhism, martyrdom, or exile. A group of Christians on the Grotō Islands near Nagasaki chose instead to go underground and became known as the Hidden Christians (*kakure kirishitan*).[1] In order to survive, they imitated Buddhism by reinterpreting its symbols while adding some uniquely Christian symbols. Using the altar statues of Kannon (Buddhist goddess of mercy), they created a syncretic Maria-Kannon. Fear of detection confined them to worship in their homes and the lack of communication between the *kakure kirishitan* groups led to many variations in their worship on the islands of Gotō, Sotome, and Ikitsuki.

Christmas was celebrated on different days—December 23 by some and December 24 by others. On this occasion, the group would gather in the home of the *chōkata*, the highest-ranking member of the *kakure kirishitan* hierarchy, who was the keeper of the calendar. A group recitation and six-hour fast was observed, followed by a feast of fish, meat, and sake. Sundays had no special significance, except for the first and last Sundays of the year. On specified festival days, the faithful would gather in a designated home to recite verses and eat *mochi*. Celebrants observed traditional rituals by sitting on the floor in two rows facing each other with heads bowed and hands resting on their laps.[2] This posture of folded hands distinguishes them from Buddhists in prayer. The *chōkata* and other leading roles are taken by men. Many of their prayers (*orashio*) contain Japanized Latin and Portuguese words and names along with teachings that have been transmitted from father to eldest son for nine or more generations. The recitation of the *orashio* lasts fifteen to twenty minutes.

The faithful have forgotten or misunderstood many of the teachings of their religion and the *orashio* being recited has no meaning for them.[3] Maria (Maruyo) and her son Anata Sama (Jesus) are viewed as central figures in their religion. However, although Christ is known as a man who died on the cross, there is no clear knowledge of what happened after his death. The sense of isolation of the *kakure kirishitan* became ingrained. When Japan's seclusion ended and French Catholic missionaries returned to Japan in the 1860s, many *kakure kirishitan* resisted returning to the Catholic Church. Demographic changes in Japan have caused many members of these isolated communities to move to the larger islands and their numbers are dwindling.

Unlike the Hidden Christians in Japan, the underground church in eighteenth-century China was never completely cut off from Rome. Chinese priests continued to be trained in Vatican-approved seminaries. Although European bishops were sometimes absent from regions like Sichuan and Jiangnan, the Chinese priests remained in intermittent contact through correspondence and the receipt of meager subsidies from Europe. This appears to be a fundamental reason the Chinese underground church did not become transformed in the manner of the Japanese *kakure kirishitan*.

THE FORMATION OF CHINESE JESUIT PRIESTS

Chinese priests in China were not ordained until the consecration of the first Chinese bishop in 1685, one century after the arrival of the Jesuit missionaries in China. Luo Wenzao 羅文藻 (Gregory López) (1616–1691) was a Chinese Dominican who received his seminary training in the Philippines and was ordained in 1654.[4] In 1666 while the European missionaries were confined to Canton, Luo's Dominican superiors ordered him as their sole Chinese priest to make an apostolic journey into China to minister to Christians.[5] With the permission of the Jesuit Visitor in Macau, Luis da Gama, Lopez set out from Canton in February 1667 in what became an epic two-year journey, traveling northward to Beijing and then westward to Shanxi and Shaanxi. Crisscrossing China east and west, he returned to the south, gradually visiting Christian communities throughout China and baptizing four thousand people.[6] What made Luo's achievement so remarkable is that he made this journey while the European missionaries had been confined to Beijing and Canton.

However, Luo, like many later Chinese priests, tended to favor the Jesuits' more accommodating position on the Chinese rites over the hard-line position of the Spanish Dominicans.[7] Luo's alienation from the Dominicans on this led them to oppose his consecration as bishop. Despite their opposition, Mgr. della Chiesa consecrated Luo as the vicar apostolic of Nanjing.

Joseph Dehergne, SJ, compiled a list of thirty-nine pre-1800 Chinese and Macanese Jesuits; however, his list is incomplete.[8] The first of these Jesuit ordinations in China took place in 1688 when Bishop Luo ordained three elderly catechists. All three were over fifty years old and had memorized phonetically the minimal amount of Latin needed to read the mass.[9] The most well-known member of this trio was the painter and poet Wu Yushan 吳漁山 (Wu Li 吳歷) (Simon Xavier a Cunha) (1632–1718). The second member was Liu Yunde 劉蘊德 (Blaise Verbiest) (1628–1707), who had been the second president of the Tribunal of Mathematics at Beijing but had been disgraced and lost his position.[10] He was baptized by the Jesuit astronomer Ferdinand Verbiest in 1684 and took Verbiest's name. The third member of the trio was Wan Qiyuan 萬其淵 (Paul Banhes) (1631–1700) of Jiangnan (east central China). The knowledge of Latin improved with the ordinations of those Chinese who studied at St. Joseph College in Macau. These included He Tianzhang 何天章 (François Xavier a Rosario) (1667–1736), who was born in Macau to a European father and Chinese mother and ordained in 1690.[11] Guo Tianpang 郭天龐 (João Pacheco) (1668–1724) was born to Japanese parents and studied in Macau and was ordained in 1694.[12] Gong Shangshi 龔尚實 (Thomas da Cruz) (1666–1745 or 1746) was born in Hangzhou.[13] His father, who had failed in his wish to become a Jesuit, died when Gong was a boy. Fr. Philippe Couplet sheltered the boy and took him to Macau where he studied Latin and was ordained in 1694. However, these ordinations fell short of the Jesuit model of forming highly educated priests.

The first Chinese to receive the full Jesuit formation was Zheng Manuo Weixin 鄭瑪諾維信 (1633–1673). He is more commonly known as Emmanuel de Siqueira because although he was born of Chinese parents in Macau and died in Beijing, he spent most of his life in Europe. When he was twelve years old, he accompanied the Jesuit Alexandre de Rhodes to Europe, departing Macau in 1645.[14] After completing a four-year journey, Siqueira arrived at Rome in 1650 and enrolled as a novice at Sant-Andrea College in 1651. Unlike many of the wealthy novices who arrived with large wardrobes, Siqueira had a meager number of personal possessions, reflecting his humble origins.[15] After a two-year novitiate, he entered the Collegio Romano from 1653 to 1657, followed by a three-year teaching term from 1657 to 1660 at the same institution.[16] After his magisterium at the Collegio Romano was completed, Siqueira was sent to Bologna for theological studies, but after one year, he was sent on to Portugal to finish his formation and to prepare for departure to China.[17] He completed his four-year course of theology at Coimbra and was ordained there in 1664, ten years after Luo Wenzao was ordained at Manila. This extended period of Siqueira's formation stood in stark contrast to the typically curtailed period of Jesuit formation of later eighteenth-century Chinese scholastics sent to Europe. They were returned more quickly to China because of the desperate need for Chinese priests.[18]

Siqueira returned to Macau in 1668, nearly twenty-three years after he had left. He was now thirty-five years old and a Jesuit priest and presumably poised to use his remarkable education in ministering to Chinese Christians.[19] However, the story ends tragically. During his long absence, he had lost his native facility in Chinese and had to spend a year in Macau reviving it. Unlike the seminarians at the Chinese College in Naples, Siqueira had lived in a European milieu without Chinese companions to help him maintain his Chinese fluency. After one year of a refresher course, he was ready. However, he had developed an advanced case of tuberculosis.[20] He was sent to Guangdong (Canton), and during 1670 recorded 150 new converts.

When an imperial edict ended the five years of confinement (1666–1671) of the missionaries at Guangzhou (Canton), the Guangdong viceroy was ordered to find two missionaries with special competence in applied sciences to serve the emperor in Beijing.[21] Claudio Filippo Grimaldi (Min Mingwo 旻明我) and Christian Herdtrich (En Lige 恩理格) were chosen and their departure for Beijing under official protection provided an opportunity for Jesuit superiors to attach Siqueira as secretary (*xianggong*) to the two court mathematicians. It was hoped that Siqueira as a Chinese priest could provide unique assistance in Beijing and possibly regain his health in the drier northern China climate rather than the warm, humid south. However, Siqueira's health was deteriorating rapidly. As the mandarinal junk traveled northward, it encountered bitterly cold winter weather that caused the Grand Canal to freeze over, forcing them to switch to land transport through snow-covered roads. Grimaldi also fell ill while Siqueira had to be left behind to recuperate. Eventually he recovered enough to arrive in Beijing to join the other Jesuits.

By the time Siqueira reached Beijing, he was in the last stages of tuberculosis, characterized by flushed cheeks and hacking cough and bedridden with fever. Even in his weakened condition, he ministered to the Christians around Beijing, most of whom shared the poverty of his origins. He died on May 26, 1673, at thirty-eight years of age.[22] He was buried in the Zhalan cemetery in Beijing.[23]

The European Jesuit formation of Aloys (Louis) Gao (Gao Leisi 高類思) (1732–1795?) and Etienne Yang (Yang Dewang 楊德望) (1733–1789?) is also well known.[24] Both Gao and Yang were born in Beijing. Yang's parents were André Yang and Catherine Li, apparently both baptized Christians. Gao and Yang must have been promising students because the French Jesuits of Beijing sent them to Paris. During his years in France, Yang also used the surname Laforest. They studied at La Flèche College and entered the Society of Jesus in 1759. They were seminarians at the college of Louis-le-Grand at Paris and were ordained in 1763 as secular priests rather than Jesuits because the order had been suppressed in France in 1762. After the suppression of the Jesuits, Secretary of State Henri Bertin became their generous protector. Before they returned to China in January 1765, Louis XV received them at Versailles and each received a royal stipend of 1,200 livres. In August 1764, only two months after their royal reception, the king signed an order expelling all Jesuits from France.[25]

When Frs. Gao and Yang returned to Beijing in 1766, they again became Jesuits, at least until 1773, when the pope dissolved the Society of Jesus throughout the world. Unlike their stay in Europe, where their activities are well documented, little is known of their work in China. Gao served in Beijing and Huguang province, and died sometime after 1795, possibly in Beijing.[26] Fr. Yang went to Jiangxi in 1767. In 1776 Louis XVI named him procurator of the French mission at Canton. In 1785 he was again in Jiangxi. He was betrayed and denounced to a mandarin by a Christian, whereupon he was arrested and imprisoned in May 1787. In 1789 he was in Beijing and Tartary (Manchuria). In 1790 he offered to go to Korea. The date and place of his death are thought, but not known, to have been 1798 in Jiangxi.[27]

CHINESE PRIESTS AND CATECHISTS IN SICHUAN

Because of European resistance, following Bishop Luo Wenzao's death in 1691, there were no further consecrations of Chinese bishops for 235 years, that is, until 1926.[28] Nevertheless, outstanding priests, like Andreas Li, emerged in the eighteenth century who demonstrated the spiritual and leadership abilities of a bishop, without receiving formal recognition through consecration.

Whereas most Chinese Christian communities during the eighteenth century stagnated in membership and struggled to survive, the Christians in Sichuan grew by substantial numbers between 1756 and 1815.[29] After suffering a decline from perhaps 8,000 in the early eighteenth century due to persecution and apostasies, the number of Christians in Sichuan grew steadily from 4,000 baptized converts in 1756, to 25,000 in 1792, to 40,000 in 1801, to 45,000 in 1804, and to 60,000 in 1815.[30] Their growth was led by a remarkable group of indigenous Catholics while European missionaries were sometimes completely absent from the province. Throughout the eighteenth century, a total of thirty-three Chinese priests outnumbered thirty-two European priests (twenty-seven of whom were French missionaries of the Société des Missions

Étrangères de Paris). Moreover, the ratio of Chinese to European priests increased such that by 1800, four French missionaries were serving together with twenty-one Chinese priests.[31]

The development of Christianity in Sichuan province was unique in several respects. The devastation of the Ming-to-Qing transition ca. 1644 reduced the population of Sichuan by half to around two million. This was followed by a tremendous migration from south and central China that increased the population of Sichuan to twenty or twenty-five million by 1800.[32] This massive migration created the conditions favorable for drawing migrants to Christianity as well as to the White Lotus sect with which it was often confused. However, other forces worked against the growth of Christianity and thus the growth was not constant.

Perhaps the earliest Chinese evangelist in Sichuan was the catechist (*chuandaoyuan* 傳道員) Linus Zhang Feng (Zhang Feng 張風) (1669?–1743), who was born in the Shixing district of Guangdong province.[33] He had taken a vow of celibacy as a young man and only his lack of Latin prevented him from becoming a priest. In 1702 Zhang accompanied Fr. Jean Basset (Bo Risheng 白日陞), MEP (1662–1707), and Fr. Louis-Antoine Appiani (Bi Tianxiang 畢天祥), CM, to Chongqing, where they divided Sichuan province between the MEP and the Lazarists (Congregation of the Mission). (Later the Lazarists would withdraw, leaving Sichuan completely to the MEP.) Fr. Basset and Fr. Jean-François Martin de la Balluère, MEP (Liang Hongren 梁弘仁) (1668–1715), remained in Chongqing while Zhang led the Lazarists on to Chengdu. Problems with the authorities ensued from the outset when rumors swirled that the missionaries were White Lotus adherents fleeing a failed revolt in Canton. To address these rumors, Basset, accompanied by Zhang, traveled to Xi'an to meet the governor-general of Shaanxi and Sichuan and obtained his support for the mission.

Basset was in favor of recruiting Chinese priests and he returned from Xi'an with three boys from Catholic families who had been given to him for training as priests.[34] They included Andreas Li and Antonius Dang (Dang Huairen 黨懷仁) 1695–1745), born in Wugong in Shaanxi province, both of whom would become leading priests in Sichuan. Tensions soon emerged between the European priests Basset and Balluère and their Chinese catechists. When Basset and Balluère refused to swear the oath to follow the interpretations of Ricci as required by the Chinese court, they failed to obtain the imperially required *piao* 票 (certificate) and were expelled from Sichuan in 1707.[35]

Basset and Balluère went to Macau, taking with them four boys to be trained for the priesthood. Among them were Andreas Li, Antonius Dang, and Stephanus (Etienne) Xu (Xu Dewang 徐德望) (1694–ca. 1763).[36] Xu was born in Leshanxian 樂山縣, Jiadingfu 嘉定府 in Sichuan and received the tonsure from the papal legate Tournon.³⁷ Many years later Andreas Li wrote of the hostility that some European missionaries in Macau expressed toward him and the other Chinese students. When Tournon proposed that the Chinese be admitted to minor orders, the other Europeans in Macau objected. They criticized the Chinese for pride, haughtiness, and corruption, the same complaints later voiced toward Fr. Filippo Huang. Only Balluère came to their defense, claiming that the flaws of the Chinese were also found among Europeans and gaining the assent of Tournon for the Chinese to proceed. In 1717, Li, Dang, and Xu traveled to Siam to study at the Collège Général in Ayudhya.

Seminary training for eighteenth-century Chinese priests varied by mission affiliation. The Jesuits sent several seminarians to Rome for study. The Dominicans had a preparatory school in Fujian and trained several Chinese priests at the Collegium Sancti Joannis Lateranensis in Manila.³⁸ The Congregation of the Sacred Family (Congregazione della Sacra Famiglia) trained its priests at the Chinese College in Naples. The Lazarists, with the consent of the queen of Portugal, established a seminary in Macau in 1784 at the former Jesuit College of St. Joseph, which enrolled eight students.³⁹ This seminary continued to operate until the Chinese Cultural Revolution of 1966–1976 forced its closure.⁴⁰ In 1788 at Beijing, the Lazarists also established a seminary at the St. Joseph Church (also known as the Eastern Church [*Dongtang* 東堂]). In 1805 this seminary had six seminarians. However, because of six persecutions in nine years, this seminary was moved from Beijing to the village of Sywantze in Mongolia, seventeen leagues from the Great Wall, where eight seminarians were brought in 1829.⁴¹

The MEP trained its Chinese priests at the College of St. Joseph, a seminary for training indigenous Asian clergy in Mahapram, Siam (present-day Thailand), located in the suburbs of Ayudhya (Ayutthaya), which was then the capital of Siam.⁴² The college was founded by Bishop Lambert de la Motte in 1665. In 1717, the vicar apostolic of the Sichuan-Guizhou-Yunnan diocese sent seven Chinese seminarians to study there, including Andreas Li (Li Ande 李安德), who would become its most famous Chinese graduate. During the years 1717–1727, the college thrived with fifty seminarians who were taught philosophy, theology, classics, Latin, and East Asian languages. The rector was Fr. Andrew Roost, a graduate of the theological faculty of the University of Paris (the Sorbonne). The success of the college provoked criticism from the Portuguese, who accused Fr. Roost of Jansenism. The seminarian Andreas Li demonstrated his proficiency in Latin when he defended the rector against such charges before the bishop. When Burmese invaders destroyed Ayudhya in 1767, the seminary was moved to Hon-dat in Vietnam. In 1770 it was moved to Virampatnam near Pondicherry (a French-controlled area of India). More than half of the thirty-three Chinese priests who served in eighteenth-century Sichuan studied at either Ayudhya or Pondicherry.[43]

When Balluère died in 1715, he entrusted the three seminarians, including Andreas Li, to the catechist Zhang. Andreas Li became the most famous priest in eighteenth-century Sichuan. His given name of Li Biaoshu was seldom used.[44] The use of baptismal names rather than given names and the use of Latin instead of Chinese in writing were means adopted by many members of the underground church to protect themselves from official persecution. Li was born in 1692 or 1693 in Chenggu near Hanzhong-fu 漢中府 in southwestern Shaanxi province near the Sichuan border. He claimed to have been born into a family that had been Catholic for five or six generations before his birth.[45] This means they would have been converted in the Ming dynasty and would have placed his family among the earliest Christian converts in China. In China, honoring the religion of one's ancestors played an important role in establishing Christianity. Frs. Basset and Balluère had recognized Li's spiritual potential as a young boy.[46] After studying at the MEP seminary in Siam, he was ordained in 1725 at the age of thirty-three by Bishop Louis Champion de Cicé, the vicar apostolic of Siam.[47] Then he was sent by the MEP to Fujian in 1726, where he met Bishop Pedro Sanz, OP, who would have a deep influence on him. After falling ill, he went to Guangzhou in 1731 to convalesce. When he attempted to return to Sichuan, he was forced to divert to Hubei province by Bishop Müllener, who was admitting only Lazarists to Sichuan. Later, Müllener allowed Li to enter Sichuan, but excluded Chengdu from his territory. Li served in Sichuan from 1735 until his death in 1774. Li later expressed admiration for Müllener, who lived in great austerity, dressed in rags, and ate the least expensive food.[48]

The vicars apostolic of early eighteenth-century Sichuan were, in succession, Johannes Müllener (1693–1742), Luigi Maggi (d. 1744), and Joachim Enjobert de Martiliat (1706–1755). Suspicions of Catholics being linked to the White Lotus sect led to a persecution in 1747 in which Martiliat and other Europeans were forced to leave Sichuan for Macau. French missionaries in Macau blamed Andreas Li and Giovanni Battista Gu (Gu Ruohan 谷若翰) for their flight.[49] European control of Chinese clerics then lapsed for a decade until the arrival in 1756 of the vicar apostolic François Pottier, who also promoted the formation of Chinese priests.

Müllener devoted a great deal of effort to fostering Chinese priests. Mgr. Appiani said that Müllener sacrificed "the bread from his own mouth" in order to nurture a dozen young boys and men.[50] Müllener at one point cared for eight young men, whom he taught to read and speak Latin. Although most of them were still young, three of them had made great progress. All three had been given to God by their parents. He gave Minor Orders to the twenty-five-year-old and the two others were soon to receive the tonsure. In the mission, there were more than fifteen others, but they were still very young. Müllener was unable to receive such a large number because he was alone and without confreres. Because it required his absence for a year to visit all the missions, the students who remained in the house under the direction of a Chinese teacher forgot much of what they had learned in the preceding year. In response to his pleas for help, three Lazarists (Frs. Gandon, Monet, and Trogneux) were sent from France and arrived in China at the end of 1733. However, insuperable obstacles forced them to return to France.

Müllener trained and ordained three Chinese priests in the years 1723–1731. His first and most notable student was Paulus Sou, CM (Su Hongxiao 蘇鴻孝) (ca. 1692–ca. 1770), who was from Shundexian 順德縣 in Guangdong province. Müllener brought him to Sichuan in 1711 and tonsured him in 1719. He was sent to Rome to study at the Propaganda College.[51] After returning to Sichuan, he was ordained by Müllener in 1723 and became a Lazarist in 1725.[52] He worked mainly in Sichuan and Huguang provinces. Su had a strong influence on Müllener, although other priests criticized Su for being so obsessed by worldly matters that he failed to go to confession and to say mass. Müllener sent his second student to Guangzhou in 1718, but the boy, who was coughing up blood and suffering from tuberculosis, died in June 1719. Müllener also trained and ordained Stephanus Siu (Xu Dewang 徐德望) (1694–?).[53] Fr. Xu was a native of Sichuan who was trained at the seminary in Siam. He served there until 1739 and after ten years in Huguang, he returned to Sichuan to serve from 1749 until 1756.[54] Müllener also trained and ordained Petrus Zhu (Zhu 朱) (?–1732).

THE FORMATION OF CHINESE UNDERGROUND PRIESTS

Andreas Li began writing a remarkably detailed diary in 1742, of which the text from 1746 to 1764 survives.[55] He wrote the diary in Latin, in part because he was sending the diary to Europeans, and in part to prevent Chinese officials from reading it, given the constant danger of persecution. Each year Li sent the latest section of the diary by courier to Macau and the courier would return with Li's small subsidy of silver from the MEP. Li lived in an austere manner and gives careful accounts of his expenses. In the 1740s Li and his fellow Chinese priest Antonius Dang were each paid eighty taels a year and the catechist Linus Zhang was paid thirty taels a year, much less than the 120 taels paid to each of the French missionaries.[56] By 1781 the Chinese clergy were no longer receiving subsidies from the MEP, but were supported entirely by Chinese Catholics.

Li's diary describes a wide range of pastoral activities, including his contacts with Christians, non-Christians, and officials as well as the details of his expenses, the religious instruction of children, baptisms, and the distribution of the eucharist. He traveled extensively from his home base in Chengdu to visit Christians throughout Sichuan, many of whom were suffering from illness and persecution. He served 130 *chrétientés* (small Catholic communities) spread over an area the size of France. Most of these *chrétientés* numbered sixty to eighty Christians, although some exceeded five hundred.[57] They were located in rural areas.

When the French missionary Urbain Lefebvre (1725–1792) traveled to Sichuan in 1754, he stayed as a guest at the home of Andreas Li in Chengdu. However, at that time Catholics in Sichuan were under suspicion for being involved in rebellious sects. Consequently, shortly afterward soldiers raided Li's home and imprisoned him as well as Lefebvre, Stephanus Xu, and a lay guide who had brought Lefebvre to Sichuan.[58] Lucio Li escaped arrest by fleeing to Shaanxi. Andreas Li was sentenced to being flogged with a hundred blows. The sentence was eventually reduced to forty blows and to wearing a cangue for one month.[59] Lefebvre was expelled to Macau and returned to Europe. In 1761–1762 trouble again occurred involving Christians around Chengdu. Li was condemned and ordered to present himself at the governor's office wearing a cangue. He was then sixty-two years old.[60] His feet became badly infected and at one point in the interrogation he fainted.

Li's diary contains endless complaints about the behavior of his Christians.[61] The Christians who lived with Li in the churchyard in Chengdu were querulous and contentious, engaging in drunkenness, fighting, and shouting obscenities. Li complained that the loud prayers they shouted in the manner of the banned White Lotus sect might attract unwanted attention from the authorities. There was suicide and infanticide by Christians. Li attributed these instances of infanticide to saving the honor of an unwed girl and to the fear of raising a girl who might not be able to find a marriage partner.[62]

The Christians' knowledge of their faith was poor and Li repeatedly claimed they were deists rather than Christians.[63] He attributed their poor knowledge to poverty, illiteracy, ignorance, the lack of priests, and the poor quality of the catechists. Because of the inferior quality of most catechists, Li proposed changing the title of *huizhang* 會長 (community leaders) to *zuzhang* 祖長 (ancestors). As for Chinese priests, Li wondered why the Chinese College in Naples was able to produce better quality priests than the MEP seminary in Siam. In 1764 he founded the first seminary in Sichuan in a mountain hut on Fenghuangshan 鳳凰山 near Chengdu; however, the lack of funds limited the number of seminarians.[64] In 1780 a French MEP priest named Thomas Hamel (Liu 劉) established a seminary at Longqi 龍溪 in

Yunnan province near the border of Sichuan.[65] In 1787 or 1788 the seminary was moved to nearby Luoranggou 落讓溝 in the vicinity of Xuzhou 叙州 (today Yibin 宜賓) in Sichuan. Over a period of thirty-two years, Fr. Hamel trained twenty-seven Chinese priests.

By 1762 Li's tireless energy was ebbing. He was seventy years old and still suffering from his chronic foot infection. He wrote in his diary that he was like "an old ox, totally exhausted, wounded in the legs, burdened with age, and unable to plow any longer."[66] Shortly after 1763 he retired because of deafness, but continued to serve by running a seminary for boys. He died in 1774.

The regional distribution of Chinese priests outside of the allowable residential centers in Beijing and Macau tended to follow the membership of their religious orders. Chinese priests trained at the Chinese College in Naples tended to go to Beijing and the provinces of Shanxi, Shaanxi, and Huguang. However, the first missionary of the Chinese College, Giovanni Battista Gu (Gu Yaowen 谷耀文), went to Sichuan after losing his classmate Giovanni Evangelista Yin (Yin Ruowang 殷若望). Fr. Yin is mentioned in the diary of Fr. Andreas Li.[67] After the demise of the Jesuits, the lower Yangzi River region of Anhui and Jiangsu was served in the eighteenth century mainly by Lazarists (Vincentians). Fujian province was served mainly by Spanish Dominicans. Sichuan was a disputed area between the Lazarists and the MEP (Missions Étrangères de Paris) until the Lazarists withdrew.

The indigenization of Catholicism in Sichuan was more a result of the development of Chinese clergy and lay leadership than of developments in theological doctrine. Church leadership in the eighteenth century rested primarily on outstanding Chinese priests and catechists who rose to the challenge of keeping the faith alive in the face of great adversity. By contrast, European priests were either absent because of forced expulsions or were rendered ineffective by divisiveness over Rites Controversy issues and rivalries with other religious orders that impeded the mission, such as Bishop Johannes Müllener's attempt to exclude MEP priests from Sichuan in order to limit the province to Lazarists. Moreover, MEP numbers declined at the end of the eighteenth century because of revolutionary conditions in France. In 1785 twenty-seven missionaries were in prison in China.[68]

Eventually Li was joined by three other Chinese priests: Antonius Dang, Stephanus Xu, and Paulus Su (Su Hongxiao 蘇宏孝), CM.[69] Stephanus Xu and Paulus Su had studied in Europe. Because of widespread Chinese skepticism toward celibacy, Chinese priests sometimes claimed to be widowers with children. Fathers Andreas Li, Su, and Dang all adopted sons.[70] Their sons were both helpful and troublesome. Li's adopted son was Laurentius Ly Veng-hoaen and the adopted son of Fr. Paulus Su was Petrus Pe.[71]

Most of the catechists were illiterate, working-class Chinese whom the Europeans looked down upon as mediocre types.[72] Disputes broke out. Appiani viewed his Chinese Christians as poor, ungrateful, rebellious, and xenophobic. He held them in low regard as unsociable creatures who shared similar vices with the ancient Romans described by St. Augustine in *The City of God*. But as a priest, he regarded them as worthy of salvation. When the catechist Zhang asked about similarities between Confucianism and Christianity, Balluère dismissed the question as stupid. And yet the Chinese catechists were more successful than the Europeans in recruiting converts. When in 1707 Basset and Balluère, along with all the members of the MEP, were expelled, they were forced to leave the Sichuan mission in the hands of Zhang. For the first time, the Christian communities in Sichuan were under Chinese leadership.

Lucus Augustinus Li (Li Shiyin 李世音) (1719–1798) was another notable priest in eighteenth-century Sichuan. He was born in Fujian and trained at the MEP Collège de Saint Joseph in Siam and ordained at Macau in 1748. Although both Andreas Li and Lucas Li reported to superiors in the Société des Missions Étrangères (Paris), they were unable to become members of that society because membership was limited to French priests.[73] Lucas Li arrived in Sichuan in 1749 and worked there tirelessly for almost forty years. He wrote a diary in Latin in 1749–1753 that has been translated into French.[74] By 1770 he was going blind, but he continued to travel to Christian communities in western Sichuan until 1778. He died at Chengdu in 1798. As the eighteenth century progressed, the role of Chinese priests and catechists increased, such that by 1804 there were eighteen Chinese priests and only four European missionaries in Sichuan.

CHRISTIAN VIRGINS (CHASTE WOMEN) IN SICHUAN

Unmarried Catholic women played an important role in the growth of Christianity in Sichuan. Because of the segregation of the sexes in China, it was extremely difficult for male priests to minister to women. As a result, a group of laywomen emerged who served as "baptizers" (*quanxi xiansheng* 權洗先生) and female catechists (*nü chuanjiao xiansheng* 女傳教先生).[75] These unmarried Catholic women consecrated their lives to serving the church and are referred to as "Virgins," known under the various names of *tongzhen* 童貞 (consecrated virgins), *zhennü* 貞女 (chaste women), and *guniang* 姑娘 (old mothers). They took private vows of chastity and lived with their families. They taught basic Catholic doctrines to women and children, performed baptisms, organized communal devotional activities, supervised collective prayers, cared for the local chapels, and helped the sick and dying.[76]

The Christian Virgins were not based on a European model of sisters, but were rather a hybrid blending of Christian theology with the Confucian ideal of a "chaste woman" (*zhennü*).⁷⁷ Catholic sisterhoods had previously emerged in Japan, where they constituted a large part of the secret church that survived after the expulsion of Christianity.⁷⁸ They performed the rites of baptism. A Chinese sisterhood had first emerged in China in the form of the seventeenth-century Beatas in Fujian. Bishop Maggi of Sichuan had begun the process of defining the rules for a sisterhood and Bishop Martiliat finished Maggi's effort in 1744 by defining twenty-five rules that established the Institute of Christian Virgins.⁷⁹

The arrival in 1772 of the French missionary Fr. Jean-Martin Moÿe, MEP (1730–1793), in Sichuan provided the impetus for the transformation of the Christian Virgins from a sheltered, contemplative group into an evangelizing force. Fr. Moÿe reorganized the Christian Virgins in the 1770s. He challenged the consecrated virgins to come out of their isolation to instruct and evangelize women and girls.⁸⁰ Martiliat's original twenty-five rules were expanded at the end of the eighteenth century by the addition of seven rules that dealt with proselyting and teaching.⁸¹

In Europe, Moÿe had founded the Sisters of Providence in Lorraine to offer free education to village children. He was deeply impressed by the faithfulness of Chinese women and believed that they surpassed Chinese men in dedication, although most of them had to memorize the prayers because they were illiterate. Because Moÿe believed in the potential of the Christian Virgins to contribute to the Church, he assigned them to missionary work and to help initiate schools for girls. He modified the rule that Bishop de Martiliat had first made for the Christian Virgins. A fellow priest named Fr. Jean François Gleyo, MEP, was initially skeptical of Moÿe's project, but later had a vision in which he proposed that the Institute of the Virgins should be consecrated to the Blessed Virgin. Moÿe enlarged the role of the Virgins by making them into female catechists (*nü chuanjiao xiansheng* 女傳教先生).

Because of the high rate of infant mortality in Sichuan, Möye trained the Virgins to be "baptizers" (*quanxi xiansheng* 權洗先生) of abandoned and moribund children in order to bestow eternal life on these poor children. In 1778 there was a severe famine in eastern Sichuan and many starving peasants flocked to a camp outside of Chongqing where the officials were distributing rice.⁸² Moÿe sent Christian Virgins to the camp to baptize moribund children.⁸³ In his 1878 study of infanticide and the work of the Holy Childhood in China, the Jesuit Gabriel Palatre related a somewhat hagiographical account of the work of the Christian Virgins in the 1778–1779 famine in eastern Sichuan.⁸⁴ Palatre wrote:

> In 1778, eastern Sichuan was subjected to a horrible famine, and the following year the plague added new suffering to those who were already desolated in

this unfortunate country. Mr. Moÿe, of the Congregation of Foreign Missions, at that time exercised an apostolic ministry at Chongqing. He foresaw, said his biographer, that children would constitute a large number of the victims of this double calamity, and he believed that it was his obligation to gather the abundant harvest that was being prepared for Heaven. The famine and the plague struck everywhere at the time, and it was necessary to regulate, to organize this ministry of charity, in order that it might produce all the effects that it would be able to expect. . . . At this conjuncture, he remembered these pious women, these fervent virgins who were the glory and the ornament of their Christian communities, and he decided to use them for the holy work of the baptism of moribund children. They responded with a generous eagerness to his appeal. A great number were seen descending from the mountain into the plain and into the towns of the scourge that raged with the most fury. Mr. Moÿe needed to provide for their subsistence, but often his need was anticipated by the charity of their families. As frugal and as mortified as they were zealous and courageous, they carried no other provisions than some cakes of maize, and they proceeded to make several journeys from their homes, seeking the sick or abandoned children and administering baptism. . . . It happened often that the pious themselves were possessed of a spirit which they were unable to account for that led them to their sick infants who they prayed to baptize. . . . Sent by Mr. Moÿe, they travelled through the towns, the villages, and even the secluded places, where they wandered among families fleeing the contagion, and where very often due to misfortune, abandoned children were lying.

But it was in the large city of Chongqing-fu that the harvest was the most abundant. The inhabitants of the countryside, pressed by the famine, flocked there from all parts, and the mandarins soon extracted themselves from the obligation of feeding all of the famished population. They established a type of camp, a half-league from the city, and they made distributions of rice to the immense multitude who gathered there each day with an immense number of children. A great many of these unfortunates met with death at the end of their suffering. The children, if they followed their parents, were not at all sheltered and often perished in the most cruel abandonment. The Christian women [i.e., Virgins], with the virtuous wife of banker Luo in mind, betook themselves every day, or every other day to where the dead were soon replaced by other multitudes, who came to die there. The [officials'] assistants initially rejected these women, saying to them: "Don't deny, without doubt, that you want to eat the rice of the poor." In reply to them, they said that they came only to distribute the remedies for sicknesses, whereupon they were allowed to enter and circulate freely in the midst of the crowd of the famished or pestilent. The mandarins and their assistants were affected by a charity that they admired without comprehending. They protected them and admitted them into the enclosure of the camp and in this way facilitated for them, without knowing it, the accomplishment of their pious mission. The majority of the children, who they baptized one day, were dead the next day. The plague became so horrible in this camp, that they were no longer burying the cadavers. Some were scarcely covered with a handful of dust. The air was foul and the stench was frightful. Nothing would stop these courageous women, and they did not at all interrupt their work of charity.[85]

Sometimes Palatre mentioned names of individual Christian Virgins:

> In two journeys to Chongqing, in a westerly direction, a Virgin by the name of Catherine Luo gave an example of courage and zeal without equal. ... She made an exact catalogue of the children who she baptized, to the number of about two-thousand, with the aim of enabling their education, if they survived. But when she returned to find them, she learned that they were all dead.[86]

Palatre also described the dangers that the Christian Virgins confronted:

> In the month of April 1779, in ending the visits of the Christian communities from the mountains, Mr. Moÿe sent some Christian [Virgins] to Ho-tcheou. ... During the passage they baptized about two hundred children, and more than a thousand in the city itself. He sent at the same time two pious women into a marketplace where the mortality was frightful among the adults, and even more so among the children. One of these courageous Christians had baptized in different places as many as fifteen hundred children. When she administered the sacrament of regeneration to a sick child of a guardsman, the condition of the little neophyte worsened, whereupon he remarked to his father that all those who the woman had baptized were dead. Immediately the guardsman, accompanied by a crowd of men who aroused his fury, rushed up to the Christian, overpowered her with injuries and the threat of death. These furious people surrounded her and cried, vying with one another: "Bring her in chains and lead her to the tribunal." "There is no need for chains," she replied, "I will go first and you follow me." God did not allow that a hand be placed upon her. All were content with demanding that she declare, by a written statement signed by her hand, that she vouched for the life of the child. She explained to them that life and death were enabled by God alone, but that she hoped that God would preserve this child by the favor of the Christians and she made the sign of the cross. In speaking thusly, she demonstrated outwardly an imposing courage, and inwardly her heart was filled with joy. The child not being dead at the end of fifteen days, she was freed. She betook herself to several towns and to Yang-tchang, about forty leagues from Chongqing.
>
> Several of these intrepid messengers of charity extended their journeys to more than a hundred leagues to the south and to the north and even farther toward the east. In spite of the incursions of brigands who they encountered more than once and the violence of pagans who drove them away, the inevitable dangers of navigation on the rivers, in the midst of the multitude of travelers, they had no misfortune to complain of, and the gates of heaven were opened by the legions of angels. Mr. Moÿe in the report that he addressed to the Sacred Congregation [of Propaganda Fide] estimated at thirty-thousand the number of children who were thus baptized in his district, during the plague and famine in the years 1778 and 1779.[87]

Bishop Pottier, vicar apostolic of Sichuan province, feared that the youthful Virgins as teachers were too young, that their leadership of the prayers of the assembly when men were present would offend local opinion and expose them to dangers from the scandalized populace, and that this would consequently bring persecution to the church. Consequently, he consulted Rome. The Congregation of Propaganda Fide responded in 1784, approving the creation of girls' schools managed by the consecrated Virgins. They were not to take vows before the age of twenty-five and the vows were renewable in three-year periods. In addition, they were neither to live in community nor to wear religious garb. Their parents had to provide their support, which limited the membership of the Virgins to more prosperous families. In 1793, the vicar apostolic of Sichuan, Jean-Didier de Saint-Martin, MEP (1743–1801), added the restriction that Virgins had to be forty years old to instruct catechumens and they could instruct men only in life-threatening circumstances.[88] Membership in the Virgins provided personal development, a relatively independent lifestyle, and status. Those who taught girls could only teach in their family home or in a home approved by a priest. The Virgins were prohibited from preaching or reading publicly to the congregations. The Virgins played an important role in the development of Christianity in Sichuan for 150 years. They were able to develop in a distinctly Chinese manner because of their isolation from European ecclesiastical control. However, by the mid-nineteenth century, some vicars apostolic began to import European women religious to guide and control the Virgins and this diminished their distinctively Chinese character.[89]

CHINESE PRIESTS IN JIANGNAN

The Chinese College of Naples sent most of their missionaries to northwestern China (mainly Shanxi and Shaanxi provinces) and, to a lesser extent, to Beijing, Huguang, and Guangdong. The Chinese priests of the Missions Étrangères de Paris were active in the western province of Sichuan. These missionary sites were chosen in part because their remote locations helped the priests to avoid detection and arrest. Northwestern China was the historical cradle of Chinese civilization and Xi'an in Shaanxi province had been the Chinese capital for more than a thousand years during the Zhou, Han, Sui, and Tang dynasties. However, the arid loess plains of the northwest were subject to floods and famines, which made agriculture precarious and limited population growth.

Unlike the northwestern region, east central China was a lush region with abundant rainfall, navigable rivers, and coastal seaports. Until around AD

1000, it had been an undeveloped frontier, but by the seventeenth century, it was becoming the cultural and economic center of China. The heart of this region lay in Jiangnan (lower Yangze River region), which was divided after 1667 into the two provinces of Jiangsu and Anhui.[90] The three provinces of Jiangsu, Anhui, and Henan were part of the Nanjing diocese. To their south lay Zhejiang province, which Rome divided into two apostolic vicariates that, after the dissolution of the Jesuits, were assigned to the Lazarists (Vincentians). To the west lay Jiangxi province with three apostolic vicariates assigned to the Lazarists.[91]

Initially, the Jesuits had been active in this east-central region, but their suppression left only a few former Jesuit priests, including most notably Gottfried von Laimbeckhoven, SJ (Nan Huairen 南懷仁) (1707–1787), the Bishop of Nanjing. Mgr. Laimbeckhoven was a remarkable leader who, although privately in disagreement with Rome's ruling against the Chinese rites, nevertheless remained obedient as a bishop of the church.[92] Laimbeckhoven served as Bishop of Nanjing from 1752 to 1787. He endured enormous difficulties, including promulgating to his confreres the papal brief *Dominus ac Redemptor* of 1773, which dissolved his own religious order.[93] Because of delays in the transmitting of the brief to China, Laimbeckhoven did not promulgate the brief until 1775.[94]

The Qianlong emperor's anti-Christian policies forced Bishop Laimbeckhoven into an itinerant mode of survival. During the 1770s and 1780s he was forced to take refuge during the day and travel at night to avoid detection.[95] The difficulty of finding accommodations was compounded by magistrates offering cash payments to informers. Persecutions and other difficulties reduced Laimbeckhoven to ministering to thirty thousand Christians with the assistance of only one Chinese priest, the Jesuit John Yao (Yao Ruohan 姚若翰) (1722–1796), who would eventually be the last Jesuit in Jiangnan.[96] In 1783 Laimbeckhoven ordained four young Chinese candidates for the priesthood who had been sent to him from Beijing by the Jesuit Fr. José de Espinha (Gao Shensi 高慎思), with two of these priests designated to assist Laimbeckhoven.[97] As Laimbeckhoven's death approached, Yao arrived just in time to administer the last rites. Laimbeckhoven was buried on May 22, 1787, in the small parish of Tangjiaxiang 湯家巷 near Songjiang, which bordered the Huangpu River.[98] His body was carried by Christians to the Catholic cemetery of Baiheshan 白鶴山 in Suzhou, where in 1877 a modest tombstone was erected and engraved with an epitaph in Latin and Chinese.[99]

The experience of Bishop Laimbeckhoven and his small band of assisting priests in east-central China is often characterized as a heroic attempt to keep the faith alive in the midst of overwhelming obstacles. The Nanjing diocese was a leading area in the instances of heroism by native priests during eighteenth-century persecutions in China.[100] But while Laimbeckhoven has received a considerable amount of attention, historians have uncovered very little information about the Chinese priests who assisted him. Consequently, these priests remain shadowy figures. This is evident in the case of Laimbeckhoven's faithful assistant, Fr. John Yao. In spite of Yao's important services, we know only a few facts about him. The few documents that have been recovered include a three-page biography (*xiaoji* 小記).[101]

Fr. Yao was born to non-Christian parents in Huijun 徽郡 (Hui prefecture) in Shexian 歙縣 (She district) in Anhui province in 1722.[102] He initially worked as a merchant at Raozhou 饒州 in the neighboring province of Jiangxi. In 1761, at the age of thirty-nine, he had a life-changing experience when he met a Catholic priest named Fr. Deng 鄧 and took his first vows. Since he was unmarried, he divided his property between his two sisters. In 1763, at forty-one years of age, Yao went to Beijing. In 1765 he was sent to Henan province, where Mgr. Laimbeckhoven conferred the tonsure and four minor orders on him. After studying moral theology, he became a priest in the following year at the relatively mature age of forty-four.

After spending some time in Beijing, he returned to Jiangsu province and acquired a reputation for pious acts and dedicated service in the face of great obstacles. He demonstrated a particular concern for the poor and during the famine of 1781 he went to Chongming 崇明, on an island at the mouth of the Yangzi River. There he distributed alms and founded four new churches. Then he led a group of Chongming Christians northward to the mainland, where they established the first Christian church at Haimen 海門 in 1790–1792. Exhausted by his efforts and anticipating his death, Fr. Yao returned to Suzhou. He died in 1796 at the age of seventy-four and was buried at the Christian cemetery of Baiheshan 白鶴山, where his stone tomb was inscribed with the simple epitaph "The grave of the honorable Yao Ruohan" (Yao-gong Ruohan zhi mu 姚公若翰之墓).

Among the European religious orders of that time, the Lazarists developed the largest contingent of Chinese priests. In comparison with the Jesuits, the Lazarists were less well funded, less educated, and more dedicated to serving the poor. During the eighty years from 1790 to 1870, eighty-one Chinese priests (an average of one priest per year) were formed by the Lazarists and served mainly in the east-central provinces of Jiangxi, Jiangsu, Anhui, and Zhejiang, as well as the northeastern provinces of Zhili and Mongolia.[103] Initially, they were formed at the Beijing seminary established by the Lazarists Nicolas-Joseph Raux (Luo Guangxiang 羅廣祥) (1754–1801) and Jean-Joseph Guislain (Ji Deming 吉德明) (1751–1812). This seminary produced some outstanding Chinese clergy from 1788 until 1826, when the Chinese authorities forced it to close.[104] Lazarist seminarians were then sent to the Macau seminary from 1827 to 1856, although they were ordained in Manila. Five outstanding seminarians were also sent to France for study in 1828–1831.[105]

In 1827, when imperial authorities closed the Beitang (North Church) in Beijing, the Lazarist Fr. Mattaeus Xue (Xue Maduo 薛瑪竇) sought refuge first in the Nantang (South Church).[106] However, by 1829 danger caused him to flee to the north to Xuanhua 宣化. Fr. Xue moved the Lazarist base to the old Christian community at Xiwanzi 西灣子 in northern Zhili province, beyond the Great Wall. From 1846 to 1870, most Lazarists went through their formation at the Xiwanzi and Anjiazhuang 安家莊 seminaries. These seminaries were located northwest of Beijing in Zhili (today Hebei) province.[107]

Fr. Xue's remarkable leadership was disregarded by Rome in 1835, with the arrival of a much younger French replacement named Joseph-Martial Mouly (Meng Zhensheng 孟振生), CM (1807–1868). Although it is impossible to pinpoint the shift from Chinese leadership of an underground church to a treaty church, certain events stand out as pivotal in terms of having symbolic significance. One of these events was the arrival of Mouly. The replacement of the fifty-four-year-old Xue, who had clearly proven his leadership abilities, by a twenty-eight-year-old European priest who had less than one year of experience in the China mission was striking and justifiable only by a Vatican perspective that had a low opinion of Chinese priests. Mouly's appointment reflected Rome's bias against the Chinese and represents an appalling demonstration of Eurocentrism that began to undermine the sacrifices of the underground Chinese priests. When in 1846 Mouly was also appointed administrator of the diocese of Beijing, the Beijing Christians objected and refused to recognize his appointment.[108] Mouly then excommunicated the dissident Christians along with several priests, causing a split to develop in the diocese.[109] During his thirty-three years in China (1835–1868), Mgr. Mouly was a leader in transforming the Catholic Church from an underground church led largely by Chinese priests into a treaty-church led by Europeans.

NOTES

1. Christal Whelan, "Religion Concealed: The Kakure Kirishitan on Narushima," *Monumenta Nipponica* 47, no. 3 (1992): 371–73.

2. Whelan, "Religion Concealed," 376–78.

3. Whelan, "Religion Concealed," 379–80.

4. Nicolas Standaert, *Handbook of Christianity in China*, vol. 1, *635–1800* (Leiden: Brill, 2001), 463.

5. Francis A. Rouleau, SJ, "The First Chinese Priest of the Society of Jesus: Emmanuel de Siqueira, 1633–1673," *Archivum Historicum Societatis Iesu* 28 (1959): 30–32.

6. Rouleau, "First Chinese Priest," 41.
7. Benno M. Biermann, OP, *Die Anfänge der neueren Dominikanermission in China* (Münster: Aschendorffschen Verlagsbuchhandlung, 1927), 131–33.
8. Joseph Dehergne, *Répertoire des Jésuites de Chine de 1552 à 1800* (Rome: Institutum Historicum Societatis Iesu, 1973), 406.
9. Rouleau, "First Chinese Priest," 4.
10. Louis Pfister, SJ, *Notices biographiques et bibliographiques sur les Jésuites de l'ancienne mission de Chine, 1552 à 1773*. Variétés sinologiques 59 (Shanghai: Imprimerie de la Mission Catholique, 1932–1934), 402–3.
11. Pfister, *Notices biographiques*, 410.
12. Dehergne, *Répertoire*, 192; Pfister, *Notices biographiques*, 457.
13. Dehergne, *Répertoire*, 68; Pfister, *Notices biographiques*, 411–12.
14. Rouleau, "First Chinese Priest," 6–8, corrects the claim in Pfister, *Notices biographiques*, 381, that Siqueira accompanied the Jesuit Martini to Europe in 1651, clarifying that Martini's companion was another Chinese boy.
15. Rouleau, "First Chinese Priest," 13–14.
16. Rouleau, "First Chinese Priest," 14–15.
17. Rouleau, "First Chinese Priest," 17–20.
18. Rouleau, "First Chinese Priest," 15.
19. Rouleau, "First Chinese Priest," 36–41.
20. Rouleau, "First Chinese Priest," 40.
21. Rouleau, "First Chinese Priest," 43–45.
22. Rouleau, "First Chinese Priest," 47–50.
23. Edward J. Malatesta and Gao Zhiyu, eds., *Departed, Yet Present, the Oldest Christian Cemetery in Beijing* (Macau: Instituto Cultural de Macau & Ricci Institute, University of San Francisco, 1995), 270–71.
24. Pfister, *Notices biographiques*, 920–25; Fang Hao, 方豪, *Zhongguo Tianzhujiao shiren wu chuan* 中國天主教世人物傳 (Biographies of historical personages in the Chinese Catholic Church), 3 vols. (Hong Kong: Xianggong Gongjiao Zhenli Xuehui, 1973), III:160–62.
25. Joseph Dehergne, SJ, "Voyageurs chinois venus à Paris au temps de la marine à voiles et l'infuence de la Chine sur la littérature française du XVIIIe siècle," *Monumenta Serica* 23 (1964): 379–86.
26. Dehergne, *Répertoire*, 133.
27. Dehergne, *Répertoire*, 301.
28. D. E. Mungello, *The Catholic Invasion of China: Remaking Chinese Christianity* (Lanham, MD: Rowman & Littlefield, 2015), 18; 43–44.
29. Robert Entenmann, "Chinese Clergy and Their European Colleagues in Sichuan, 1702–1800," in *Silent Force: Native Converts in the Catholic China Mission*, ed. Rachel Lu Yan and Philip Vanhaelemeersch (Leuven, Belgium: Ferdinand Verbiest Institute, 2009), 75.
30. Robert Entenmann, "Chinese Catholic Clergy and Catechists in Eighteenth-Century Szechwan," in *Actes du Vie Colloque International de Sinologie. Chantilly 1989*, ed. Edward J. Malatesta, SJ, and Yves Raguin, SJ (Taipei: Ricci Institute, 1995), 393; Jean Charbonnier, "Chinese Catholics," in *Handbook of Christianity in China*, vol. 2, *1800 to Present*, ed. R. G. Tiedemann (Leiden: Brill, 2010), 215.

31. Robert Entenmann, "A Mission without Missionaries: Chinese Catholic Clergy in Sichuan, 1746–1756," in *Sinicizing Christianity*, ed. Zheng Yangwen (Leiden: Brill, 2017), 33.

32. Entenmann, "Chinese Catholic Clergy," 390–91.

33. Robert Entenmann, "Linus Zhang Feng (1669?–1743): A Catholic Lay Evangelist in Early Qing Sichuan," in *China, New Faces of Ethnography*, ed. Bettina Gransow, Pal Nyiri, and Shiaw-Chian Fong (Münster: Lit. Verlag; Piscataway, NJ: Transaction Publishers, 2005), 138.

34. Joseph Ruellen, "Introduction," in *Sichuan: Chronique d'une mission au XVIIIe siècle. Journal d'André Ly 1746–1764* (Paris: Éditions You Feng, 2015).

35. Joseph de Moidrey, SJ, *La Hiérarchie catholique en Chine, en Corée et au Japon (1307–1914)* (Shanghai: T'ou-sè-wè Orphanage, 1914), 124.

36. Fang Hao, III:129–30. See also Joseph van den Brandt, *Les Lazaristes en Chine 1697–1935. Notes biographiques* (Beiping: Imprimerie des Lazaristes, 1936), 3.

37. Entenmann, "Chinese Clergy," 78.

38. R. G. Tiedemann, "The Controversy over the Formation of an Indigenous Clergy and the Establishment of a Catholic Hierarchy in China, 1846–1926," in *Light a Candle: Encounters and Friendship with China*, ed. Roman Malek, SVD, and Gianni Criveller, PIME (Nettetal: Steyler, 2010), 341.

39. Henri Crapez, CM, "Notes d'histoire sur le clergé chinois et les Lazaristes de 1697 a 1900," *Collectanea Commissionis Synodalis* 10 (1937): 671–72.

40. Philippe Pons, *Macao*, trans. Sarah Adams (London: Reaktion Books Ltd., 2002), 46.

41. Crapez, "Notes d'histoire," 678–79.

42. Jean-Pierre Charbonnier, *Christians in China: A.D. 600 to 2000*, trans. M. N. L. Couve de Murville (San Francisco: Ignatius Press, 2007), 278; Robert Entenmann, "Andreas Ly on the First Jinchuan War in Western Sichuan (1747–1749)," *Sino-Western Cultural Relations Journal* 19 (1997): 6.

43. Entenmann, "Chinese Catholic Clergy," 396.

44. Henry Serruys, "Andrew Li, Chinese Priest, 1692 (1693?)–1774," *Neue Zeitschrift für Missionswissenschaft* 32, no. 2 (1976): 39–41.

45. Andreas Li, *Journal d'André Ly, prêtre chinois, missionnaire, et notaire apostolique 1746–1763* (Paris: Alphonse Picard et Fils, éditeurs, 1906), 452; 457; 458.

46. Anton Borer, SMB, "Das Tagebuch André Ly's als Quelle der Missionspastoral," *Neue Zeitschrift für Missionswissenschaft* 1 (1945): 194.

47. Li, *Journal d'André Ly*, 458.

48. Serruys, "Andrew Li," 138.

49. Entenmann, "Mission without Missionaries," 38.

50. Crapez, "Notes d'histoire," 670.

51. Entenmann, "Chinese Clergy," 79–80.

52. Brandt, *Lazaristes en Chine*, 3.

53. Entenmann, "Mission without Missionaries," 37.

54. Entenmann, "Mission without Missionaries," 39.

55. Andreas Li, *Sichuan. Chronique d'une mission au XVIIIe siècle. Journal d'André Ly 1746–1764*, trans. Colette Douet (Paris: Éditions You Feng, 2015). The original Latin manuscript is held in the archives of the Missions Étrangères de Paris.
56. Entenmann, "Chinese Catholic Clergy," 403.
57. Entenmann, "Chinese Catholic Clergy," 400–1.
58. Entenmann, "Mission without Missionaries," 46–47.
59. Serruys, "Andrew Li," 54; 136.
60. Li, *Journal d'André Ly*, 452.
61. Serruys, "Andrew Li," 130.
62. Serruys, "Andrew Li," 143.
63. Serruys, "Andrew Li," 130–31.
64. Tiedemann, "Controversy," 342–43.
65. Entenmann, "Chinese Catholic Clergy," 397–98.
66. Serruys, "Andrew Li," 136.
67. Armand Olichon, *Journal d'André Ly, prêtre chinois, missionnaire, et notaire apostolique 1746–1763*, ed. Adrieu Launay, MEP (Paris: Alphonse Picard, 1906), 143.
68. Johannes Jennes, CICM, *Four Centuries of Catechetics in China.* 中國教理講授史, English trans. Albert Van Lierde; Chinese trans. T'ien Yung-cheng 田永正, CICM (Taipei: Tianzhujiao Huaming Shuju, 1976), 95.
69. Fang Hao, III:129–30. See also Brandt, *Lazaristes en Chine*, 3.
70. Entenmann, "Chinese Catholic Clergy," 402–3.
71. Olichon, *Journal d'André Ly*, 135; 137; 143; 147.
72. Entenmann, "Linus Zhang Feng," 140–41.
73. Entenmann, "Mission without Missionaries," 39.
74. Fr. Li Shiyin's diary has been translated from Latin into French by Joseph Ruellen, MEP, annotated by Robert Entenmann, and published in four parts in the *Sino-Western Cultural Relations Journal* 33 (2011): 62–77 (October 1749–September 1750); 34 (2012): 45–58 (September 1750–October 1751); 35 (2013): 57–77 (November 1751–November 1752); and 36 (2014): 59–70 (January–August 1753).
75. R. G. Tiedemann, "Catholic Communities of Women (Foreign)," in *Handbook of Christianity in China*, vol. 2, *1800 to Present* (Leiden: Brill, 2010), 526.
76. Xiaojuan Huang 黃曉鵑, "Christian Communities and Alternative Devotions in China, 1780–1860" (PhD diss., Princeton University, 2006), 237.
77. Eugenio Menegon, "Ancestors, Virgins, and Friars: The Localization of Christianity in Late Imperial Mindong (Fujian, China), 1632–1863" (PhD diss., University of California–Berkeley, 2002), 320–27.
78. Jo Ann Kay McNamara, *Sisters in Arms: Catholic Nuns through Two Millennia* (Cambridge, MA: Harvard University Press, 1996), 609–10.
79. Ji Li 紀李, "Chinese Christian Virgins and Catholic Communities of Women in Northeast China," *Chinese Historical Review* 20, no. 1 (May 2013): 21.
80. Robert Entenmann, "Christian Virgins in Eighteenth-Century Sichuan," in *Christianity in China from the Eighteenth Century to the Present*, ed. Daniel H. Bays (Stanford, CA: Stanford University Press, 1996), 184–89; Charbonnier, *Christians in China*, 309–12.

81. Li, "Chinese Christian Virgins," 22.

82. Gabriel Palatre, SJ, *L'infanticide et l'œuvre de la Sainte-Enfance en Chine* (Shanghai: Mission catholique à l'orphelinat de Tou-sè-wè, 1878), 138–40.

83. Georges Goyau, *Jean-Martin Moye, missionaire en Chine 1772–1783* (Paris: Alsatia, 1937), 97.

84. Palatre, *L'infanticide*, 138–40. Palatre was drawing this material from a biography titled "Vie de M. l'abbé Moÿe, de la Société de Missions Étrangères," 354–68.

85. Palatre, *L'infanticide*, 138–39.

86. Palatre, *L'infanticide*, 139.

87. Palatre, *L'infanticide*, 139–40.

88. Charbonnier, "Chinese Catholics," 230–32.

89. Tiedemann, *Handbook*, II:526–27.

90. Huang, "Christian Communities," 112.

91. To the west of Jiangxi lay Huguang province (divided into Hubei and Hunan). Hubei province was divided into three apostolic vicariates assigned to the Franciscans while Hunan province contained three apostolic vicariates assigned to the foreign missions of Parma and Milano. Finally, to the north lay Shandong province with three apostolic vicariates—two assigned to the Franciscans and south Shandong assigned to the German missionaries of Steyl (Gesellschaft des Göttlichen Wortes or SVD). Joseph de la Servière, SJ, *Histoire de la mission du Kiang-nan*. 2 vols. (Shanghai: Tóu-sè-wè Orphanage, 1914), I:5.

92. Stephan Puhl and Sigismund Freiherr von Elverfeldt-Ulm, *Gottfried von Laimbeckhoven SJ (1707–1787), Der Bischof von Nanjing mit Faksimile seiner Reisebeschreibung*, ed. Roman Malek, SVD (Nettetal: Steyler Verlag, 2000), 44–45.

93. Servière, *Histoire*, I:5.

94. Nicolas Standaert, "The Chinese Mission without Jesuits: The Suppression and Restoration of the Society of Jesus in China," *Ching Feng* 16, no. 1–2 (2017): 82–83.

95. Lars Peter Laamann, *Christian Heretics in Late Imperial China: Christian Inculturation and State Control, 1720–1850* (London: Routledge, 2006), 66–67.

96. Pfister, *Notices biographiques*, 910–11.

97. Servière, *Histoire*, I:11; Puhl and Elverfeldt-Ulm, *Laimbeckhoven*, 54.

98. Pfister, *Notices biographiques*, 769.

99. Servière, *Histoire*, I:11, writing in 1914, said Laimbeckhoven's grave in Suzhou had a modest gravestone inscribed in both Latin and Chinese. However, Puhl and Elverfeldt-Ulm, *Laimbeckhoven*, 62–64, reproduces several photographs of the gravesite dating from 1938 to 1997 that indicate that the cemetery was damaged during the Cultural Revolution and has since been restored.

100. Johannes Beckmann, SMB, "Die Lage der katholischen Missionen in China um 1815," *Neue Zeitschrift für Missionswissenschaft* 2 (1946): 222.

101. Xiaoji 小記 (short biography) of Fr. John Yao (Yao Ruohan), *Feng Tianxue Xu Qiyuan xingshi xiaoji* 奉天學徐啟元行實, Zikawei Library 540.3, cited in Adrian Dudink, "The Zikawei (徐家匯) Collection in the Jesuit Theologate Library at Furen 輔仁 University (Taiwan): Background and Draft Catalogue," *Sino-Western Cultural Relations Journal* 18 (1996): 26.

102. Xiaoji 小記 (short biography) of Yao, 1–3. See also Pfister, *Notices biographiques*, 910–11, 18 and Dehergne, *Répertoire*, 302.

103. Compiled from Brandt, *Lazaristes en Chine*, 8–79.

104. Charbonnier, "Chinese Catholics," 226–27.

105. Joseph Li 李 (aka Chen 陳) went to France in 1828–1831; Matthieu Zhao 趙, Matthieu Lü 呂, François Qiu 邱 (aka Fang 方), and Antoine Tan 譚 went to France in 1830–1831.

106. Tiedemann, *Handbook*, II:226–27.

107. Jean Charbonnier, MEP, *Guide to the Catholic Church in China 1989* (Singapore: China Catholic Communication, 1989), 43; 52–53.

108. Tiedemann, *Handbook*, II:128–29.

109. Louis Wei Tsing-sing, *La politique missionnaire de la France en Chine 1842–1856* (Paris: Nouvelles Éditions Latines, 1960), 467.

Chapter Six

European and Chinese Forms of Martyrdom

SACRIFICE AND MARTYRDOM AMONG CHINESE PRIESTS AND CATECHISTS

The expulsion of most European missionaries from China after 1724 had created an opportunity for leadership by Chinese priests and catechists. This period lasted until approximately 1870, when European missionaries again began to outnumber the Chinese priests. As the Chinese assumed a leading role in the Church, they became the prime targets of anti-Christian persecution. As native Chinese, they had a better understanding than Europeans of Chinese culture and Chinese ways of thinking, as well as the language. This allowed them to temper the application of the rigid Rites Controversy rulings from Rome and to mitigate their negative consequences.

Because of China's great size, Catholic missions were organized on a regional basis that largely followed China's provincial divisions. The first three dioceses created in China were subject to the Portuguese *Padroado* and established in 1690 under the patronage of the king of Portugal as dependencies of the archbishop of Goa (Hindustan).[1] These were (1) the diocese of Macau, which covered the provinces of Guangdong and Guangxi as well as Hainan Island; (2) the diocese of Nanjing, which covered the double province of Jiangnan (Jiangsu and Anhui) and Henan; and (3) the diocese of Beijing, which covered Zhili and Shandong. However, Portugal lacked the resources to sponsor enough missionaries. Consequently, beginning in 1659, Propaganda Fide began to appoint apostolic vicars to circumvent Portuguese influence and concentrate control of the China mission in the hands of the Vatican. This was done by creating titular bishops of extinct sees in the Middle East and North Africa who were appointed solely by the pope and were technically not residential bishops of sees within Portuguese territory.[2] The apostolic vicar of Sichuan also administered Guizhou and Yunnan.[3] The apostolic vicar of Fujian also administered Zhejiang and Jiangxi and the apostolic vicar of Shanxi administered Shaanxi, Gansu, and the double province of Huguang (Hubei and Hunan).

Following the 1724 proscription of Christianity, there was a divergence in the Chinese throne's treatment of Christian priests. This was the result of the Yongzheng emperor's decision to allow Christians to be active in Beijing and to grudgingly tolerate their presence in the Guangzhou-Macau region while banning Christian proselytizing in the provinces.[4] The presence of missionaries in the capital was allowed for the sake of diplomacy and commerce. Nevertheless, small numbers of European missionaries and a growing number of Chinese priests continued to thwart the imperial will in the provinces.

Because of the 1724 proscription, the physical edifices of the churches in the provinces became less important in the lives of Christians. The Yongzheng emperor had proposed that Christian churches (*Tianzhu tang* 天主堂) be converted to places of public use (*gongsuo* 公所).[5] These conversions were done gradually; in the case of the two churches in Licheng 厯城 county in Jinan 濟南 prefecture in Shandong province, they involved converting churches to a foundling hospital and a charitable school.[6] In some cases Christians were employed to care for other church properties, including houses and land. The famous Baroque-style church in Hangzhou, built in 1663, was converted to a *Tianhou* temple 天后宫 in 1730.

Only in Beijing were impressive structures allowed to continue to function as churches. In 1605 the early Jesuit missionary Matteo Ricci, with the help of Fr. Sabatino de Ursis, had bought a plot of land at the Xuanwumen 宣武門 (Gate of Proclaimed Military Strength) along the southern wall surrounding the Tartar Imperial City, only three miles from Tiananmen.[7] He built a small chapel there in 1610. In 1650 Fr. Adam Schall built an impressive church on this site with the financial assistance of the Shunzhi emperor.[8] The church was 25.5 meters long and 14.5 meters wide and was named the Church of the Immaculate Conception (Wuchan shitai shengmu wei zhubao 無玷始胎聖母為主保). It was later renamed the Nantang (South Church) when other churches were built in Beijing.[9] When the Nantang was destroyed by two earthquakes and a fire in 1775, the Qianlong emperor is said to have contributed 20,000 taels to its rebuilding, although Filippo Huang mentioned the Qianlong emperor giving only 10,000 taels for the rebuilding of the Nantang.[10]

When Bishop Gaetan Pires-Pireira, the last foreign resident remaining in Beijing, died in 1838, the Nantang was closed. To save it from confiscation, the Catholics signed over the property deed to the Russian Ecclesiastical Mission, who preserved it until 1860, when it was confiscated by the Anglo-French forces and restored to Catholic ownership.[11] It was reopened and renovated in 1860. During the Boxer Rebellion (1900), it was stormed by a mob and burned to the ground. Hundreds of Chinese Christians who had taken refuge in the church were massacred or burned alive. The church was rebuilt in 1904. During the Cultural Revolution (1966–1976), the church was closed and used as a toy factory. In 1971 it was reopened for services, but attendance was limited to diplomats, foreign tourists, and overseas Chinese. Finally, in 1979, it was formally reopened to the Chinese people.

INDIGENOUS CHINESE CATHOLIC LEADERSHIP

Ultimately neither impressive physical structures like the Nantang nor scholarly and well-funded European missionaries were the most essential elements needed for the survival of Christianity in China. Far more essential were the Chinese Catholics themselves and their indigenous leadership. Denied appointment to formal leadership roles as Chinese bishops by European clerics, Chinese priests and catechists assumed the informal leadership roles that rested on their willingness to suffer and die for their beliefs. Martyrdom has been a core element of Christianity from its very beginning. The often-cited quotation of the early Christian writer Tertullian (ca. 155–ca. 240) is relevant here—"The blood of the martyrs is the seed of the church."[12] However, one needs to distinguish the more general sense of martyrdom from the formal category of sainthood in which one dies for one's Christian beliefs at the hands of those who hate Christianity.[13] In his book *China's Saints*, Anthony Clark emphasizes the historical similarities between the Christian martyrs of the early church in western Europe and the Chinese Christian martyrs of the seventeenth to twentieth centuries.[14] However, the classic European model is not a perfect fit with the East Asian model and it has impeded our understanding of the spirit of martyrdom that was very much alive in the eighteenth-century Chinese church.

The classic image of martyrdom among Europeans presents apostasy as the polar opposite of martyrdom. Some seventeenth-century Japanese Christians famously duplicated this classic image of European martyrdom, but Japanese culture complicated the response of many Japanese, as has been perceptively treated in Shusaku Endo's novel, *Silence*. Eighteenth-century Chinese Christians also expressed martyrdom in a way that was misread by European priests to indicate a lack of commitment to the faith by Chinese priests and laypersons. While there were indeed instances among Chinese Christians of the heroic martyrdom in the extreme sense that involved suffering and death, the more pervasive model of Chinese martyrdom involved extended suffering that expressed itself in long-term commitment rather than death. Fr. Andreas

Li was deeply influenced by the martyr's death of Bishop Sanz in Fujian in 1747.[15] However, the effect upon Li seems to have involved an intensification of his willingness to suffer in a way that led to death by gradual exhaustion rather than a dramatic culminating act. The historian Lars Laamann captures the Chinese sense of martyrdom by explaining the apostasies of eighteenth-century Chinese Christians as a form of temporary withdrawal and a tactical retreat for the sake of survival rather than a complete rejection of Christianity.[16] To purists who insist on martyrdom culminating in death inflicted by the enemies of Christianity, one can perhaps best respond by pondering the complicated ramifications of the silence of God heard by Endo's apostates.

Because the Jesuits had been highly intellectual by both nature and training, they had built their apostolate on knowledge of the arts and sciences and their technical application, as in calendar making. The Jesuits placed a great priority on learning not only to speak, but also to read Chinese. This enabled them to gain the acceptance of Chinese literati. By contrast, the Lazarist successors of the Jesuits were more inclined toward pastoral work among the poor, most of whom were illiterate. The Chinese who were trained as priests in the eighteenth century came from less elite social backgrounds and were less oriented toward literary culture than the prominent seventeenth-century Chinese converts. The eighteenth-century seminary training of Chinese priests tended to focus on teaching Latin and theology. Unlike European missionaries who had the assistance of Chinese catechist-secretaries to write letters and compile records for them, the Chinese priests and catechists were forced to function with minimal financial support. Practical matters were paramount and they lived in a state of perpetual transience in order to minister to their widely dispersed flocks while evading official interrogations. Such circumstances did not promote scholarship. Consequently, the surviving written accounts of their activity are limited.

These surviving accounts of eighteenth-century Catholic priests—written either as letters in Italian, as journals in Latin, or as brief biographies in Chinese—focus on practical matters and their struggles to survive. They give detailed accounts of the number of baptisms and communicants that they administered; they make pleas for financial support; they voice complaints about the immoral behavior of parishioners; they describe their attempts to evade detection by hostile officials; and they describe the interrogations and torture that they underwent. The subtleties of the Rites Controversy were of no compelling interest to priests who were struggling to serve their flocks and to prevent their members from apostatizing in the face of government persecutions. Consequently, the Rites debate did not play a major role in their discussions, except in defending themselves against the complaints of European missionaries who criticized Chinese priests for applying a lax theological standard in such matters. The Chinese priests and catechists devoted themselves to their ministry, but in such an atmosphere there was, ironically, a feeling that the fate of the Church did not depend on their efforts, regardless of how strenuous they were. Fr. Andreas Li, despite his remarkable years of devoted service, was convinced that the development of the Church in China depended not on human effort but on the will of God.[17]

Historically the pattern of martyrs differs from the acts of great heroes in history, whether of a biblical figure like David, of a European warrior like Charlemagne, or of a Chinese warrior like Guan Yu. The latter were heroic warriors of stature said to have exhibited great strength and courage in defense of noble causes. Christian martyrs, by contrast, tend to lack physical strength, but demonstrate physical endurance. Physically, Christian martyrs are often old and weak. Women and children along with ascetic, fasting men populate their ranks.[18] They undergo a combat that is more spiritual than physical and involves a triumph of the will over the body. And their actions often lack a practical goal. Martyrs often die for their faith without knowing the results of their sacrifices.

In 1754 in Sichuan, a dispute over an unpaid debt between a non-Christian, Li Guishu, and his Catholic cousin, Gabriel Wang, escalated into the accusation that the Christians were plotting a revolt.[19] Because of the possibility of a White Lotus connection, the governor-general of Sichuan Huang Tinggui 黃廷桂 (1691–1759) ordered an investigation.[20] Seventy Christians, including Fr. Andreas Li and his coworker Fr. Stephanus Xu, were arrested together with the French missionary Urbain Lefebvre, MEP, who had illegally arrived in Sichuan with his guide, Jacobus Ouang. When Li was brought for his interrogation with the governor-general, his neck was said to be so tightly chained that his face was turning purple. Lefebvre said that with their rosaries taken from them, the chain links served as the beads of rosaries in their prayers.

Fr. Lefebvre's notes present this account of the governor-general's interrogation: "Asked about the Christians, Andreas Li refused to name them and, when he was asked how long he had practiced Christianity, he said that his ancestors were Christians."

The most striking part of his interrogation was this condemnation by the governor-general: "You are more than sixty years old and educated," the mandarin said to him. "However, you have neither honors nor a distinguished title. We, as you can see, are important in the empire and we have dignities of respect and rank, from which you can conclude that everything in your religion is vain and irrational." Father Andreas replied, "The Christian religion does not promise a transitory and earthly happiness, but rather eternal blessedness for those who worship the true God, follow his commandments, and listen to the voice of their conscience."[21] Li added, "Among human beings, to ignore those who have given us birth is a great crime. Would there be a crime more horrible than denying my God in order to escape punishment? If I would deny the God who I love with all my heart and all my soul, I would suffer torments more atrocious than those you want to inflict on me. I would ask your excellency to do me the honor of condemning me! (*Qing da laoye chang xing* 請大老爺賞刑)."[22] Li added, "I was kneeling before Governor Huang and he looked at me menacingly, and three times he said to me in an ironic tone, angry and full of reproach: 'You old Christian! (*lao Tianzhujiao* 老天主教).'"[23]

The approaching night brought an end to the interrogation. They remained outside with their captive companions in the midst of soldiers and hangers-on, waiting for their judgment. Lefebvre provided this elaboration:

> In their turn, Mr. Andreas and Jacques Ouang were called in order to be interrogated, either together or separately. Sometimes they were dismissed, sometimes they were recalled, according to the caprice of the mandarins. The instrument of torture (*kia-kouen*) [*jiagun* 夾棍, i.e., ankle press] is there all prepared for use.[24] The interrogators of Mr. Andreas and of J. Ouang take almost all of the rest of the day. The judges spend little time interrogating the other companions. They pour out insults against Christianity in the presence of Mr. Andreas, who is charged to respond. For example, one of the judges said to him "Are you not ashamed to practice this perverse religion of Europeans, which destroys the submission of children to their parents?" In replying, Mr. Andreas cited the fourth precept of the Decalogue [which commands that we honor parents]. "I do not believe," said the judge, "that you can delude me by your words. I cite for you, myself, from extracts of horrible books of your religion. I have read that your religion teaches that children should be regarded by their parents as bricks from their mold. But does a brick, once made, depend on its mold? By no means! Where is therefore, according to your religion, the holy and necessary submission of children in regard to their parents?" Mr. Andreas responded by citing a book by Fr. Adam Schall, the famous court mathematician who in treating Christianity geometrically, was trying to explain precisely the thesis attacked by that mandarin. Mr. Andreas said: "The piety and the submission of children in regard to their parents, he said, are natural rights, since God formed parents in order to create children, as the workman uses a mold in order to make a brick."[25]

Ultimately, because the rumor of a revolt was found to be fabricated out of personal animosity, the accuser was punished with a beating of twenty strokes of the bastinado, but the Christians were given even greater punishments, with some sentenced to forty strokes and two months in the cangue and others given twenty-five strokes and one month in the cangue. The governor-general of Sichuan implemented the command from Beijing and expelled Fr. Lefebvre to Macau.[26] Li was sentenced to one hundred strokes, but because of his age and infirmities and the dignity he had displayed in voicing his arguments, he was freed. Li's familial ties played a role in his defense. Withholding the truth that he was supported by other Christians, Li claimed that his adopted son Petrus Pe supported him. Moreover, during the interrogations, Li made an important point that he did not convert to Christianity, but rather received the religion by family tradition from his ancestors, who date to the Ming dynasty, and that his family had been Christian for five or six generations before his birth.[27] This argument commanded respect in Chinese culture and it helps to explain the faithfulness of many Chinese Catholics to their church through the years. It was an act of filial piety and provided him with a filial basis for being a Christian. The sentences of the other prisoners were reduced as well. The punishments issued were fairly lenient and reflected the special circumstances of local authority in Sichuan. Periodic persecutions in Sichuan continued. Andreas Li later wrote to the MEP procurator to relate the persecution of June 1761 and praise the behavior of the deacon, Charles Yen.[28]

MENDICANT MARTYRDOMS

The willingness of the Jesuit missionaries to adapt Christianity to Chinese culture is often portrayed as admirable by historians. Conversely, the Vatican's rejection of Jesuit accommodation in the Chinese Rites Controversy rulings of *Ex illa die* (1715) and *Ex quo singulari* (1742) has been condemned and blamed for its damaging effects on the development of Christianity in China. However, the Jesuit cultivation of the Chinese court and the literati elite, although admirable in many ways, turned out to have built the church in China on an overly narrow base of the population. Consequently, when the Kangxi and Yongzheng emperors turned against Christianity and the eminent converts withdrew under a wave of political suspicion, it faced a crisis of survival. As the eighteenth century progressed, the Society of Jesus became a waning force in China and was finally dissolved by the papal ruling *Dominus ac Redemptor* in 1773. In fact, what survived was an underground church in which literacy, unlike in the Jesuit model, was not a dominating factor. Aside from the Latin language and liturgy taught to Chinese seminarians, other qualities took precedence. Ironically, a more influential model for the underground church came from the mendicant orders, and particularly the Dominicans. Although their hard-line approach, which extols martyrdom, is intellectually less admirable than the Jesuit approach, its less accommodating stance was better suited to the underground Church's survival.[29]

The Dominicans arrived in China in 1587. After almost one hundred years of missionary experience in the Americas, they traveled in a western direction across the Pacific Ocean.³⁰ While the Jesuits were sponsored by the Portuguese crown, the Dominicans were supported by the Spanish monarchs. Since Portugal and Spain were maritime competitors, the Dominicans were forbidden either to use the Portuguese trade routes around the Cape of Good Hope or to reside in the Portuguese enclave of Macau. Of the three mendicant orders, the Dominicans differed from the Franciscans and Augustinians in preparing for entry into China by studying the Chinese language in the Chinatown district of Parian in Manila. They learned Chinese characters and one of the Min dialects in order to catechize the working classes in Parian, who had emigrated from Fujian.³¹ In the process, they learned about Chinese popular culture. For the Dominicans in the Philippines, the island of Formosa (Taiwan) offered easy, albeit dangerous, access via trade routes to the province of Fujian. Fujian was chosen as the Dominican mission field in part because the population of Fujian province spoke the Min dialect that the Dominicans had learned in the Philippines.³²

In 1632 the Dominicans established a mission station in the small town of Fuan, which lay inland from the coast of northern Fujian. The Dominican missionary style was much more confrontational than the Jesuit style. While most Jesuits sought to accommodate Christianity to Chinese culture, the Dominicans preached the Gospel in a more direct manner and with less concern for offending Chinese sensibilities. They were far more open in displaying the crucifix than the Jesuits. The Dominicans complained that the Jesuits hid the crucifix from public view and avoided mentioning the Passion and death of Christ.³³ The Jesuits had de-emphasized displaying the crucifix and the Crucifixion, delaying it to one of the final teachings given to neophytes. This was done out of deference to the literati's sensibility, which disdained the slave-like connotations associated with corporal punishments like crucifixion. This tendency to de-emphasize highly sensitive teachings like the crucifix contributed to the creation of an accommodating theological form of Christianity, which has been characterized as "Confucian monotheism."³⁴

Some Franciscan missionaries followed their fellow mendicant Dominicans in their approach. The Franciscan Father Michael Fernández-Oliver (Nan Huaide 南懷德) was a leader in organizing lay societies of Chinese Christians during his thirty-year apostolate (1695–1725) in Shandong.³⁵ The most fervent of these confraternities (congregations) was the Confraternity of the Passion of Christ (*Ku hui* 苦會), in which meetings of men were held in a darkened and closed church. The members would meditate on the sufferings of Christ at the time of his crucifixion and engage in penitential practices, such as fasting and self-flagellation. During the meeting of the confraternity, each member would come forward and kiss the image of the crucified Lord Jesus (*a besar le s. imagen de N. Señor crucificado*).³⁶ Many Chinese were responsive to these practices. For Fernández-Oliver, it was no coincidence that this highly emotional ceremony of kissing the crucifix was instituted in Jinan on the same day that the latest anti-Christian persecution began in March 1700 in Cochin. He believed that this tender act of spiritual intimacy was a fitting reaction to the threat of physical violence from hostile outsiders.

Dominican practices came into conflict with Jesuit practices that accommodated local customs.[37] This led to clashes of the Dominican followers with the local gentry and officials, which led to a transformation of Christianity into a new local religion. This conflict between the Jesuit and Dominican forms of Christianity continued. As the eighteenth century unfolded and the Jesuit approach of accommodation was destroyed by papal rulings, it lost relevance to persecuted Christians while the Dominican approach became more influential within the underground church.

The Dominican Father Francisco Fernandez de Capillas, OP (Liu Fangji 劉方濟), who was decapitated at Fuan in 1648, is recognized by the Catholic church to be the "*Protomartyr Sinensis.*"[38] However, Fr. Capillas became the subject of great controversy when he was included in the list of martyrs elevated to sainthood by Pope John Paul II in 2000. The official Chinese press accused Capillas of causing the people to revolt.[39] Specifically, he was accused of sexually abusing women by encouraging them to delay or avoid marriage in emulation of the virginity of Mary. It was implied that he had also seduced them.

The Jesuits also claim to have had a protomartyr in Francisco Martins (Martines), SJ (Huang Mingsha 黃明沙). Martins was born in Macau in 1569 and underwent his novitiate and training in Jiangxi. He was denounced by a fellow Christian as a spy for the Jesuit Fr. Lazzaro Cattaneo, who was accused of sedition.[40] He was interrogated and subjected to torture by the *jiagun* 夾棍 (ankle press) and later sent to the *haidao* 海道 (admiral of the sea), who subjected him to severe flagellation, which led to his death in Guangzhou (Canton) in 1606. However, the Jesuits did not cultivate martyrdom in the way the Dominicans did. The mentality of these old Dominicans is explained by a Dominican scholar who wrote:

> The greatest wish that the old Dominican missionaries sought was what the normal person, who shrinks back from it as from the greatest evil, does not understand—martyrdom. To be sure—this must be emphasized—they did not intentionally prize the rage of the heathen: that would have been wrong. They often would have been able to do that, but then their communities would have been without shepherds, and the mission would have found its end. More often they fled if they could, and sought to avoid the persecution of the enemy. When they, on the other hand, by God's providence fell into the hands of the enemy, they rejoiced in their hearts, and happily bore, whatever happened to them.[41]

The Yongzheng emperor's edict of 1724 proscribing Christianity was made in reaction to several anti-Christian movements, of which the conflict in Fujian between Dominican missionaries and local officials was the latest. Anti-Christian officials were ascendant in the new emperor's court. The senior court official Zhang Pengge 張鵬翮 (1649–1725) submitted three memorials in early 1723 calling for the prohibition of Christianity in China and the expulsion of the missionaries, except in Beijing.[42] In December 1723, when a local official reported that the missionaries were unlawfully constructing a new church, Gioro Manbao (覺囉滿保) (1673–1725), the governor-general of Zhejiang and Fujian, submitted a request to the throne that Christianity be abolished in China.[43] Recent research indicates that the Yongzheng emperor encouraged the submission of these memorials for the prohibition of Christianity.

A climactic event for Christians in Fujian came with the execution of five Dominicans in 1747 and 1748. Their evangelism was a popular movement focused on the visible crucifix and animated preaching rather than on intellectual arguments.[44] Their leader was Pedro Sanz, OP (Bai Duolu 白多祿) (1680–1747), the vicar apostolic of Fujian. Perhaps fate marked him for martyrdom when he survived the death of his mother and twin sister at his birth. He was ordained in 1704 and assigned in 1708 to the Dominican priory of Saragossa, where he was director of the Confraternity of the Holy Rosary. He practiced, as was common among his fellow friars, a rigid spiritual discipline. He was pious and charitable and called an "angel of love and virtue." He departed Spain in the company of forty-two Dominican missionaries and traveled by way of Mexico to the Philippines, where he arrived in 1713, and entered China in 1715. In Fujian he established three lay organizations to foster piety and increase the number of converts. He organized a group of tertiary Dominicans, a Christian group who occupied an intermediate position between the laity and the priesthood. The first of these was the Catholic Literary Association, which included many literati converts and grew to six hundred members.[45] This Third Order of Saint Dominic took vows and followed the same rules as the friars. He also created a subordinate group of women within the Third Order who engaged in study to function as female catechists.[46] They took a vow of chastity but lived with relatives instead of in community. The members of this Third Order were referred to as *xiunü* 修女, anticipating the contemporary term for nuns.

Sanz was named superior of the Dominican mission in 1717, but the anti-Christian atmosphere became so hostile that he was forced to go into hiding in 1723, staying in a convert's home during the daytime and leaving only at night to administer the sacraments. In 1730 he was consecrated bishop at Guangzhou (Canton). Bishop Sanz was a fearless missioner. At his recommendation, the Dominican missions opened the priesthood to native Fujianese and admitted two or three Chinese novices to the Colegio de Santo Tomás in Manila in 1732.[47] They were the first Chinese Dominicans ordained in Manila since the Fuan native Bishop Gregorio Luo Wenzao had been ordained there in 1654. In spite of the growing anti-Christian atmosphere, Sanz is said to have baptized five hundred new Christians by 1738 and confirmed four thousand by 1740. He was protected by native Christians, some of whom were tertiary Dominicans. Weakened by hunger and body ailments, Sanz finally turned himself in to Chinese authorities in 1746 at the age of sixty-six.[48] What was notable during these events was the sacrifices that converts—many of them tertiary Dominicans—made in risking their own lives to hide Sanz. Juan Alcobar was taken prisoner first and soon afterward Franciscano Serrano, Francisco Díaz, and Joachim Royo, along with the Apostolic Vicar Pedro Sanz, were incarcerated.[49] Eventually Sanz, four other Dominican priests, and five Chinese converts were taken to Fuzhou bound with heavy chains. After a great deal of torture, Sanz was beheaded on May 26, 1747. The other four martyred priests were strangled in the dungeon in Fuzhou on October 28, 1748.

The martyrdom of Bishop Sanz had a profound impact on Andreas Li of Sichuan, who had previously worked with Sanz in Fujian.[50] On October 4, 1747, on the Feast of Saint Francis of Assisi, Li wrote this in his journal:

> In celebrating the Holy-Sacrifice [i.e., mass], I have rendered to God my humble acts of thanks, from which, in his mercy, he has designed to make Pierre Sanz, bishop and martyr, as our patron and protector. A relic of his blood was brought to me. I have presented it for the kisses and veneration of Christians present at the mass. If my sins are an obstacle, I hope, by the example of the holy Bishop, who I will be able to follow in my turn to become the testimony of Christ, in offering my life and my blood.[51]

Clearly, the actions of the Dominican Bishop Sanz became an inspiring model for Andreas Li.

Bishop Sanz's martyrdom has remained an object of controversy. His name appeared on the list of 120 Catholic martyrs who were killed in China in the years between 1648 and 1930 and who were canonized by Pope John Paul II in 2000.[52] Official spokesmen for the Chinese Foreign Ministry and the Chinese Catholic Patriotic Association (representing the Chinese state-recognized church as opposed to the underground Catholic Church loyal to Rome) criticized the Vatican on the grounds that these so-called martyrs and saints were, in fact, criminals allied with Western imperialists.[53] The official Chinese position was that they had been justly executed for violating Chinese laws.

CHINESE CHRISTIAN MARTYRDOMS

Chinese accounts of Christian sacrifice and martyrdom were composed for distribution to sustain and inspire Christians. Due to the destruction of Chinese archives and the inaccessibility of old collections, these accounts, such as the previously described account of the life of Fr. John Yao (Yao Ruohan 姚若翰), are only now being discovered. A slightly more detailed account presents a somewhat formulaic, but striking picture of the catechist Laurentius Zhou (Zhou Laolengzuo 周老楞佐). The account is written in a tone that is notably similar in spirit to the Dominican martyrdoms of 1747 and 1748, although it did not end in Laurentius's death.

> Laurentius was a resident of Beijing who wished to throw off the fetters of this world and devote his entire energy to reverently serving the Lord of Heaven. In particular he sought and received from his family permission not to marry, but rather to live as a [celibate] catechist. Their love clearly grasped that this was a matter that lay not with themselves, but rather with their son, and so in even the least particular they would not thwart him, but on the contrary take joy in the purity of his intention.
>
> Consequently, Laurentius quickly sought the great grace of his Spiritual Father, who, having recognized and tested his virtue, willingly granted his request. Laurentius reverently practiced this holy profession until the first year of Qianlong [note: 1736 may be an error and the intended reign year may be the first year of Yongzheng, i.e., 1724], when the command was issued prohibiting the Holy Teaching, i.e., Christianity.[54] Laurentius in his youth at 26 years of age, applied himself with even more diligence to holy works. He prepared for great contention. His numerous gentile friends encouraged him either to cease practicing, or to pretend to apostatize the Holy Religion, and thus to evade the coming calamity. Laurentius replied, saying, "The command prohibiting religion: have you read it or not? Can the Emperor prohibit serving the Lord of Heaven? The Emperor himself serves him! The present incident is merely on a par with the way in which in former times the wealthy Governor-General Gioro Manbao 覺囉滿保 of Fujian promulgated a false memorial to the effect that the Christians were engaged in rebellion.[55] The enemies of our religion obstinately persist in accusing us of engaging in rebellion and continue to memorialize to the same effect. That is why the Emperor only prohibits engaging in rebellion. How can he prohibit the Holy Teaching itself? The Holy Teaching commands that we love the Lord of Heaven, and that we love other people as our neighbors. He commands that we be filial children and remember our deceased parents, and within our Church we teach the same, compared with those outside our Church, and earnestly hold to the Emperor's instructions. Now of these commands of the [Holy] Teaching, is there even one that should be prohibited? What need is there to pretend [that one has turned one's back on Christianity]? We Catholics would be better to suffer innumerable deaths than to turn our backs even for a

moment on the favor of the Lord of Heaven and we would even want to sacrifice our life to making it clear that the Holy Catholic Church is the true teaching."

After a few days, the officials arrested Laurentius, and ordered him to apostatize. Laurentius firmly refused. The officials decided to give him the bastinado. During this torture, he said to one official, "This torture is my joy, so you can understand that my religion is true and incapable of being rejected. I welcome death in order to prove the truth of the Church's teachings." The official replied, "You delight in death, and I delight in following the Imperial decree!" So he commanded an increase in the level of torture, until the soldiers became envious of Laurentius's courage! They left him alone, lying on the floor, and departed. But, afraid, they said, "We still have the larger bastinado-poles to cause him even more pain." Laurentius [upon their return] then mocked them, saying, "Even should you use an iron rod to break my bones, and knives to slice up my body, you would certainly still fail to get me to reject the Holy Teaching. I urgently desire to be the Lord of Heaven's holy believer, even unto death!" The officials heard these words and ordered that he be sent home.

Having heard of her son's glorious struggle, his mother felt great joy, and eagerly awaited his arrival at the gate. [When he arrived,] she eagerly embraced him, showed great affection to him, and wept tears to eulogize the beauty [of his actions]. She exclaimed, "My son! Before entering the house, go to the chapel, and thank the Lord of Heaven for giving you this victory of the great and merciful Truth!"

In Jiangnan, the Changshu 常熟 native Tang Ruose 唐若瑟 and other Christians were put to the torture unto death. Unfortunately, I have not seen detailed records of their cases.[56]

In this unsophisticated account, the defiant resistance of Zhou Laurentius and Tang Ruose is glorified. It is unclear when the author recorded it and it is likely that the account was passed down orally for many years before being committed to writing.

In his journal, Fr. Andreas Li recorded on April 16, 1748, that he admitted to Holy Communion a man whom Fr. Jean-Hyacinthe de Verthamon had absolved from excommunication. This man, Joseph Van, commonly known as "Toothless [*vulgo dentibus carentem nuncupatum*]," had been interrogated as a suspected Christian and out of fear of torture and punishment, had signed a statement of apostasy before the magistrate of Huayang.[57] But he had second thoughts and snatched the statement out of the hands of the official.

There is a pattern duplicated in the lives of the Chinese priests Giovanni Gu, Andreas Li, Filippo Huang, Li Shiyin (Lucas Augustinius Li), and Yao Ruohan. They each lived relatively long lives of sixty-two, eighty-one (or eighty-two), sixty-five, seventy-nine, and seventy-four years, respectively. Each one is said to have worked tirelessly in ministering to Christians, exhausting themselves in service to their flocks. All of them suffered from a lack of funds. Andreas Li suffered from a chronic foot infection and grew deaf at the end of his life. Filippo Huang suffered from an ulcerated leg, swollen extremities, hand tremors, and tuberculosis. Li Shiyin served tirelessly and went blind. Yao Ruohan exhausted himself in service to the poor and starving.

Because of the restrictions on Christian priests in eighteenth-century China, catechists who were religious teachers (*chuandaoyuan* 傳道員) played a very important role. Unlike the secretary-catechists (*xianggong* 相公) Tommaso Wu (Lucio Wu's father) and Gioacchino Wang (Wang Yajing 王雅敬), who married and had children, many of the teacher-catechists aspired to be priests. Catechists like Linus Zhang Feng of Sichuan were celibate and lacked only the knowledge of Latin to become priests. Zhou Laurentius of Beijing appears to have been in a similar situation. Celibacy was practiced by both Chinese priests and many catechists. Celibacy blended with Chinese filiality; Yao Ruohan and Zhou Laurentius both felt an obligation to secure their parents' permission to be celibate.

The asceticism, sacrifices, and martyrdoms of Christian missionaries that was manifested so heroically by the Dominican missionaries found striking echo among Chinese priests. The Naples Holy Congregation missionaries Giovanni Yin and Gennaro Amodei both had frail bodies and devout hearts. In fact, their physical weaknesses seem to have been essential ingredients that sublimated themselves into spiritual strength. Some European priests criticized Chinese priests for their tendency to engage in commercial transactions. However, Europeans contributed to this commercial tendency by making a practice of offering less financial support to Chinese priests than to European missionaries in China. In fact, there were few substantial differences in the willingness of European Dominican missionaries and Chinese priests of the eighteenth-century underground Church in China to suffer for their faith.

NOTES

1. Henri Crapez, CM, "Notes d'histoire sur le clergé chinois et les Lazaristes de 1697 a 1900," *Collectanea Commissionis Synodalis* 10 (1937): 667.

2. Nicolas Standaert, *Handbook of Christianity in China*, vol. 1, *635–1800* (Leiden: Brill, 2001), I:290; 576.

3. Johannes Beckmann, SMB, "Die Lage der katholischen Missionen in China um 1815," *Neue Zeitschrift für Missionswissenschaft* 2 (1946): 218.

4. Eugenio Menegon, "Yongzheng's Conundrum: The Emperor on Christianity, Religions, and Heterodoxy," in *Rooted in Hope: China—Religion—Christianity. Festschrift in Honor of Roman Malek, SVD,* ed. Barbara Hoster, Dirk Kuhjmann, and Zbigniew Wesolowski, SVD (Abingdon, Oxon, UK: Routledge, 2017), 311f.

5. Xiaojuan Huang 黃曉鵑, "Christian Communities and Alternative Devotions in China, 1780–1860" (PhD diss., Princeton University, 2006), 36.

6. Huang, "Christian Communities," 32.

7. Thierry Meynard, SJ, *Following the Footsteps of the Jesuits in Beijing* (Saint Louis: Institute of Jesuit Sources, 2006), 2–6, and *Guide to the Catholic Church in China 1989*/中國天主教指南 1989 (Singapore: China Catholic Communication, 1989), 22–25.

8. The source of this information is a fragment titled "Beijing Tianzhutang" 北京天主堂 (The Beijing Christian Church), in *Xujiahu cang shulou Ming-Qing Tianzhujiao wenxian* 徐家匯藏書僂明清天主教文獻 (Chinese Christian Texts from the Zikawei Library), edited by Nicolas Standaert, Adrian Dudink, Huang Yilong, and Chu Pingyi, 5 vols. (Taipei: Fang chi 方濟 Publishers, 1996), 4:1842–43. This fragment is from a work by the scholar and bibliophile Zhu Yicun 朱彝尊 (1629–1709), who began his well-known history of Beijing and its environs, the *Rixia jiuwen* 日下舊聞, in 1686. The work was completed in 1687, supplemented by his son, Zhu Kuntian 朱昆田 (1652–1699), and printed in 1688 in 42 *juan*. It was revised and supplemented by order of the Qianlong emperor in 1774 and printed in 160 *juan* ca. 1782 as *Qinding Rixia jiuwei kao* 欽定日下舊聞考. Fang Chao-ying, *Eminent Chinese of the Ch'ing Period* (Washington, DC: Government Printing Office, 1943), 183; Adrian Dudink, "The Zikawei (徐家匯) Collection in the Jesuit Theologate Library at Fujen 輔仁 University (Taiwan): Background and Draft Catalogue," *Sino-Western Cultural Relations Journal* 18 (1996): 34.

9. There were four main churches in Beijing. For a description of these churches, see Anthony E. Clark, *China Gothic: The Bishop of Beijing and His Cathedral* (Seattle: University of Washington Press, 2019), 77–81.

10. Huang to Fatigati, October 4, 1775, in Giacomo Di Fiore, *Lettere di Missioneri della Cina (1761–1775)* (Napoli: Istituto Universitario Orientale, 1995), 372.

11. L. C. Arlington and William Lewisohn, *In Search of Old Peking* (Beijing: Henri Vetch, 1935), 163.

12. Tertullian, *The Apology* (Whitefish, MT: Kessinger, repr. 2004), 50.

13. Anthony E. Clark, *China's Saints: Catholic Martyrdom during the Qing (1644–1911)* (Bethlehem, PA: Lehigh University Press, 2011), 18–19.

14. Clark, *China's Saints*, 20.

15. Chinese Regional Bishops' Conference, ed., *Les 120 nouveaux saints martyrs de Chine* (Taipei, 2000), 66.

16. Lars Peter Laamann, "Apostasy and Martyrdom in Eighteenth-Century China," *International Journal for the Study of the Christian Church* 15, no. 4 (2016): 282–84.

17. Anton Borer, SMB, "Das Tagebuch André Ly's als Quelle der Missionspastoral," *Neue Zeitschrift für Missionswissenschaft* 1 (1945): 195.

18. Bruno Chenu, Claude Prud'homme, France Quéré, and Jean-Claude Thomas, *The Book of Christian Martyrs* (New York: Crossroad Publishing, 1990), 4–5.

19. Robert Entenmann, "The Lefebvre Incident of 1754," in *A Voluntary Exile: Chinese Christianity and Cultural Confluence since 1552*, ed. Anthony E. Clark (Bethlehem, PA: Lehigh University Press, 2014), 63–67.

20. Rufus O. Suter, "Huang T'ing-kuei," in *Eminent Chinese of the Ch'ing Period*, ed. Arthur Hummel (Washington, DC: Government Printing Office, 1943), 349–50.

21. Andreas Li, *Journal d'André Ly, prêtre chinois, missionnaire, et notaire apostolique 1746–1763* (Paris: Alphonse Picard et Fils, éditeurs, 1906), 458.

22. Li, *Journal d'André Ly*, 459.

23. Li, *Journal d'André Ly*, 459.

24. For drawings and a description of the *jiagun*, see Philip A. Kuhn, *Soulstealers: The Chinese Sorcery Scare of 1768* (Cambridge, MA: Harvard University Press, 1990), 14–17.

25. Armand Olichon, *Aux Origines du Clergé chinois. Le Prêtre André Ly missionnaire au Se-tchoan (1692–1775)* (Paris: Bloud & Gay, 1933), 342–43.

26. Olichon, *Origines du Clergé*, 343–44; Entenmann, "Lefebvre Incident," 68–71.

27. Li, *Journal d'André Ly*, 452; 457; 458.

28. Charles Ruellen, MEP, "Histoire de séminaristes chinois au XVIIIe siècle," *Missions Étrangères de Paris, Asie et Océan Indien* 529 (2017): 37.

29. In the great debate between Jesuit and mendicant approaches in China, the defenders of Jesuit accommodation have dominated scholarship. However, there are articulate defenders of the mendicant position, e.g., James S. Cummins, "Two Missionary Methods in China: Mendicants and Jesuits," *Archivo Ibero-Americano* 38, no. 149–52 (1978): 33–108. Also see J. S. Cummins, *A Question of Rites: Friar Domingo Navarrete and the Jesuits in China* (Aldershot, UK: Scolar Press, 1993).

30. Fidel Villarroel, OP, "The Chinese Rites Controversy: Dominican Viewpoint," *Philippiniana Sacra* 28, no. 82 (1993): 13.

31. Villarroel, "Chinese Rites Controversy," 14–17; 23.

32. The Fuzhou dialect along with the dialects of Amoy and Swatow are part of the Min-speaking part of China, which is centered in Fujian and northeastern Guangdong provinces. The Taiwanese dialect is very similar to that of Amoy. The mountainous terrain and lack of navigable rivers make it most accessible by sea. See S. Robert Ramsey, *The Languages of China* (Princeton, NJ: Princeton University Press, 1987), figure 6 and pp. 107–8.

33. These complaints constituted the first of twelve points presented by Fr. Juan Bautista Morales, OP, to the Jesuit Visitor Fr. Manoel Dias in 1639. Villarroel, "Chinese Rites Controversy," 28.

34. Erik Zürcher, "Confucian and Christian Religiosity in Late Ming China," *Catholic Historical Review* 83 (1997): 623–25.

35. D. E. Mungello, *The Spirit and the Flesh in Shandong, 1650–1785* (Lanham, MD: Rowman & Littlefield, 2001), 80–81.

36. Michael Fernández-Oliver, "Epistola ad P. Emmanuelem de la Bañeza, Ji'nanfu, September 1, 1703," in *Sinica Franciscana*, vol. VIII, *Relationes et epistolas primorum Fratrum Minorum Italorum in Sinis qui a. 1684–92 missionem ingressi sunt*, ed. Fortunatus Margiotti, OFM. 2 parts (Rome: Segreteria della Missioni, 1975), part 2, 854–55.

37. Eugenio Menegon, *Ancestors, Virgins, & Friars: Christianity as a Local Religion in Late Imperial China* (Cambridge, MA: Harvard University Press, 2009), 61.

38. Benno M. Biermann, OP, *Die Anfänge der neueren Dominikanermission in China* (Münster: Aschendorffschen, 1927), 82. Also see Chinese Regional Bishops' Conference, *120 nouveaux saints*, 65–66.

39. D. E. Mungello, *The Catholic Invasion of China: Remaking Chinese Christianity* (Lanham, MD: Rowman & Littlefield, 2015), 96–97.

40. Joseph Dehergne, *Répertoire des Jésuites de Chine de 1552 à 1800* (Rome: Institutum Historicum Societatis Iesu, 1973), 167; Louis Pfister, SJ, *Notices biographiques et bibliographiques sur les Jésuites de l'ancienne mission de Chine 1552–1773* (Shanghai: Imprimerie de la Mission Catholique, 1932–1934), 49–50.

41. Biermann, *Anfänge der neunen*, 79.

42. Laamann, "Apostasy and Martyrdom," 60.

43. Huang, "Christian Communities," 27.

44. Clark, *China's Saints*, 67–70.

45. Clark, *China's Saints*, 70.

46. Clark, *China's Saints*, 71.

47. Menegon, *Ancestors, Virgins, & Friars*, 127.

48. Clark, *China's Saints*, 73.

49. Biermann, *Anfänge der neunen*, 221.

50. Henry Serruys, "Andrew Li, Chinese Priest, 1692 (1693?)–1774," *Neue Zeitschrift für Missionswissenschaft* 32, no. 2 (1976): 48.

51. Li, *Journal d'André Ly*, 174–75.

52. Chinese Regional Bishops' Conference, *120 nouveaux saints*, 66.

53. Mungello, *Catholic Invasion*, 94–96; 117–20.

54. I am grateful to Dr. Adrian Dudink for suggesting this correction. The possibly mistaken reference to the first year of the Qianlong emperor's reign in 1736 instead of the intended reference to the first year of the Yongzheng emperor's reign—the proscription of Christianity occurred on January 12, 1724, at the beginning of the Yongzheng emperor's reign—might be attributable to the relatively low level of historical knowledge then held by Chinese Christian authors.

55. On Gioro Manbao, see Fang Chao-ying, "Shih Shih-p'iao," in *Eminent Chinese of the Ch'ing Period*, ed. Arthur Hummel (Washington, DC: Government Printing Office, 1943), 655.

56. Translated by the author with assistance from Jonathan Chaves, Ad Dudink, and Robert Gimello. Anonymous manuscript, "*Laolengzuo Zhongguo xiansheng*" 老楞佐中國先生 (The Chinese Catechist Laurentius), in *Xujiahui shulou Ming-Qing Tianzhujiao wenxian* 徐家匯書樓明清天主教文獻 (Chinese Christian texts from the Zikawei Library), ed. Nicolas Standaert (Zhong Mingdan 鍾鳴旦), Adrian Dudink (Du Dingke 杜鼎克), Huang Yilong 黃一農, and Zhu Pingyi 祝平一, 5 vols. (Taipei: Fangqi 方濟 Press, 1996), 3:1372–75.

57. Robert Entenmann, "Andreas Ly on the First Jinchuan War in Western Sichuan (1747–1749)," *Sino-Western Cultural Relations Journal* 19 (1997): 10.

Conclusion

The Chinese Rites Controversy may be over, resolved by a combination of changes in Chinese society and increasing flexibility by the Vatican.[1] However, the issues underlying the Rites Controversy remain. These problems include the resistance of Catholic traditionalists to accepting the unique contextuality of the Chinese church. These issues first clearly emerged in the eighteenth century when most European missionaries were expelled from China, and Chinese priests and catechists effectively took control of the Chinese church in areas outside of Beijing and the Guangzhou-Macau region. These Chinese priests and catechists did not challenge the hierarchical structure of the Catholic Church. Baptisms were performed and the rites of the Eucharist were celebrated. However, ordinations had to be conducted by European bishops located in places peripheral to China because these required the sanction of a bishop and there were no Chinese bishops between the death of Bishop Gregory Luo Wenzao in 1691 and the consecration of six Chinese bishops by Pius XII in 1926.

The aspirations of Catholicism to become a truly universal church have been impeded by the shift in dominant images from the early pacifist Jesus of Nazareth to the Teutonic warrior-king of Christ the King (*Christus Rex*) that developed in the early Middle Ages. Beginning with the fifteenth-century discovery voyages, European missionaries carried this warrior-king image to Asia, Africa, and the Americas.[2] This image of Jesus as a powerful and triumphant king became the basis of a rationalization for European massacres, exploitation, and the destruction of Asian, African, and American native cultures. Europeans had developed their Christology in a way that assumed it was context-free and promoted a false sense of universality, assuming that their Christology was applicable to all times and places.[3] But Asian Christologies have rejected the idea of one standard and instead have emphasized the differing visions of Christ's message. In their attempt to adapt the image of Christ to the Asian world, they have rejected the European universalist-positivist image and instead have embraced a proliferation of contextual Christologies.

Drawing upon the widespread continuing influence of Confucianism in East Asia, numerous Christians have proposed that the image of the sage, *shengren* 聖人, be adopted in presenting Jesus as a crucified and risen sage.[4] Although it is largely unknown to contemporary scholars, three hundred years ago the Jesuit missionary and Figurist Joseph de Prémare (Ma Ruose 馬若瑟) (1666–1736) had anticipated these claims and argued that the original meaning of sage (*shengren*) in the Chinese classics (*jing* 經) had meant saint, holy man (sanctus vir).[5] Although Confucians had applied the term of sage (*shengren*) to Confucius, Prémare believed that the original meaning was closer to Christ. Unfortunately, Prémare's interpretation was rejected as too radical by both the Catholic Church and by early Sinologists, while his major work on this theme lay unread as a manuscript on a shelf of a Paris library for many years.[6]

In summarizing the influence of Christianity on China in his classic study *A History of Christian Missions in China*, Kenneth Scott Latourette (1864–1968) wrote, "the Anti-Christian Movement was unmistakable evidence that the new religion was important enough to evoke widespread and violent opposition."[7] Latourette was referring to the anti-Christian movement of the 1920s in China, but the point could also be applied to anti-Christian movements of the period of the first underground church in China in the eighteenth century. Anti-Christian movements in China have a long history that dates from Shen Que's 沈榷 three memorials, composed at the time of the Nanjing Incident (1616–1617), in which he attacked Christianity as an alien teaching in China.[8] Shen's three essays were included in Xu Changzhi's 徐昌治 anti-Christian classic *Poxieji* 破邪集 (Exposing Heterodoxy Collection) (1640).[9] The *Poxieji* contains almost sixty essays, memorials, and other writings by forty Confucian and Buddhist scholars, most of which were composed in the years 1635–1639.[10] Other notable anti-Christian movements followed, stimulated by Yang Guangxian's attack on the Jesuit court astronomers and their religion in his *Budeyi* 不得已 (1664), the Yongzheng emperor's expulsion order of 1724, the Tianjin Incident of 1870, the Righteous Fists (Boxer) Movement of 1900, the rise of Chinese nationalism in the 1920s, the Cultural Revolution (1966–1976), and most recently Xi Jinping's anti-Christian policies.[11] A thread running through all of these movements was an attack on Christianity as an alien teaching in China. However, Christianity was not the sole object of attack. Demographic changes during the Qing dynasty had fostered the growth of secret brotherhoods of Buddhist, Daoist, Muslim, and

Christian affiliations and they all were attacked by the Qing government as heretical beliefs (*xiejiao* 邪教).[12]

In his well-known treatment of the anti-Christian tradition, Paul Cohen emphasized the crucial role of the Chinese sense of heterodoxy (*yiduan xieshuo* 異端邪說) versus orthodoxy or "the right way" (*zhengdao* 正道), but he rightly notes that this distinction involved a broader concept than its Western counterpart, which was more religious and theological.[13] Cohen claimed that the division between orthodoxy and heterodoxy in China "centered on intercultural lines."[14] At different times in China, the orthodoxy-heterodoxy lines were drawn between Daoists and Confucians opposing Buddhism and later between Confucians and Buddhists against Christians (as is reflected in the contributors to the anti-Christian collection *Poxieji*). But in both cases, the object of the attack was "the heterodoxy of a new foreign invader." Cohen briefly admits that the Chinese notion of heterodoxy involved a "political threat," but he did not develop this political aspect. Cohen's book on Chinese antiforeignism was based upon his doctoral dissertation composed in the early 1960s.[15] In the almost sixty years since his research, the contours of modern Chinese history have filled out considerably.

Viewed from today's vantage point, one could argue that the dominant reason for the existence of the eighteenth-century underground church was an authoritarian element that has been part of China since the famous first emperor Qin Shi Huangdi (221–210 BC). It was embraced by the Manchu rulers in the eighteenth century and now by the Chinese Communist leader Xi Jinping today. In the eighteenth century, the Kangxi emperor refused to accept the claims of authority of the Papal Legate Tournon and insisted that all Christian missionaries in China submit to follow the approach defined by Matteo Ricci. In the twenty-first century, the ongoing negotiations between President Xi's government and the Vatican indicate a Chinese refusal to accept the universal nature of the Catholic Church and an insistence that the Catholic Church in China be subjugated in certain aspects to Chinese authorities.

This program of subjugation of religion is apparent today in Xi Jinping's recent attempt to "Sinicize" religion by removing crosses from 1,700 Christian churches in Zhejiang province and by the mass detentions of Uighur Muslims in Xinjiang province.[16] From the perspective of China's long history and the persistent pattern of Chinese authoritarianism in this regard, Catholics are viewed as a threat to the existence of the state. Consequently, it is unlikely that the Chinese rulers will relinquish this attempt to control Catholics in China. And yet the Christians' resistance today, as in the eighteenth century, is strong. It is more likely that both the anti-Christian tradition in China and the underground church will continue to exist. One wonders if the blood of the martyrs will, once again, become the seed of the church in our own time.

NOTES

1. George Minamiki, SJ, *The Chinese Rites Controversy from Its Beginnings to Modern Times* (Chicago: Loyola University Press, 1985), 183–203.

2. Jonathan Tan Yun-Ka 陳連佳, "Jesus, the Crucified and Risen Sage: Constructing a Contemporary Confucian Christology," in *The Chinese Face of Jesus Christ*, vol. 3b, ed. Roman Malek, SVD (Sankt Augustin & Nettetal, Germany: Institut Monumenta Serica, 2007), 1485.

3. Tan, "Jesus, the Crucified and Risen Sage," 1488–89.

4. Tan, "Jesus, the Crucified and Risen Sage," 1496–99; 1506–7.

5. D. E. Mungello, *The Silencing of Jesuit Figurist Joseph de Prémare in Eighteenth-Century China* (Lanham, MD: Lexington Books, 2019), 54.

6. Prémare's major work was *Selecta quaedam Vestigia praecipuorum Christianae relligionis dogmatum ex antiquis Sinarum libris eruta* (Certain selected vestiges of the principal Christian religious teachings extracted from ancient Chinese books), 1725. See Mungello, *Silencing*, 45–59.

7. Kenneth Scott Latourette, *A History of Christian Missions in China* (London: Society for Promoting Christian Knowledge, 1929), 840.

8. John D. Young, *Confucianism and Christianity: The First Encounter* (Hong Kong: Hong Kong University Press, 1983), 59–65.

9. Lienche Tu Fang, "Chen Ch'üeh," in *Dictionary of Ming Biography 1368–1644*, ed. L. Carrington Goodrich, 2 vols. (New York: Columbia University Press, 1976), II:1177–79.

10. For summaries of the *Poxieji*, see Paul A. Cohen, *China and Christianity: The Missionary Movement and the Growth of Chinese Antiforeignism 1860–1870* (Cambridge, MA: Harvard University Press, 1967), 21–24; Jacques Gernet, *Chine et christianisme. Action et réaction* (Paris: Éditions Gallimard, 1982), 20–22.

11. Yang Guangxian 楊光先, *Budeyi* 不得已 (I cannot do otherwise), in *Tianzhujiao dongchuan wenxian xubian* 天主教東傳文獻續編 (A continuation of a collection of writing from the Eastern mission of the Catholic Church), 3 vols. From the Vatican Library collection. (Taibei: Student Bookstore, 1966), 1069–1332.

12. Lars Peter Laamann, "Apostasy and Martyrdom in Eighteenth-Century China," *International Journal for the Study of the Christian Church* 15, no. 4 (2016): 280.

13. Cohen, *China and Christianity*, 19.

14. Cohen, *China and Christianity*, 20.

15. According to *WorldCat Dissertations and Thesis List of Records* (online), Cohen's book *China and Christianity: The Missionary Movement and the Growth of Chinese Antiforeignism, 1860–1870* was first published by Harvard University Press in 1963 and was based on Cohen's doctoral dissertation at Harvard.

16. Ian Johnson, "China Suppresses Christianity from the Top Down," *New York Times*, May 22, 2016; Austin Ramzy and Chris Buckley, "'Show Absolutely No Mercy': Inside China's Mass Detentions," *New York Times*, November 17, 2019.

Bibliography

Arlington, L. C., and William Lewisohn. *In Search of Old Peking*. Beijing: Henri Vetch, 1935.
Bangert, William V., SJ. *A History of the Society of Jesus*. Rev. ed. St. Louis: Institute of Jesuit Sources, 1986.
Bartlett, Beatrice S. *Monarchs and Ministers: The Grand Council in Mid-Ch'ing China, 1723–1820*. Berkeley: University of California Press, 1991.
Beckmann, Johannes, SMB. "Die Lage der katholischen Missionen in China um 1815." *Neue Zeitschrift für Missionswissenschaft* 2 (1946): 217–23.
Biermann, Benno M., OP. *Die Anfänge der neueren Dominikanermission in China*. Münster: Aschendorffschen Verlagsbuchhandlung, 1927.
Borer, Anton, SMB. "Das Tagebuch André Ly's als Quelle der Missionspastoral." *Neue Zeitschrift für Missionswissenschaft* 1 (1945): 194–203.
Chan, Albert, SJ. *Chinese Books and Documents in the Jesuit Archives in Rome: A Descriptive Catalogue*. Japonica-Sinica I–IV. Armonk, NY: M. E. Sharpe, 2002.
Charbonnier, Jean-Pierre. *Christians in China: A.D. 600 to 2000*. Translated by M. N. L. Couve de Murville. San Francisco: Ignatius Press, 2007.
Chenu, Bruno, Claude Prud'homme, France Quéré, and Jean-Claude Thomas. *The Book of Christian Martyrs*. New York: Crossroad Publishing, 1990.
Chinese Regional Bishops' Conference, ed. *Les 120 nouveaux saints martyrs de Chine*. Taipei, 2000.
Chou Chin-sheng. *An Economic History of China*. Originally published in Chinese as *Zhongguo jingji shi* 中國經濟史 (1959). Translated by Edward H. Kaplan. Bellingham: Western Washington State College, 1974.
Chuanjiao zhinan 傳教指南 (A guide to the missions), Hejian Shengshitang 河間勝世堂. Hejian, 1905.
Clark, Anthony E. *China Gothic: The Bishop of Beijing and His Cathedral*. Seattle: University of Washington Press, 2019.
———. *China's Saints: Catholic Martyrdom during the Qing (1644–1911)*. Bethlehem, PA: Lehigh University Press, 2011.

Cohen, Paul A. *China and Christianity: The Missionary Movement and the Growth of Chinese Antiforeignism, 1860–1870.* Cambridge, MA: Harvard University Press, 1963.
Conner, Patrick. "China and the Landscape Garden: Reports, Engravings and Misconceptions." *Art History* 2, no. 4 (December 1979): 429–39.
Couling, Samuel. *The Encyclopedia Sinica.* Shanghai: Kelly and Walsh, 1917.
Courant, Maurice. *Catalogue des livres chinois . . . de la Bibliothèque Nationale.* Paris: Leroux, 1910.
Crapez, Henri. "Notes d'histoire sur le clergé chinois et les Lazaristes." *Collectanea Commissionis Synodalis* (Peiping) 10 (1937): 666–83; 767–85.
Criveller, Gianni. "The Chinese Priests of the College for the Chinese in Naples and the Promotion of the Indigenous Clergy (XVIII–XIX Centuries)." In *Silent Force: Native Converts in the Catholic China Mission,* ed. Rachel Lu Yan and Philip Vanhaelemeersch, 147–82. Leuven: Ferdinand Verbiest Institute, 2009.
Cummins, J. S. *A Question of Rites: Friar Domingo Navarrete and the Jesuits in China.* Aldershot, UK: Scolar Press, 1993.
———. "Two Missionary Methods in China: Mendicants and Jesuits." *Archivo Ibero-Americano* 38, no. 149–52 (1978).
D'Arelli, Francesco. "The Chinese College in Eighteenth-Century Naples." *East and West* 58, no. 1–4 (December 2008): 283–312.
Dehergne, Joseph, SJ. "Les Chrétientés de Chine de la periode Ming (1581–1650)." *Monumenta Serica* 16 (1957): 1–136 & map.
———. "La Mission de Pékin vers 1700." *Archivum Historicum Societatis Iesu* 22 (1953): 314–38.
———. "Les Missions du nord de la Chine vers 1700." *Archivum Historicum Societatis Iesu* 24 (1955): 251–94.
———. *Répertoire des Jésuites de Chine de 1552 à 1800.* Rome: Institutum Historicum Societatis Iesu, 1973.
———. "Voyageurs chinois venus à Paris au temps de la marine à voiles et l'infuence de la Chine sur la littérature française du XVIIIe siècle." *Monumenta Serica* 23 (1964): 372–97.
Di Fiore, Giacomo. "Carità e reclusione nell'Europa del Settecento. Le disavventure carcerarie di due cinesi al seguito di Jean-François Foucquet e di Matteo Ripa." In *Scritture di Storia (Historical Writings),* edited by Università degli Studi di Napoli "L'orientale," 49–89. Napoli: Edizione Scientifiche Italiane, 2005.
———. "Un cinese a Castel Sant'Angelo." *La conoscenza dell'Asia e dell'Africa in Italia nei secoli XVIII e XIX.* Vol. 2. Napoli: Istituto Universitario Orientale, 1985, 219–86.
———. *Lettere di Missioneri della Cina (1761–1775).* Napoli: Istituto Universitario Orientale, 1995.
Elenchus Alumnorum decreta et documenta quae spectant ad Collegium Sacrae Familiae Neapolis. Shanghai: T'ou-sè-wè Orphanage Printers, 1917.
Entenmann, Robert. "Andreas Ly on the First Jinchuan War in Western Sichuan (1747–1749)." *Sino-Western Cultural Relations Journal* 19 (1997): 6–21.

———. "Chinese Catholic Clergy and Catechists in Eighteenth-Century Szechwan." In *Actes du Vie Colloque International de Sinologie. Chantilly 1989*, edited by Edward J. Malatesta, SJ, and Yves Raguin, SJ, 389–410. Taipei: Ricci Institut, 1995.

———. "Chinese Clergy and Their European Colleagues in Sichuan, 1702–1800." In *Silent Force: Native Converts in the Catholic China Mission*, edited by Rachel Lu Yan and Philip Vanhaelemeersch, 75–94. Leuven: Ferdinand Verbiest Institute, 2009.

———. "Christian Virgins in Eighteenth-Century Sichuan." In *Christianity in China from the Eighteenth Century to the Present*, edited by Daniel H. Bays, 180–94. Stanford, CA: Stanford University Press, 1996.

———. "The Lefebvre Incident of 1754." In *A Voluntary Exile: Chinese Christianity and Cultural Confluence since 1552*, edited by Anthony E. Clark, 59–76. Bethlehem, PA: Lehigh University Press, 2014.

———. "Linus Zhang Feng (1669?–1743): A Catholic Lay Evangelist in Early Qing Sichuan." In *China: New Faces of Ethnography*, edited by Bettina Gransow, Pal Nyiri, and Shiaw-Chian Fong, 138–46. Münster: Lit. Verlag; Piscataway, NJ: Transaction Publishers, 2005.

———. "A Mission without Missionaries: Chinese Catholic Clergy in Sichuan, 1746–1756." In *Sinicizing Christianity*, edited by Zheng Yangwen, 33–54. Leiden: Brill, 2017.

Fang Hao 方豪. *Zhongguo Tianzhujiao shiren wu chuan* 中國天主教世人物傳 (Biographies of historical personages in the Chinese Catholic Church). 3 vols. Hong Kong: Xianggong Gongjiao Zhenli Xuehui, 1973.

Fatica, Michele. "Per una Mostra Bibliografica ed Iconografica su Matteo Ripa, il Collegio dei Cinesi e il Real Collegio Asiatico (1682–1888)." In *Matteo Ripa e il Collegio dei Cinesi. La Missione Cattolica in Cina tra I Secoli XVIII–XIX*, edited by Michele Fatica and Francesco D'Arelli, 1–38. Napoli: Istituto Universitario Orientale, 1999.

———. "Il processo di canonizzazione di Matteo Ripa, fondatore del Collegio dei Cinesi di Napoli. L'iter di un fallimento." In *Scrivere di santi. Atti del II Convegno di studio dell'Associazione italiana per lo studio della santità, dei culti e dell'agiografia, Napoli, 22–25 ottobre 1997*, edited by G. Luongo, 303–23. Roma: Pubblicazioni dell'Università Cattolica del Sacro Cuore, 1998.

Fatica, M., and V. Carpentiero. "Per una storia del processo di canonizzazione di Matteo Ripa: Problema di filologia e di agiografia." In *La conoscenza dell'Asia e dell'Africa*. Vol. III, edited by Aldo Gallota and Ugo Marazzi, 73–110. Napoli: Istituto Universitario Orientale, 1984.

Fatica, Michele, and Francesco D'Arelli, eds. *Matteo Ripa e il Collegio dei Cinesi. La Missione Cattolica in Cina tra I Secoli XVIII–XIX*. Napoli: Istituto Universitario Orientale, 1999.

Fu, Lo-shu. *A Documentary Chronicle of Sino-Western Relations (1644–1820)*. Tucson: University of Arizona Press, 1966.

Gernet, Jacques. *Chine et christianisme. Action et réaction*. Paris: Éditions Gallimard, 1982.

"Gesheng tang zhi" 各省堂誌 (A record of churches in each province). In *Xujiahu cang shulou Ming-Qing Tianzhujiao wenxian* (徐家匯藏書僂明清天主教文獻) (Chinese Christian Texts from the Zikawei Library). 5 vols., edited by Nicolas Standaert, Adrian Dudink, Huang Yilong, and Chu Pingyi. Taipei: Fang chi 方濟 Publishers, 1996.

Goodrich, L. Carrington, ed. *Dictionary of Ming Biography 1368–1644*. 2 vols. New York: Columbia University Press, 1976.

Goyau, Georges. *Jean-Martin Moye, missionaire en Chine 1772–1783*. Paris: Alsatia, 1937.

Gray, Basil. "Lord Burlington and Father Ripa's Chinese Engravings." *British Museum Quarterly* 22, no. 1–2 (1960): 40–43.

Guide to the Catholic Church in China 1989/中國天主教指南 1989 (Singapore: China Catholic Communication, 1989.

Han Qi 韩琦. 从中西文献看马国贤在宫廷的活动 (Matteo Ripa's Activities at Court Drawn from Sino-Western Documents). In *Matteo Ripa e il Collegio dei Cinesi*, edited by Michele Fatica and Francesco D'Arelli, 71–82. Napoli: Istituto Universitario Orientale, 1999.

Heyndricks, Jeroom J., CICM. "Beijing und der Heilige Stuhl—auf der Suche nach einer gemeinsamen Basis: Zwei verwundete Partner im Dialog." *China Heute* 38, no. 3 (2019): 170–83.

Huang, Pei. *Autocracy at Work: A Study of the Yung-cheng Period, 1723–1735*. Bloomington: Indiana University Press, 1974.

Huang, Xiaojuan 黃曉鵑. "Christian Communities and Alternative Devotions in China, 1780–1860." PhD diss., Princeton University, 2006.

Hummel, Arthur, ed. *Eminent Chinese of the Ch'ing Period*. Washington, DC: Government Printing Office, 1943.

Jennes, Johannes, CICM. *Four Centuries of Catechetics in China.* 中國教理講授史. English translation by Albert Van Lierde; Chinese translation by T'ien Yung-cheng 田永正, CICM. Taipei: Tianzhujiao Huaming Shuju, 1976.

Johns, Christopher M. S. *China and the Church: Chinoiserie in Global Context*. Oakland: University of California Press, 2016.

Krahl, Joseph, SJ. *China Mission in Crisis: Bishop Laimbeckhoven and His Times 1738–1787*. Rome: Gregorian University Press, 1964.

Kuhn, Philip A. *Soulstealers: The Chinese Sorcery Scare of 1768*. Cambridge, MA: Harvard University Press, 1990.

Laamann, Lars Peter. "Apostasy and Martyrdom in Eighteenth-Century China." *International Journal for the Study of the Christian Church* 15, no. 4 (2016): 275–88.

———. *Christian Heretics in Late Imperial China: Christian Inculturation and State Control, 1720–1850*. London: Routledge, 2006.

"*Laolengzuo Zhongguo xiansheng*" 老楞佐中國先生 (The Chinese Catechist Laurentius). In *Xujiahui shulou Ming-Qing Tianzhujiao wenxian* 徐家匯書樓明清天主教文獻 (Chinese Christian Texts from the Zikawei Library). 5 vols., edited by Nicolas Standaert (Zhong Mingdan 鍾鳴旦), Adrian Dudink (Du Dingke 杜鼎克), Huang Yilong 黃一農, and Zhu Pingyi 祝平一, Vol. 3, 1372–75. Taipei: Fangqi 方濟 Press, 1996.

Latourette, Kenneth Scott. *A History of Christian Missions in China*. London: Society for Promoting Christian Knowledge, 1929.
Le Comte, Louis, SJ. *Nouveaux mémoires sur l'état présent de la Chine*. 2 vols. Paris: Jean Anisson, 1697.
Leung, Beatrice. *Sino-Vatican Relations: Problems in Conflicting Authority 1976–1986*. Cambridge, UK: Cambridge University Press, 1992.
Li, Andreas. "Andreas Ly on the First Jinchuan War in Western Sichuan (1747–1749)." Translated by Robert Entenmann. *Sino-Western Cultural Relations Journal* 19 (1997): 6–21.
———. *Journal d'André Ly, prêtre chinois, missionnaire, et notaire apostolique 1746–1763*. Latin text. Introduction by Adrien Launay. Paris: Alphonse Picard et Fils, éditeurs, 1906.
———. *Sichuan. Chronique d'une mission au XVIIIe siècle. Journal d'André Ly 1746–1764*. Translated by Colette Douet. Paris: Éditions You Feng, 2015.
Li Ji 紀李. "Chinese Christian Virgins and Catholic Communities of Women in Northeast China." *Chinese Historical Review* 20, no. 1 (May 2013): 16–32.
Li, Shiyin. Diary [segments]. Translated from Latin into French by Joseph Ruellen, MEP. Annotated by Robert Entenmann. *Sino-Western Cultural Relations Journal* 33 (2011): 62–77 (October 1749–September 1750); 34 (2012): 45–58 (September 1750–October 1751); 35 (2013): 57–77 (November 1751–November 1752); & 36 (2014): 59–70 (January–August 1753).
Lin Juyuan 林铁钧. *Qingshi biannian* 清史编年 (Qing history chronicle). 北京：中国人民大学出版社, 1988.
MacInnis, Donald E. *Religious Policy and Practice in Communist China: A Documentary History*. New York: Macmillan, 1972.
Malatesta, Edward J., and Gao Zhiyu, eds. *Zhalan: Departed, Yet Present, the Oldest Christian Cemetery in Beijing*. Macau: Instituto Cultural de Macau & Ricci Institute, University of San Francisco, 1995.
Margiotti, Fortunato. "La Chiesa Cattolica al traguardo della maturità." In *Sacrae Congregationis de Propaganda Fidei Memoria Rerum. 350 anni a servizio delle missioni 1622–1972*. Vol. 3, edited by Josef Metzler, 508–40. Rom-Freiburg-Wien: Heider, 1975.
Margiotti, Fortunatus, OFM, ed. *Sinica Franciscana*, vol. VIII, *Relationes et epistolas primorum Fratrum Minorum Italorum in Sinis qui a. 1684–92 missionem ingressi sunt*. 2 parts. Rome: Segreteria della Missioni, 1975.
Mariani, Paul P. *Church Militant: Bishop Kung and the Chinese Catholic Resistance in Communist Shanghai*. Cambridge, MA: Harvard University Press, 2011.
McNamara, Jo Ann Kay. *Sisters in Arms: Catholic Nuns through Two Millennia*. Cambridge, MA: Harvard University Press, 1998.
Menegon, Eugenio. *Ancestors, Virgins, and Friars: Christianity as a Local Religion in Late Imperial China*. Cambridge, MA: Harvard University Press, 2009.
———. "Ancestors, Virgins, and Friars: The Localization of Christianity in Late Imperial Mindong (Fujian, China), 1632–1863." PhD diss., University of California–Berkeley, 2002.
———. "Bishop Bai's Cave: The Fujian Martyrs and the Politics of Martyrdom between China, the Philippines, and Europe, Eighteenth Century to the Present." In

Life and Death in the Missions of New France and East Asia: Narratives of Faith & Martyrdom. Studies in the History of Christianity in East Asia, edited by Antoni Ucerler et al. Leiden: Brill, forthcoming 2021.

———. "Christian Loyalists, Spanish Friars, and Holy Virgins in Fujian during the Ming-Qing Transition." *Monumenta Serica* 51 (2003): 335–65.

———. "Interlopers at the Fringes of Empire: The Procurators of the Propaganda Fidei Papal Congregation in Canton and Macao, 1700–1823." *Cross-Currents: East Asian History and Culture Review* 25 (December 2017): 26–62.

———. "Wanted: An Eighteenth-Century Chinese Catholic Priest in China, Italy, India and Southeast Asia." *Journal of Modern Italian Studies* 15, no. 4 (2010): 502–18.

———. "Yongzheng's Conundrum: The Emperor on Christianity, Religions, and Heterodoxy." In *Rooted in Hope: China—Religion—Christianity. Festschrift in Honor of Roman Malek, SVD*, edited by Barbara Hoster, Dirk Kuhjmann, and Zbigniew Wesolowski, SVD, 311–35; 430. Abingdon, Oxon, UK: Routledge, 2017.

Meynard, Thierry, SJ. *Following the Footsteps of the Jesuits in Beijing*. Saint Louis: Institute of Jesuit Sources, 2006.

Minimiki, George, SJ. *The Chinese Rites Controversy from Its Beginnings to Modern Times*. Chicago: Loyola University Press, 1985.

Moidrey, Joseph de, SJ. *La Hiérarchie catholique en Chine, en Corée et au Japon (1307–1914)*. Shanghai: Tousèwèi Orphanage, 1914.

Mong, Ambrose. "Catholic Missions in China: Failure to Form a Native Clergy." *International Journal for the Study of the Christian Church* 19, no. 1 (2019): 30–43.

Mungello, D. E. *The Catholic Invasion of China: Remaking Chinese Christianity*. Lanham, MD: Rowman & Littlefield, 2015.

———, ed. *The Chinese Rites Controversy: Its History and Meaning*. Monumenta Serica Monograph Series 33. Nettetal, Germany: Steyler Verlag, 1994.

———. *Leibniz and Confucianism: The Search for Accord*. Honolulu: University of Hawai'i Press, 1977.

———. *The Silencing of the Jesuit Figurist Joseph de Prémare in Eighteenth-Century China*. Lanham, MD: Lexington Books, 2019.

———. *Western Queers in China: Flight to the Land of Oz*. Lanham, MD: Rowman & Littlefield, 2012.

Olichon, Armand. *Le Prêtre André Ly missionnaire au Se-Tchoan (1692–1775)*. Paris: Bloud & Gay, 1933.

Palatre, Gabriel, SJ. *L'infanticide et l'œuvre de la Sainte-Enfance en Chine*. Shanghai: Mission catholique à l'orphelinat de Tou-sè-wè, 1878.

Pelliot, Paul. *Inventaire sommaire des manuscrits et imprimés chinois de la Bibliothèque Vaticane*. Revised and edited by Takata Tokio. Kyoto: Italian School of East Asian Studies, 1995.

Pfister, Louis, SJ. *Notices biographiques et bibliographiques sur les Jésuites de l'ancienne mission de Chine 1552–1773*. Shanghai: Imprimerie de la Mission Catholique, 1932–1934.

Plumb, J. H. *The First Four Georges*. London: B. T. Batsford, Ltd., 1956; reprinted by Fontana, 1966.

Pons, Philippe. *Macao.* Translated by Sarah Adams. London: Reaktion Books Ltd., 2002.
Puhl, Stephan, and Sigismund Freiherr von Elverfeldt-Ulm. *Gottfried von Laimbeckhoven SJ (1707–1787), Der Bischof von Nanjing mit Faksimile seiner Reisebeschreibung.* Edited by Roman Malek, SVD. Nettetal: Steyler Verlag, 2000.
Raini, Emanuele. "Catechisti e capi laici delle comunità nella storia della chiesa in Cina: Prospetto storico e documenti." *Urbana University Journal* 2 (2019): 97–156.
Ramsey, S. Robert. *The Languages of China.* Princeton, NJ: Princeton University Press, 1987.
Reil, Sebald. *Kilian Stumpf 1655–1720: Ein Würzburger Jesuit am Kaiserhof zu Peking.* Münster, Westfalen: Aschendorff, 1978.
Ricci, Matteo. *On Friendship: One Hundred Maxims for a Chinese Prince.* Translated by Timothy Billings. New York: Columbia University Press, 2009.
Ripa, Matteo. *Giornale (1705–1724).* Vol. I (1705–1711); Vol. II (1711–1716). Introduzione, testo critico e note di Michele Fatica. Napoli: Istituto Universitario Orientale, 1991 and 1996.
———. *Memoirs of Father Ripa during Thirteen Years' Residence at the Court of Peking in the Service of the Emperor of China.* Selected and translated by Fortunato Prandi. London: John Murray, 1844.
———. *Storia della Fondazione della Congregazione e del Collegio di'cinesi.* 3 vols. Napoli: Tipografia Manfredi, 1832.
Rivinius, Karl Josef. *Das Collegium Sinicum zu Neapel und seine Umwandlung in ein Orientalisches Institut.* Sankt Augustin: Institut Monumenta Serica, 2004.
Rosso, Antonio Sisto, OFM. *Apostolic Legations to China of the Eighteenth Century.* South Pasadena, CA: Perkins, 1948.
Rouleau, Francis A., SJ. "The First Chinese Priest of the Society of Jesus: Emmanuel de Siqueira, 1633–1673." *Archivum Historicum Societatis Iesu* 28 (1959): 3–49.
———. "Maillard de Tournon, Papal Legate at the Court of Peking: The First Imperial Audience (31 December 1705)." *Archivum Historicum Societatis Iesu* 31 (1962): 264–323.
Ruellen, Charles, MEP. "Histoire de séminaristes chinois au XVIIIe siècle." *Missions Étrangères de Paris, Asie et Océan Indien* 529 (2017): 34–42.
Serruys, Henry. "Andrew Li, Chinese Priest, 1692 (1693?)–1774." *Neue Zeitschrift für Missionswissenschaft* 32, no. 2 (1976): 39–55; 130–44.
Servière, Joseph de la, SJ. *Histoire de la mission du Kiang-nan.* 2 vols. Shanghai: Tóu-sè-wè Orphanage, 1914.
Smith, Seán A. "Surrogate Fathers: The Lazarists as Jesuit Successors in the Eighteenth Century, 1759–1814." *Journal of Ecclesiastical History* 69, no. 1 (2018): 57–85.
Song Liming 宋黎明. 2019. "Luo Wenzhao haishi Luo Wenzao?—wei zhongguo shouwei guoji zhujiao Luo zhujiao zhengming 罗文炤还是罗文藻?—为中国首位国籍主教罗主教正名." *Haijiaoshi yanjiu* 海交史研究 3 (2019): 40–51.
Spence, Jonathan D. *Emperor of China: Self-Portrait of K'ang-hsi.* New York: Vintage, 1975.

Standaert, Nicolas. "The Chinese Mission without Jesuits: The Suppression and Restoration of the Society of Jesus in China." *Ching Feng* 16, no. 1–2 (2017): 79–96.
———, ed. *Handbook of Christianity in China*. Vol. 1: *635–1800*. Leiden: Brill, 2001.
Strassberg, Richard. "An Intercultural Artist: Matteo Ripa: His Engravings and Their Transmission to the West." In *Thirty-Six Views: The Kangxi Emperor's Mountain Estate in Poetry and Prints*, 41–72. Washington, DC: Dumbarton Oaks, 2016.
Stumpf, Kilian, SJ. *The Acta Pekinensia of Historical Records of the Maillard de Tournon Legation*. Vol. 1: December 1705–August 1706, edited by Paul Rule and Claudia von Collani. Rome: Institutum Historicum Societatis Iesu, 2015.
Tan Yun-Ka, Jonathan 陳連佳. "Jesus, the Crucified and Risen Sage: Constructing a Contemporary Confucian Christology." In *The Chinese Face of Jesus Christ*. Vol. 3b, edited by Roman Malek, SVD, 1481–1513. Sankt Augustin & Nettetal, Germany: Institut Monumenta Serica, 2007.
Tertullian, *The Apology*. Whitefish, MT: Kessinger, repr., 2004.
Tiedemann, R. G. "The Controversy over the Formation of an Indigenous Clergy and the Establishment of a Catholic Hierarchy in China, 1846–1926." In *Light a Candle: Encounters and Friendship with China*, edited by Roman Malek, SVD, and Gianni Criveller, PIME, 337–75. Nettetal: Institut Monumenta Serica, 2010.
———, ed. *Handbook of Christianity in China*. Vol. 2: *1800 to Present*. Leiden: Brill, 2010.
van Coillie, Dries. *I Was Brainwashed in Peking*. Brussels: Nederlandse Boekdruk Industrie, 1969.
van den Brandt, Joseph, CM. *Les Lazaristes en Chine 1697–1935. Notes biographiques*. Beiping: Imprimerie des Lazaristes, 1936.
Villarroel, Fidel, OP. "The Chinese Rites Controversy: Dominican Viewpoint." *Philippiniana Sacra* 28, no. 82 (1993): 5–61.
Wakeman, Frederic, Jr. *The Great Enterprise: The Manchu Reconstruction of Imperial Order in Seventeenth-Century China*. 2 vols. Berkeley: University of California Press, 1985.
Waley-Cohen, Joanna. *Exile in Mid-Qing China: Banishment to Xinjiang, 1758–1820*. New Haven, CT: Yale University Press, 1991.
Wei, Louis Tsing-sing. *La politique missionnaire de la France en Chine 1842–1856*. Paris: Nouvelles Éditions Latines, 1960.
Whelan, Christal. "Religion Concealed: The Kakure Kirishitan on Narushima." *Monumenta Nipponica* 47, no. 3 (1992): 369–87.
Willeke, Bernward Henry, OFM. *Imperial Government and Catholic Missions in China during the Years 1784–1785*. Saint Bonaventure, NY: Franciscan Institute, 1948.
Witek, John W., SJ. *Controversial Ideas in China and in Europe: A Biography of Jean-François Foucquet, S.J. (1665–1741)*. Rome: Institutum Historicum S.I., 1982.
———. "Jean-François Foucquet: Un Controversiste Jésuite en Chine et en Europe." Actes de Colloque de Sinologie. *La Mission Française de Pékin aux XVIIe et XVIII Siècles*. Paris: Les Belles Lettres, 1976, 115–35.

Wittkower, Rudolf. "English Neo-Palladianism, the Landscape Garden, China, and the Enlightenment." *L'Arte* (Istituto Editoriale Italiano Milano) 6 (June 1969): 18–35.

Wong, Young-Tsu. *A Paradise Lost: The Imperial Garden Yuanming Yuan*. Honolulu: University of Hawai'i Press, 2001.

Wu Cuncun, *Homoerotic Sensibilities in Late Imperial China*. London: Routledge-Curzon, 2004.

Xiaoji 小記 (short biography) of Fr. John Yao (Yao Ruohan), *Feng Tianxue Xu Qiyuan xingshi xiaoji* 奉天學徐啟元行實. Zikawei Library, Shanghai 540.3.

Young, John D. *Confucianism and Christianity: The First Encounter*. Hong Kong: Hong Kong University Press, 1983.

Yu Dong, *Catalogo delle Opere cinesi Missionarie della Biblioteca Apostolica Vaticana (XVI–XVIII sec)*. Vatican: Biblioteca Apostolica Vaticana, 1996.

Yue Zhuang. "Hatchings in the Void: Ritual and Order in *Bishu Shanzhuang Shi* and Matteo Ripa's *Views of Jehol*." In *Qing Encounters: Artistic Exchanges between China and the West*, edited by Petra Ten-Doesschate Chu and Ning Ding, 142–57. Los Angeles: Getty Research Institute, 2015.

Zelin, Madeleine. "The Yung-cheng Reign." In *The Cambridge History of China*. Vol. 9, *The Ch'ing Dynasty to 1800*, edited by Willard J. Peterson, 183–229. Cambridge, UK: Cambridge University Press, 2002.

Zhu Yicun 朱彝尊. "Beijing Tianzhutang" 北京天主堂 (The Beijing Christian Church), in *Xujiahui cang shulou Ming-Qing Tianzhujiao wenxian* (徐家匯藏書僂明清天主教文獻) (Chinese Christian Texts from the Zikawei Library), edited by Nicolas Standaert, Adrian Dudink, Huang Yilong & Chu Pingyi. 5 vols. Taipei: Fang chi 方濟 Publishers, 1996, 1842–43.

Zürcher, Erik. "Confucian and Christian Religiosity in Late Ming China." *Catholic Historical Review* 83 (1997): 614–53.

Index

actor-escort ephebes (*dan*), 23, 34
Adolfine, Sr. Maria, 3
adopted sons by priests, 119, 139
Alcobar, Juan, OP, 143
Amandine, Sr. Marie, 4
Amodei, Gennaro, CCN, 24–25, 146
Amos, book of, 22
An Anna, born Jiao, 5
An Anna, born Xin, 5
An Linghua, Maria, 5
An Maria, born Guo, 5
ancestor veneration: banned by Rome, 7; Chinese tempering of ban, 133; oath to abjure, 60
ancestors and Christianity, 116, 137, 139
Andlauer, Modeste, SJ, 5
Andrada, Giuseppe, CCN, 75
ankle press (*jiagun*), 98, 141
Anti-Christian movements, 152–153
apostasy, 14, 98, 135, 136, 144–145
Appiani, Luigi Antonio, CM, 60–61, 114
aquafortis (nitric acid), 29, 31
Archimandrite, Moscovite, 93
arrogance of Chinese, 71
asceticism, 24, 31–32, 47, 146
authoritarianism, 7, 153

Bai Xiaoman, Lorenzo, 3
Balat, Teodorico, OFM, 3
Balluère, Jean-François Martin de la, MEP, 114–115, 120
baptismal names, 116
baptisms, 89; by Virgins, 120
Basset, Jean, MEP, 114, 120
bastinado, 118, 138–139, 141, 145
Bauer, Andrea, OFM, 4
Beatas, 16
beheading, 143
Bellisario, Angelo, CCN, 66, 93
Bellisario, Gàbriele, CCN, 62, 65, 66
Bertin, Henri, 113
betrayal, 44
Bi Yuan, 100, 102
bird-brain (*cervellone*), 67, 71, 76
bishops, appointment of, 16
Blasio, Michelangelo, 57
Blessed Virgin, 121. See also Queen of Martyrs
blood of the martyrs, 135, 153
blood, relic of, 143
Borgia, Duke Domenico, 56–57
Borgia, Stefano, 103–104
Boucher, Giovanni Antonio, OFM, 102
Bouvet, Joachim, SJ, 12
Boxers (Righteous Fists), 100, 152

British East India Company, 25, 45, 47
Brollo, Basilio, OFM, 58
Buddha, 12
Buddhism, 40, 70, 152–153
Bürger, Nathanael, OFM, 95, 98

Cai Wenan, Paolo, CCN, 21, 66, 68, 69, 76, 86, 88, 101
Cai, Pietro, CCN, 101, 103
Calmocco, 68
cangue, 118, 138
caning. *See* bastinado
Canton. *See* Guangzhou
Cao Guiying, Agnese, 3
Cape of Good Hope, 46
Capillas, Francisco Fernandez de, OP, 3; accused of sexual abuse, 141
Caracciolo of Santobono, Msgr., 77
Caraffa, Cardinal, 55
Caravario, Callisto, SDB, 3
Cardoso, João, SJ, 28
Carvalho, Sebastião José de, 87–88
Castel Sant'Angelo, 77–78
Castorano, Carlo di Orazio da, OFM, 38–39, 70
catechists: 37; as celibate, 144, 146; as religious teachers 33, 91, 146; as secretaries, 33, 91, 112, 136, 146; illiteracy, 120; women as, 120
Catholic Literary Association, 142
Catholicism as universal religion, 23. *See also* universal church
celebrate mass in Chinese, 104
celibacy, 144, 146. *See also* Christian Virgins
Cercì, Fr. Giuseppe, 67–67
Cerù, Fr. Giuseppe, 24
Chapdelaine, Augustus, MEP, 3
Charlemagne, 137
Charles VI, Emperor, 57
chaste women. *See zhennü*
Chen Aijie, Rosa, 4
Chen Changpin, Paolo, 3
Chen Jinjie, Teresa, 4
Chen Xianheng, Giovanni, 2

Chen Ximan, OFS, 4
Chi Zhuzi, 4
Chiara, Maria, FMM, 4
Chinese Catholic Patriotic Association (CCPA), 9, 143
Chinese College. *See* Collegio dei Cinesi
Chinese criticism of Europeans, 92–97, 115
Chinese filial piety, 94
Chinese language dialects, 55, 58
Chinese Martyrs Sanctuary, 2
Chinese-Latin dictionary, 58
chinoiserie, 13
Chongming, 126
Chongqing-fu, 122
chrétientés, 118
Christian Virgins (chaste women), 16, 120–124
Christologies, 151–152
churches, 10–11, 14, 17n7, 89, 93, 115, 127, 134–135
Cioffo, Msgr., 74
Clark, Anthony, 135
Clet, Francisco Regis, CM, 3
clocks, 44, 88, 93, 96
Coimbra, 111
Collegio dei Cinesi Napoli (CCN), 17, 21, 55–78, 87, 103
Collegio Romano, 111
Collegio de Santo Tomás, 143
Collegio Urbano (Rome), 67
Confraternity of the Passion of Christ (*Ku hui*), 140–141
Confucian disciple Zilu, 12–13
Confucian monotheism, 140
Confucians, 153
Confucius, veneration of, 7, 90, 152
Congregation of the Mission. *See* Lazarists
conjugal visits, 26
contributions from Ripa's brothers, 33
Couplet, Philippe, SJ, 111
Crescitelli, Alberico, PIME, 4
criticism of European bishops, 104

Crucifix, display of, 140, 142
Cui Barbara, born Lian, 5
Cultural Revolution, 10, 115, 152

Dai, Cassio Giuseppe, CCN, 103
Dalai Lama, 8
Damasceno, Giovanni, OESA, 88, 93, 96
Dang, Fr. Antonius, 114, 117, 119
Daoism, 12, 152–153
Datong-fu, 68, 90, 92, 98
David, 137
De la Paix, Marie, FMM, 4
De Saint Just, Marie, FMM, 4
De Sainte Nathalie, Sr. Marie, 4
deceitfulness of Chinese, 76. *See also* dissimulation of Chinese
Deci, Fr. Ignazio, CCN, 67
deists, 118
Della Chiesa, Bernardino, OFM, 38–39, 70
demographic changes, 114, 152
Demon (*Demonio*), 42, 63, 68
Deng, Fr., 126
Denn, Paolo, SJ, 5
deracination, 58
Diaz del Rincon, Francesco, OP, 2
Díaz, Franciscano, OP, 143
dissimulation of Chinese, 64. *See also* deceitfulness of Chinese
Dominicans, 110–111, 119; as model for underground church, 139–143, 146; ministry to women, 16; opened priesthood to native Fujianese, 143. *Dominus ac Redemptor* (1773), 125, 139
Donegal, p. 25–26
Dong Bodi, Patrizio, 3
donkeys, 94
Dorgon, 29
dreams, 37–38
drunkenness, 46, 92
Du Fengji, Maddalena, 5
Du Maria, born Tian, 5
Du Maria, born Zhao, 5

Du Yushi, 41, 42
ducats, 33, 89
Dufresse, Gabriel-Taurin, MEP, 3
Dutchmen, 46

Earl of Burlington, 46
Ebumi, 109
Eight Permissions, 69–70, 71
elders (*laohuizhang*), 91
Eleuths, 29
Endo, Shusaku, 135
engraving of copperplate, 28–31
Enlightenment, 87
Ermellina di Gesu, Maria, FMM, 4
Espinha, José de, SJ, 125
Eurocentrism, 27, 93, 127
European bias against Chinese priests, 92–96, 115, 127
European criticism of Chinese priests, 136
European expansion, 13–14, 151
European feelings of superiority over Chinese, 95
European racism toward Chinese, 15, 120
Eusebio di Cittadella, OFM, 95–96
Ex illa die (1715), 39, 60, 65, 69, 70, 71,139; Chinese circumvention of, 89–90
Ex quo singulari (1742), 139
expulsion of missionaries (1951), 9

famine of 1778–1779, 121–123
famine of 1781, 126
Fan Hui, Rosa, 6
Fan Kun, Maria, 5
Fancchini, Elia, OFM, 3
Fang Chao-ying, 50n76
Fantosati, Antonio, OFM, 3
Fatigati, Gennaro, CCN, 59, 70, 77, 87, 87, 96, 104
Favre, Guillaume Bonjour, OSA, 24–25, 27, 28
fen, 43
Feng De, Mattias, OFS, 4

Fernández-Oliver, Michael, OFM, 140–141
Ferrari, Orzio Maria, MEP, 43
Figuera, Juan Alcobel, OP, 2
filial piety, 73
five vows, 75
flogging. See bastinado
Fogolla, Francesco, OFM, 3
Foligno, 76
Forbidden City palace, 28, 35
forged testimonials, 73–74
Francesco, Msgr. Giuseppe della Torre, 101
Franciscans, 43, 101
French Revolution, 15
Fróes, Bishop Francisco da Purificaçâo de Rocha, 70
Fu Guilin, Maria, 5
Fujian, 140
Fukangan, 103
Funari, Fr. Onarato, 24–25

Galdo, Holy Congregation secretary, 59
Gama, Luis da, SJ, 110
Gambaro, Giuseppe Mario, OFM, 3
gambling, 77
Gandon, CM, 117
Gansu, 41
Gao, Aloys (Louis), SJ, 112–113
Gao, Tomaso, 90–91
Garden of Joyful Spring (*Changchunyuan*), 28, 33, 35, 36–38, 41
Ge Tingzhu, Paolo, 5
Geneva, 75–76
Gherardi, Giovanni, 28
Giacomantonio, Cesidio, OFM, 4
gifts (porcelain and silk), 41–42
Gioro Manbao, 142, 144
Giovanni Battista da Mandello, OFM, 100
Giovanni da Sassari, OFM, 100
Giuseppe (student), 33
Giuseppe Mattei da Bientina, OFM, 100
Gleyo, Jean François, MEP, 121

golden age of conversions, 10–11
Gong Shangshi, SJ, 111
Goville, Pierre de, SJ, 93
grape wine, 93
Grassi, Gregorio, OFM, 3
grave desecration: by Boxers, 100; in Cultural Revolution, 131n99
Gray, Basil, 46
Great Wall, 92
Grimaldi, Claudio Filippo, SJ, 112
Gu, Basilio, 36–37
Gu, Giovanni Battista, 32, 37, 42, 45, 58–63, 68, 69, 70, 71, 76, 86, 88, 93–94, 116, 119, 145–146; asceticism of, 47
Guan Yu, 31–32, 137
Guangzhou (Canton), 28
Gubeikou, 36–38
Guislain, Jean-Joseph, CM, 126
guniang (old mothers), 120
Guo Maria, born Li, 5
Guo Shilong, 27
Guo Tianpang, SJ, 111
Guo, Giacomo, 36
Guo, Matteo, 36–37
Guo, Vitale Giuseppe, CCN, 66, 69, 70, 76, 86, 88, 94, 95

Haimen, 126
Hamel, Thomas, MEP, 118–119
Hao Kaizhi, Joachim, 3
He Tianzhang, SJ, 111
Hei, catechist, 98
Herdtrich, Christian, SJ, 112
heretical beliefs (*xiejiao*), 153
heroes versus martyrs, 137
heterodoxy (*yiduan*), 12
Hidden Christians, see *kakure kirishitan*
Holy Childhood, 121
Holy Congregation. See Holy Family
Holy Family Congregation, 40, 55–58, 72, 72, 74–78, 87. See also Collegio dei Cinesi
homesickness, 63
homoeroticism, 35

homosexuality, 23–25, 33–34, 44, 63
Huang Tinggui, 137
Huang, Filippo, 33–34, 42, 45, 47, 57, 59, 63–66, 70, 71, 76, 134, 145–146; ministry in China, 85–100, served in Zhili & Shanxi, 86, 87, 88; criticism of, 94, 115
Huangyu quanlan tu, 31
huizhang (head of Christian community), 91, 118
humility of Saint Francis, 95
Hunyuan-zhou, 91

Iberian rivalry, 140
infanticide, 118, 121
Isoré, Rémi, SJ, 5
Italian language, 58, 65, 74, 87

Japanese martyrdom, 135
Jartoux (Giartù), Pierre, SJ, 31, 39
Jehol. *See* Rehe
Jesuits: accommodation, 13, 139; at court, 38; atlas, 30–31, 46; dissolution of 1773, 15; first Chinese ordinations, 111; literary apostolate of, 136; Ripa's disagreements with, 39, 41; suppression of, 85–86, 87–88, 90, 125. *See also Dominus ac Redemptor*
Ji Tianxiang, Marco, 5
Jiangnan, 125
Jiangzhou, 92
Jiao Zhengang, 102
jiaohua (transformation through education), 12
jiaoyang (civilizing mission), 12
jing (Chinese classics), 152
Ju (Zhu?), Fr. Pablo, 66

kakure kirishitan, 109–110
Kangxi emperor, 11–12, 27, 29–30, 39–42, 70, 153
Ke, Paulus, 65
Kielmansegg, Charlotte Sophia, 46
King George I, 46

kissing the crucifix, 140–141
Korean War, 9

La Magna, Fr. Domenico, CCN, 71, 72
Laamann, Lars, 136
lack of funds. *See* subsidies
Laimbeckhoven, Gottfried von, SJ, 125
Lang Fu, Paolo, 4
Lang, born Yang, 4
Lantrua, Giovanni da Triora, OFM, 2
Latin language, 58, 59, 74, 87, 117, 139
Latourette, Kenneth Scott, 152
Lazarists (Vincentians), 114, 119, 125; pastoral apostolate of, 61, 136
Lecari, Cardinal Niccolò, 77
Lefebvre, Urbain, MEP, 118, 137–138
Leibniz, Gottfried, 12
Li Chien-yi, 1
Li Guishu, 137
Li Quanhui, Pietro, 6
Li Quanzhen, Raimondo, 6
Li Veng-hoaen, Laurentius, 119
Li, Cristofaro, 37
Li, Fr. Andreas, 96, 113–120, 135–139, 143, 145–146
Li, Fr. Lucas Augustinus, 120, 145–146
Li, Giuseppe Lucio, CCN, 66–68, 70, 76, 86, 92, 118
Li, Jacobus, CCN, 65
Liborio, 56
Lin Zhao, Agatha, 3
Liu Hanzuo, Paolo, Fr., 3
Liu Jinde, Paolo, 5
Liu Ruiting, Fr. Thaddeus, 3
Liu Wenyuan, Pietro, 3
Liu Xi, 101
Liu Yunde (Blaise Verbiest), SJ, 111
Liu Ziyu, Pietro, 4
Liu, Dominico, 103
Liu, Filippo, 103
Liu, Pio Martino, the younger, 68–69, 76, 86, 88, 89, 92, 98, 102, 103
Liu, Pio the elder, 68–69, 86
Liu, Simone Carlo, 103
London, 46–47

Louis XV, 113
Lu Tingmei, Jérôme, 3
Lu, Monica, 1
Luigi Landi da Signa, OFM, 100
Luo Tingyin, 2
Luo Wenzao (Gregorio Lopez), OP, 55–56, 110–111, 143, 151
Luo, Catherine, 122–123
Luo, Fr. Matthew, 104

Ma Taishun, Giovanni Battista, 6
Ma, Emanuele, 103
Macartney, Lord George, 65
Macau, 26, 87–88, 90
Maggi, Luigi Maria, OP, 69, 71, 95,116, 121
Magni, Francesco Maria, OFM, 92
male tears, 31, 63
Mangin, Léon Ignatius, SJ, 6
Mao Zedong, 8, 9
maps, 30–31, 116
Martiliat, Joachim Enjobert de, MEP, 121
Martins, Francisco, SJ, 141
martyr-saints, list of 121, 1–6
martyrdom, 1–6, 31–32, 47, 60, 90, 135–145, 153
martyrs, 1–6, 135–137, 153. See also blood of the martyrs, Chinese Martyrs Sanctuary, martyr-saints, Queen of Martyrs, 57
Medici, Andrea, 64, 66–67
Meiling Mountain, 43
mendicant model of martyrdom, 139–143
MEP Collège de Saint Joseph, Siam, 120
Mezzabarba, Carlo Ambrogio, 41, 69–70
Min dialect, 140
Miralta, Fr. Archangelo, 64
Monet, CM, 117
Monte Casino, 72
mortifications, dietary, 32
Motte, Lambert de la, MEP, 115

Mouly, Joseph-Martial, CM, 127
Mourão, João, SJ, 11, 41
Moÿe, Jean-Martin, MEP, 121–123
mules, 91, 94, 98
Müllener, Johann, CM, 60–61, 66, 71, 116
Muslims, 8, 100, 152, 153

Nanjing diocese, 125
Nantang, 89, 134–135
Naples, 22, 40, 47
Nardi, Fr. Carlo, 73
Néel, Giovanni Pietro, MEP, 2
Neiwufu Zao Ban Wai, 41
Nurhaci, 11

official church, 9
Olivantani brothers, 58
Orphan of Zhao, 13
orthodoxy (*zhengdao*), 153
Ouang, Jacobus, 137–138

pacifist image of Jesus, 151
Padroado, 23, 85, 100, 133
Palatre, Gabriel, SJ, 121
Palladini, Fr. Emiliano, 87, 89, 90, 92–95
Pantoja, Diego de, SJ, 98
Parian district in Manila, 140
patacas, 89
Patriotic church. See official church
Pe, Petrus, 119, 139
Pearl River, 45
Pedrini, Teodorico, CM, 11, 26–28, 37, 39, 41
Perboyre, Jean Gabriel, CM, 1, 2
Perroni, Domenico, OMD, 24, 42
Petra, Cardinal, 60, 67
Philippines, 110. See also seminaries, Manila
piao (certificate), 61, 114
Piazza de Trinità 73
Pignatelli, Cardinal, 58
Pires-Pireira, Gaetan, 134
Pisani, Giuseppe, CCN, 56

plague, 67
pontifical galleys, 76
Pope Alexander VI, 24
Pope Benedict XII, 55
Pope Benedict XIII, 58
Pope Benedict XIV, 69, 70, 77, 78
Pope Clement XI, 24, 55
Pope Clement XII, 69, 72
Pope Francis I, 16
Pope Innocent XII, 86
Pope John Paul II, 1, 143
Pope Pius XII, 151
Pottier, François, MEP, 96, 116, 124
Poxieji, 152–153
Prandi, Fortunato, 25
Prémare, Joseph de, SJ, 43, 152
Propaganda Fide, 7, 23, 42, 44, 55–58, 60, 64, 66, 69, 71, 72, 75, 76, 77–78, 85, 86, 92, 94, 100, 103–104, 123, 133; college of, 117
Protestant hostility, 25
Protestant house churches, 17n7
Protestantism, 45

Qi Yu, Maria, 5
Qianlong emperor, 88, 101, 144; contributes to rebuilding Nantang, 89, 134
Qianmen Gate, 34
Qin Chunfu, Simon, 4
Qin Elizabetta, born Bian, 5
Qin Lu, 102
Queen of Martyrs (Mary), 57

Raux, Nicolas-Joseph, CM, 126
Real Collegio Asiatico, 69, 78
rebellion, 144
Red Guards, 10. *See also* Cultural Revolution
Rehe (Jehol), 29, 33, 35
rheumatism, 78
Rhodes, Alexandre de, SJ, 111
Ricci, Matteo, SJ, 10, 61, 98, 114, 134, 153
Riccio, Nicolò, CCN, 69

rigid theological views, 70
Ripa, Caterina, 67
Ripa, Fr. Giuseppe, 73
Ripa, Lorenzo, 67
Ripa, Matteo: 21–47; influence of, 104; love of Giovanni Gu, Yin Giovanni & Paolo Cai, 76; paternal bond with Lucio Wu, 74–75; wisdom of, 100.
Rites Controversy, 15, 39, 67, 69, 119, 136, 151
Rome, 76; as a bureaucratic maze, 40, 63. *See also* Vatican bureaucracy
Roost, Andrew, MEP, 115
Royo, Joachim, OP, 2, 143
Ruspoli, Cardinal Bartolomeo, 56
Russian Ecclesiastical Mission, 134
Russian Orthodox Church, 93

Sacripanti, Cardinal Giuseppe, 56
Saint-Martin, Jean-Didier de, MEP, 124
San Biagio, Giuseppe, 57
San Paolo College, Macau, 88
Sanguozhi yanyi, 33
Sant-Andrea College, Rome, 111
Sanz, Pedro, OP, 2, 116, 142–143
scent: fragrant, 31
Schall, Adam, SJ, 100, 134, 138
scudi, 89
Scy (Xi?), Lorenzo, 37
secret brotherhoods, 152
sedition, 141
seeds of martyrdom, 90, 146, 153
seminaries: Anjiazhuang, 127; Ayudhya (Ayutthaya), Siam, 86, 115; Beijing, 15, 115, 126; Hon-dat, Vietnam, 115; Macau, 15, 115, 126–127; Manila, 86, 127, 143; Naples, 15; Rome, 86; Sichuan, 118–119; Sywantze, Mongolia, 115; Virampatnam near Pondicherry, 115–116; Xiwanzi, 127
Senigallia, p. 73, 75
sensibility, 31, 35, 37
Serrano del Rincon, Francis, OP, 2
Serrano, Franciscano, OP, 143

Shanxi, 90–98
Shen Jihe, Tommaso, OFS, 3
Shen Que, 152
Shen Yu, 29–30
shenfu (father) prohibited, 103
sheng (saint for Confucius), 90
shengren (sage), 152
Shunzhi emperor, 100, 134
Sichuan, 113–117
Sigismondo a S. Nicola, OESA, 88, 92, 94, 96
Sinicization, 35. 153
Sinophile, 104
Siqueira, Emmanuel de, SJ. *See* Zheng Manuo Weixin
Sisters of Providence, Lorraine, 121
slander, 39
slowing pace of conversions, 14
Société des Missions Étrangères de Paris (MEP), 113–114, 119
sodomy, 34–35
Songgotu, 35–36
Spence, Jonathan D., 50n76
Spinelli, Archbishop Giuseppe, 77
Spinelli, Cardinal, 74
St. Claire cloister, Macau, 16
St. Joseph Church (*Dongtang*), Beijing, 115
St. Joseph College, Macau, 111
State Administration for Religious Affairs (SARA), 8, 9
Staunton, George, 65
strangulations, 143
Su Maoxiang, 10
Su, Paulus, CM, 117, 119
subsidies, 88–89, 90, 92, 93, 98, 117
Sunu clan, 11
supercargo, 45
surgeon, 45

taels (*liang*), 33, 43, 89
Taglialatela, Vincenzo, CCN, 40
Taiyuan-fu, 90, 93
Tang Ruose, 145
Tartars (Mongols), 92

Teresiano, Fr. Rinaldo Maria, 60
Tertullian, 135
Thilisch, Franz, SJ, 28
Third Order of Saint Dominic, 142
Thirty-Six Views of Jehol, 29–30, 46–47
Three-Self Patriotic Movement, 17n7
Tibet, 8
tongzhen (consecrated virgins), 120
Tournon, Papal Legate, 7, 14, 15, 23, 27–28, 40, 44, 115, 153
treaty church replaces underground church, 127
Treaty of Nanjing, 8
treaty ports, 8
Tribunal of Mathematics, 111
Trogneux, CM, 117

Uighurs, 8, 153
underground church: after 1957, 9; Bishop Laimbeckhoven, 125; Dominicans in Fujian, 142–143; eighteenth century, 15, 17, 153; Gao Tomaso, 90–91; Great Persecution, 100–103; Huang Filippo, 97–98; in Japan, 109–110; Li, Fr. Andreas, 137–139; origins of, 7, 134; Zhou Laurentius, 144–145
Ungar, Giuseppe. *See* Wu, Lucio
universal church, 23, 92–93, 151–153
universal truth (*zhengdao*), p. 13
Ursis, Sabatino de, SJ, 134

Van Coillie, Fr. Dries, 9
Van, Joseph, 145
Vatican bureaucracy, 56–57
Vatican Library, 77
Verbiest, Ferdinand, SJ, 111
Versiglia, Luigi, SDB, 3
Verthamon, Jean Hyacinthe de, 145
vicars apostolic, 85, 131n91, 133–134
Vienna, 57, 63
violence, threat of, 97
virginity of Mary, emulation of, 141
vocation (spiritual), 65, 73

Wan Qiyuan (Paul Banhes), SJ, 111
Wang Bing, Lorenzo, 3
Wang Cheng, Lucia, 5
Wang Erman, Pietro, 4
Wang Kuiji, Giuseppe, 5
Wang Kuixin, Giovanni, 5
Wang Luqi, Lucia, 4
Wang Mande, Marta, 3
Wang Maria, born Li, 5
Wang Rui, Giovanni, OFS, 4
Wang Tianqing, Andreas, 4
Wang Tommaso, 86
Wang Yumei, Giuseppe, 5
Wang Zuolong, Peter, 6
Wang, Anna 4
Wang, Gabriel, 137
Wang, Gioacchino, 42, 45–47, 60–63, 146
warrior-king image of Christ, 151
White Lotus sect, 14, 102, 137
whoremonger and merchant, 92–93
will of God, 137
Wittkower, Rudolf, 46
women baptizers, 120
Wu Anbang, Pietro, OFS, 4
Wu Anju, Paolo, 5
Wu Gaosheng, Pietro, 2
Wu Mantang, Giovanni Battista, 5
Wu Wanshu, Paolo, 5
Wu Wenyin, Giovanni, 6
Wu Xuesheng, Martino, 2
Wu Yushan (Wu Li), SJ, 111
Wu, Lucio, 23, 32, 37, 42, 44–47, 57, 59, 63–66, 70, 71, 78, 85, 86–87; flight of, 72–77; pseudonym Giuseppe Ungar, 74; Wu, Pietro Andrea, 92
Wu, Tommaso, 33, 37, 42, 73, 146

xenophobia, 8
Xi Jinping, 7, 8, 16, 152, 153
Xie, Bartolomeo, 101
Xinjiang province, 153
Xinjiang, 8
xiunü (prototype of nuns), 142

Xu Changzhi, 152
Xu Guangqi, 10
Xu, Gaetano, 103
Xu, Stephanus (Etienne), CM, 114–115, 117, 118, 119, 137
Xue, Mattaeus, CM, 127

Yan Guodong, Giacomo, 4
Yan Tingyun, 10
Yang (Forest), Etienne, SJ, 112
Yang Guangxuan, 152
Yang, Tommaso, 36
Yao Ruohan. *See* John Yao
Yao, John, SJ, 125–126, 144, 145–146
yellow human bondage, 78
Yen, Charles, 139
Yi Zhenmei, Lucia, 3
Yili, 69, 102, 103
Yin, Giovanni Evangelista, 32, 36–38, 42, 59–62, 86; asceticism of, 47, 146; death of, 63, 119; father of, 37–38; mother of, 38, 46, 57; prophetic powers, 38, 57–58; martyrdom, 60; submissive, 70
Yinlu (sixteenth prince), 41–42
Yinreng, 35
Yintang, 11, 41
Yinti, 41
Yinxiang (thirteenth prince), 41
Yinzhen. *See* Yongzheng emperor
Yongzheng emperor, 7, 11; as imperial heir, 36; converted churches to public places, 134; edict of 1724 Proscribing Christianity, 134, 142, 144, 152; edict of May 28, 1727, 12–13; hostility toward Christianity, 40; usurpation accusation, 18n16, 50n76
Yuan Gengyin, Giuseppe, 5
Yuan Zaide, Fr. Giuseppe, 3

Zeng Xuekong, 102
Zeng, Francesco, 102
Zeng, Francesco, 102
Zhalan cemetery, 98–99, 112

Zhang Banniu, Petro, OFS, 4
Zhang Dapeng, Giuseppe, 2
Zhang Huailu, 6
Zhang Huan, Giovanni, OFS, 3
Zhang Kui, 30
Zhang Pengge, 142
Zhang Rong, Francesco, OFS, 3
Zhang Tianshen, Giovanni, 3
Zhang Wenlan, Giuseppe, 3
Zhang Zhihe, Filippo, OFS, 4
Zhang, Giovanni Evangelista, 88
Zhang, Jingguang, Giovanni, 4
Zhang, Linus Feng, 61, 114, 117, 120, 146
Zhang, Teresa, born He, 4
Zhao Maria, 6
Zhao Maris, born Guo, 6

Zhao Mingxi, Giovanni Battista, 6
Zhao Mingxzhen, Pietro, 6
Zhao Quanxin, Giacomo, 4
Zhao Rosa, 6
Zhao, Domenico, 64, 66–67, 70, 76
Zhao, Simone, 64, 66, 67, 86
Zheng Manuo Weixin, SJ, 111–112
Zheng Xu, Maria, 5
zhennü (chaste women): Christian, 120–121; Confucian, 120. Zhou Laurentius, 144–146
Zhu Gui, 29
Zhu Rixin, 5
Zhu Wurui, Giovanni Battista, 6
Zhu, Mary, born Wu, 4
Zhu, Petrus, CM, 117

www.ingramcontent.com/pod-product-compliance
Lightning Source LLC
Chambersburg PA
CBHW022013300426
44117CB00005B/172